ISLAMIC PSYCHOANALYSIS AND PSYCHOANALYTIC ISLAM

This pioneering volume brings together scholars and clinicians working at the intersection of Islam and psychoanalysis to explore both the connections that link these two traditions, as well as the tensions that exist between them.

Uniting authors from a diverse range of traditions and perspectives, including Freudian, Jungian, Lacanian, Object-Relations, and Group-Analytic, the book creates a dialogue through which several key questions can be addressed. How can Islam be rendered amenable to psychoanalytic interpretation? What might an 'Islamic psychoanalysis' look like that accompanies and questions the forms of psychoanalysis that developed in the West? And what might a 'psychoanalytic Islam' look like that speaks for, and perhaps even transforms, the forms of truth that Islam produces?

In an era of increasing Islamophobia in the West, this important book identifies areas where clinical practice can be informed by a deeper understanding of contemporary Islam, as well as what it means to be a Muslim today. It will appeal to trainees and practitioners of psychoanalysis and psychotherapy, as well as scholars interested in religion and Islamic studies.

Ian Parker is a Psychoanalyst in Manchester, and **Sabah Siddiqui** is a Researcher and author of *Religion and Psychoanalysis in India* (Routledge, 2016). They are both members of the Discourse Unit and the Manchester Psychoanalytic Matrix.

ISLAMIC PSYCHOANALYSIS AND PSYCHOANALYTIC ISLAM

Cultural and Clinical Dialogues

Edited by Ian Parker and Sabah Siddiqui

Routledge
Taylor & Francis Group

LONDON AND NEW YORK

First published 2019
by Routledge
2 Park Square, Milton Park, Abingdon, Oxon OX14 4RN

and by Routledge
52 Vanderbilt Avenue, New York, NY 10017

Routledge is an imprint of the Taylor & Francis Group, an informa business

British Library Cataloguing-in-Publication Data
A catalogue record for this book is available from the British Library

Library of Congress Cataloging-in-Publication Data
A catalog record has been requested for this book

ISBN: 978-0-367-08671-8 (hbk)
ISBN: 978-0-367-08674-9 (pbk)
ISBN: 978-0-429-02369-9 (ebk)

Typeset in Bembo
by Swales & Willis Ltd

CONTENTS

FOREWORD

Ian Parker

This book emerges from the international conference Islamic Psychoanalysis/ Psychoanalytic Islam which was organised by the College of Psychoanalysts in the UK – a professional body open to different traditions in psychoanalysis. We were fortunate to have the support of the Centre for Interdisciplinary Research in Arts and Languages at the University of Manchester and Manchester Psychoanalytic Matrix. There were speakers and participants from Brazil, Germany, Greece, India, Iran, Ireland, Italy, Mexico, Turkey, the USA, and the UK. The idea for the conference sprung from a conversation with a psychoanalyst who visited us from Brazil last year, João Gabriel Lima da Silva. João was working on the impact of Christianity on psychoanalysis in Brazil. This is a particular cultural context in which psychoanalysis is very widespread and in which leading psychoanalysts have often come from ecclesiastical backgrounds, to the point where it has been claimed that youngest sons of the middle classes now go into training as psychoanalysts instead of as priests. It prompted a thought about the way that culture frames psychoanalysis, including the way that certain psychoanalytic ideas themselves become thinkable. João pointed out that Christian themes in some forms of psychoanalysis are powerful but go unnoticed by many practitioners.

This would seem to require us to make those connections explicit so that we could interrogate them, perhaps in a project called 'Christian Psychoanalysis/ Psychoanalytic Christianity'. But we wanted to do something more radical than that. There have already been explorations of the link between Christianity and psychoanalysis, some of them concerning the question of adaptation, adaptation of psychoanalysis to society, beginning with Sigmund Freud's own attempt to make psychoanalysis more acceptable to his host culture by nominating the son of a Christian pastor, Carl Jung, as first President of the International Psychoanalytical Association. Jungians, as well as Freudians, have since tried to disentangle them- selves from the consequences of that, including the complicity of Jung with antisemitism. As we know, Jung was willing to become President of the International General Medical Society of Psychotherapy under the control of the Nazis in 1933, while Freud's books were burnt, and his work condemned as being a 'Jewish science'.

If we just track back for a moment, we can see a number of questions embedded in that claim that psychoanalysis is a 'Jewish science', including the attempts to reclaim Freud as someone grounded in a particularly marginalised sub-culture, as a Jew in what was then the Austro-Hungarian Empire. Now, it does seem problematic to reduce psychoanalysis, whether that is done by its friends or its enemies, to a particular kind of culture. Freud himself was a secular Jew, and even his later writings on Moses and monotheism refused a religious narrative, they rather look designed to provoke Jews as well as gentiles. And, despite his tactical endorsement of Jung, he held true to psychoanalysis as a critique of every culture, including the way that overly rationalist versions of the Western Enlightenment were being installed in Europe. That critique of rationality was to be crucial to the work of the psychoanalytic social theorists of the Frankfurt School, of course.

A Japanese psychoanalyst commenting on the supposed colonial role of psychoanalysis in the East once asked whether it was really indeed the case that Freud was European. What he was getting at was Freud's place as, we could say to use a Scottish term, 'outwith' culture, both of the dominant Christian culture of the time and of his own Jewish culture. And this Japanese analyst was also getting at the status of psychoanalysis not as part of a culture, but as 'liminal' to it, simultaneously part of it and as reflexively critical of it, both in it and at a distance from it. We can see this liminal status of psychoanalysis in Japan where some analysts are part of the very marginal Christian sub-culture there and are able to use that position to reflect on dominant cultural assumptions about childcare, dependency, and the development of the self. We can also see it in the work of analysts who forge a link between Freud's ideas and Japanese Buddhism, using that link to open up contradictions between common-sense Buddhism and a deeper reading of it as a metaphysical frame to grasp the evanescence of subjectivity.

If we take the buried, hidden nature of culture inside different contradictory forms of psychoanalysis around the world seriously, and if we treat psychoanalysis as such as something that is never actually psychoanalysis 'as such' but is always necessarily internally divided, then that gives a different vantage point on the relationship between religion, any religion, and psychoanalytic theory and psychoanalytic practice. It means that we tell the story (well, stories) of the emergence and development of psychoanalysis in a different way, and it means that we see other possible combinations of psychoanalysis with other cultural forms in a different light. So, even as we elaborate a narrative about the entanglement of psychoanalysis with culture, we have to bear in mind those complications. Take this narrative, for example, as one that we came up with, with João's help, to frame this research project.

The unconscious was invented by Freud at a particular cultural-historical moment, and it was invented in such a way as to construct and then seem to unlock the self constructed in the nuclear family. Elements of the theory of subjectivity that Freud patched together, and patched together differently in different writings, drew on Judaism, not deliberately but as a function of his engagement as an outsider with the Christian culture around him and around his family and sub-cultural networks. And that meant that there was indeed something 'Jewish' about this science of subjectivity and clinical practice that was able to function, not a prescription for how individuals should be but as a critical description which aimed at the transformation of who they could be. I am summarising and condensing a range of reflections on the early nature of the psychoanalytic movement as possibly, in some way, rooted in the position of the Jews who comprised it. Notice here, also, the political stakes of Freudian theory and practice. It does not confirm but subverts taken-for-granted forms of life. In that sense, the Nazis were right to see it as a threat to order, as a threat to the capitalist order they were dedicated to saving from 'Jewish Bolshevism' or 'Judeo-Bolshevism', their specific formulation to describe the enemy.

Psychoanalysis did then break into mainstream culture in the West, through sensationalist mistranslations of Freud's work into English, through the arrival in the United States, and other parts of the world, of psychoanalysts, many of them Jewish, fleeing Nazism, and through the popularisation of themes of the ego and the id and dreams and the unconscious through literature and film which was suited to its more surrealist aspects. And, paradoxically, at the very moment that Christian culture was becoming secularised, psychoanalysis as a secular practice had to adapt itself to that culture. That adaptation to US culture, which then became one of the transmission belts for the popularisation of psychoanalysis throughout much of the rest of the world, involved the suppression of many of Freud's colleagues' links with the political left, what was referred to as 'the repression of psychoanalysis'. What was accepted, though, was rendered acceptable and tailored to a culture that was still by default Christian.

Some forms of psychoanalysis fared better than others, and one complaint levelled against Jacques Lacan in France, who became popular in a culture that was ostensibly secular, but still suffused with Christian imagery and institutions, was that he Christianised psychoanalysis. Then we come in a loop back to where I started, for it was that Lacanian psychoanalysis that pitted itself against the predominantly Jewish International Psychoanalytical Association and that arrived in Brazil to become so influential there. Of course, things play out differently in other parts of the world, and that is where the suspicion that psychoanalysis is part of a colonial and then postcolonial globalisation of Western culture takes root. Whether or not Freud himself was or was not really European, and whether or not psychoanalysts endorsed either the ideological compromise formation sometimes named as 'Judeo-Christian' culture, which is actually one in which Judaism is explicitly or implicitly assumed to have been superseded by Christianity, or the tradition of the Western Enlightenment that likes to pretend that it has transcended both Judaism and Christianity, is rather beside the point.

The point is that psychoanalysis is hosted by and carries with it a complex series of debates around these questions, a package structured by those oppositions, and Western cultural preoccupations. Then the standard mode of engagement with the rest of the world and with other cultures by psychoanalysis tends to be structured by, and work alongside, so-called 'transcultural psychiatry' or 'intercultural psychotherapy'. That is, when psychoanalysts reflect on the dangers of the colonial imposition of their frame of reference as if it was a worldview, they often replace it with an attempt to translate their practice into the terms used in other cultures or respectfully accede to other frameworks. Incidentally, Freud himself never saw psychoanalysis as a worldview, but as closest to the worldview of science, which, given the role that scientific rationality has played in versions of the Western Enlightenment, does not solve but rather gives another twist to the problem. Coming back to the question of transcultural psychiatry or intercultural psychotherapy, this is precisely one of the reasons why we did not frame the title of this book in terms of a simple combination of psychoanalysis and Islam, as if the task was simply one of conjoining the two, respecting each, and leaving both intact.

Instead, for all of the problems of recuperation, the neutralisation and absorption of versions of psychoanalysis by its host cultures – something I have stressed so far in my narrative about the development of psychoanalysis in relation to Judaism and Christianity – we first of all hold to the critically reflexive and even subversive nature of psychoanalysis. And, just as psychoanalysis worked because it was inside as well as outside its host cultures, our bet is that something more radical can be produced by active engagement now with Islam as something that operates adjacent to and against 'Judeo-Christian' culture and secular forms psychoanalysis, 'outwith' both. Just as Islamic science, the mathematics and medicine of the Islamic Golden Age, was crucial to the development of what we like to think of as 'Western' science, so we wager that asking what Islamic psychoanalysis and psychoanalytic Islam might look like forces a question not about others, the rest of the world, but about us.

I say 'us' advisedly. This conference took place in Britain in 2017 with international visitors to help us work on these questions at times of the increased segregation of communities, of what we often refer to using the psychologised shorthand term 'Islamophobia'. When we discussed the idea for this conference in the College of Psychoanalysts there was some anxiety. Someone suggested that it might be provocative, and another suggested that we invite the police. We discussed, along the way, how this might be complemented by another conference which engaged with the neuropsychological turn and concern with an evidence-based practice called 'Scientific Psychoanalysis/Psychoanalytic Science'. That too would serve to force a question through the compression of terms, to make visible connections that usually operate outside our immediate awareness, but operate nonetheless.

The conjunctions and compressions that we posed in the title of the conference and now this book are designed to avoid either the usual attempts to give psychoanalytic readings of Islam or to invite Islamic scholars to tell us what is wrong with psychoanalysis. Rather, the task is much more difficult, and perhaps it is impossible, and none the worse for being impossible – remember that psychoanalysis is an impossible profession – to do at least two things. First, and there are political stakes to this, to welcome into psychoanalysis Islamic traditions and reflections on tradition, not as complementary but as intimately part of the project of psychoanalysis as a critical description and transformation of contemporary subjectivity. And, second, to ask whether the next historic wave of psychoanalytic work, after the first two waves of Jewish and Christian-inflected theory, will come from Islam as a growing cultural force.

CONTRIBUTORS

Maryam Aslzaker is a Psychoanalytic Psychotherapist. She graduated in Clinical Psychology from the University of Social Welfare and Rehabilitation Sciences. She is Assistant Professor of Clinical Psychology in Shahid Beheshti University of Medical Sciences (SBUM) where she teaches psychotherapy and developmental psychopathology to postgraduate students of Clinical Psychology. She has been in the Persian translation team for analytic books such as *The Patient and the Analyst* by Joseph Sandler and *Freud and Beyond* by Stephen Mitchell.

Robert K. Beshara is a Critical Psychologist, interested in theorising subjectivity vis-à-vis ideology through radical qualitative research (e.g., discourse analysis). In addition to being a scholar-activist, he is a fine artist with a background in film, theatre, and music. He holds two terminal degrees: a Ph.D. in Psychology: Consciousness and Society from the University of West Georgia and an M.F.A. in Independent Film and Digital Imaging from Governors State University. He currently works as an Assistant Professor of Psychology at Northern New Mexico College. For more information, kindly visit: www.robertbeshara.com

Julia Borossa is an Associate Professor, and the Director of the Centre for Psychoanalysis, Middlesex University. She is the author of *Hysteria* (2001) and the editor of *Sandor Ferenczi: Selected Writings* (1999) and (with Ivan Ward) of *Psychoanalysis, Fascism, Fundamentalism* (2009). Her numerous essays on the histories and politics of psychoanalysis have appeared in edited collections and journals including the *Journal of European Studies* and the *Journal of Postcolonial Writing*. She is a group analyst and a member of the College of Psychoanalysts-UK.

Forough Edrissi received her Ph.D. in Clinical Psychology from Shahid Beheshti University of Medical Sciences (SBUM), she wrote her doctoral dissertation on

'Efficacy of tuning in to kids program on parent socialization and anxiety symptoms in preschool children'. She works as a Psychoanalytic Psychotherapist in private practice in Tehran and the focus of her studies is on Object Relation schools. She is the author and translator of some papers and books.

Nathan Gorelick is Associate Professor of English at Utah Valley University. His work has appeared in several journals of literary theory and Continental philosophy, including *Continental Thought and Theory, CR: The New Centennial Review, Discourse, Theory & Event, Umbr(a): A Journal of the Unconscious*, and *SCTIW Review* – the journal of the Society for Contemporary Thought and the Islamicate World. He was also managing editor of the 2009 issue of *Umbr(a)* on Islam and psychoanalysis. He is a founding member of the Buffalo Group for the Application of Psychoanalysis, the only non-clinical research circle of the École freudienne du Québec.

Shifa Haq is an Assistant Professor (Psychology-Psychotherapy) at the School of Human Studies, Ambedkar University Delhi. She also works as a Psychoanalytic Psychotherapist at the Centre of Psychotherapy and Clinical Research, Ambedkar University Delhi. Her research interests include mourning in the context of disappearances in Kashmir, gender, and psychoanalysis.

Gohar Homayounpour is a Psychoanalyst, member of the International Psychoanalytic Association, Training and Supervising Psychoanalyst of the Freudian Group of Tehran, a Lecturer at Shahid Beheshti University, and author of *Doing Psychoanalysis in Tehran* (MIT Press, 2013). She is also a member of the scientific board of the Freud Museum in Vienna.

Farshid Kazemi is a Ph.D. Candidate at the Department of Islamic and Middle Eastern Studies, University of Edinburgh, UK. He received his B.A. in English Literature from the University of British Columbia, Canada. His monograph uses Lacanian psychoanalytic theory and feminist film theory to theorise the structure of desire and sexuality in post-revolutionary Iranian cinema.

Zehra Mehdi works on communal violence, political identity, and psychoanalysis in the twenty-first century, India. Her ongoing doctoral research at the Department of Religion, Columbia University, New York, is on the politics of gender, Muslim identity, and Nationalism in North India. Her Ph.D. explores the links between a gendered narrative of religion in Post Partition India and its political manifestations and psychic identifications. She is also a psychoanalytical psychotherapist trained in India and writes on how questions of religious difference enter the clinic, with a particular focus on transference and counter-transference processes. She has published papers in the *American Journal of Applied Psychoanalytic Studies*, as well as with Karnac, Palgrave Macmillan, Rowman, and Littlefield.

Ian Parker is a Psychoanalyst and Researcher in Manchester, with Visiting Professorships at the University of Manchester and universities in Belgium, Brazil, South Africa, and Spain. His books include *Lacanian Psychoanalysis: Revolutions in Subjectivity* (Routledge, 2011). He was co-founder (with Erica Burman) of the Discourse Unit (www.discourseunit.com). He is editor of the *Lines of the Symbolic in Psychoanalysis* book series for Routledge.

Chiara Sebastiani (University of Bologna, CIPA, IAAP) is a Sociologist, Political Scientist and Jungian Analyst based in Rome. Her current interests focus on the relationship between the urban environment, religion and the psyche: on this, she has presented papers at several international conferences. Among her works: 'Psiche nella città' (with A. Connolly, in *La Psiche nell'Epoca dell Tecnica*, Milano: Vivarium, 2007); 'The Gendered Dimension of Public Spaces: a Cross-Cultural Perspective' (*Temperanter*, n.1/2, 2011); *Una città una rivoluzione. Tunisi e la riconquista dello spazio pubblico* (Cosenza: Pellegrini Editore, 2014); *La sfida delle parole* (Bologna: Editrice Socialmente, 2014). She has translated and edited, in Italian, Max Weber's *Sociology of Religion* (*Sociologia delle religioni*, a cura di Chiara Sebastiani, Torino: Utet, vol. 2, 2008). She currently coordinates and supervises a Jungian developing group in Belarus.

Sabah Siddiqui is a Researcher at the University of Manchester. Her research is on the subjects and the ghosts of contemporary mental health discourse that is informed by postcolonial, feminist, and psychoanalytic methods. She was trained clinically as a Psychodynamic Psychotherapist in Delhi and has authored the book *Religion and Psychoanalysis in India: Critical Clinical Practice* (Routledge, 2016). Sabah co-edited a special issue for the *Annual Review of Critical Psychology* in 2018 on *Sex and Power in the University*. She would like to believe that instead of disciplines, she is more interested in methodologies.

Eva Tepest completed her bachelor's degree in Arab Studies at Leipzig University, Germany, and Ain Shams University, Cairo, Egypt, as well as a master's degree in Middle Eastern Studies at Lund University, Sweden and University College of London Qatar. She is currently a Freelance Writer and Journalist based in Berlin. Her research interests include gender and sexuality non-conforming identities, politics of the Syrian uprising, and feminist and social movements in North Africa and West Asia.

Amal Treacher Kabesh is an Associate Professor at the School of Sociology and Social Policy, University of Nottingham, and author of *Postcolonial Masculinities: Emotions, Histories and Ethics* (Ashgate, 2013) and *Egyptian Revolutions: Repetition, Conflict, Identification* (Rowman and Littlefield, 2017).

INTRODUCTION

Sabah Siddiqui

The coming together of Islam and psychoanalysis should be cataclysmic . . . if popular discourse on either topic is anything to go by. At the Islamic Psychoanalysis/ Psychoanalytic Islam Conference at the University of Manchester on the 26th and 27th of June 2017, we had a different experience. Some 100 participants from 11 countries participated in a convivial discussion on psychoanalysis in Islamicate countries, Islam through a psychoanalytic lens, the practices of psychoanalytically-trained Muslim therapists, and the psychoanalysis of Muslim analysands.

In the months preceding the conference, in a casual conversation, I found out that a friend was concerned that whether holding this event was 'safe'. She had asked me if we had requested for extra 'security' on the days of the conference. It was not obvious to me who would be needing security and from whom. We had not arranged for extra security from the police or the university. Were we trying to protect our delegates, the university, society, or the state? Who should we have been looking out for? Certainly, psychoanalysts are not the most loved in psychology departments, but their presence has never incited the university community to violence. She was surely referring to the other aspect of the title: Islam, a topic that features far more in the public opinion of the UK and beyond than psychoanalysis. Would the mention of Islam draw out a predictable violence?

In our experience, the organising of the conference of the College of Psychoanalysis, London, met with no challenges to safety at the University of Manchester, to our person or to the event. We applied for funding and administrative support and received both. In the months leading up to the conference, if I spoke about the event within the university, the response I met with was usually polite disinterest: it was to be another conference in the busy calendar of an internationally acclaimed university. Once the call for the conference was out, one of our biggest concerns was whether all our international delegates for the conference would be able to secure a visa for permission to enter the United Kingdom. In fact, not everybody did, and the names of delegates who were unable to attend due to travel restrictions were remembered and repeated at the conference. After the conference, I remembered the conversation I had on the safety of holding a conference on such a topic with a sense of amusement, and of relief, but also a little bit of disappointment. The university is a space that academizes speech, and the conventions of academic writing and presenting cool hot tempers: the measured speech of conference delegates, the hallowed references to scholarship, and the control of time-keeping and the chairing of sessions keeps unbridled passion in check. We sat and spoke and ate. There were several calls to make this discussion a regular occurrence, but when we parted ways at the end of the two days, after sixteen papers presented and four plenary sessions, for the moment, we had had enough of all talk concerned with Islam and psychoanalysis. Some of the attendees who had travelled far to be there spoke about their plans to tour the United Kingdom or meet friends and family residing here. My friend, if she had attended the conference, may have been bored with the lack of violence.

Some of the disparity between expectation and reality may stem from the conflation between the terms of 'Islam' and 'Muslim'. Quite naturally, the talk about Islam refers to Muslims. Yet we need to be cautious when one is used to refer to the other. In 2010, according to the Pew Research Center, Islam had a global following of 1.6 billion people, spread across the world, who self-identified as Muslims. An immediate association of 'Muslim' is with 'Arab' but as the Pew Research Center report states,

> Muslims are concentrated in the Asia–Pacific region, where six-in-ten (62%) of all Muslims reside. Many Muslims also live in the Middle East and North Africa (20%) and sub-Saharan Africa (16%). The remainder of the world's Muslim population is in Europe (3%), North America (less than 1%) and Latin America and the Caribbean (also less than 1%).
>
> *(2012: 21)*

Despite its historical origin being in present-day Saudi Arabia, the largest number of Muslims reside in Indonesia. By region, it is South Asia that has the highest number of Muslims spread between Pakistan, India, and Bangladesh. Although the language of the Quran is Arabic, by the geographical spread of the adherents of Islam, it is obvious that the first language of most Muslims in the world is not Arabic. Furthermore, the original language of the Quran is old Arabic, the parlance of which is not common amongst Arabic speakers today. To add to this, there are several internal schisms within Islam with Sunnism and Shi'ism being two major divisions (Sufism and Kharijism are two other ideological schisms within Islam), which then further break down into smaller sub-sects. Each sect differently interprets the discursive traditions of Islam. While any attempt to describe Islam in its entirety is challenging, it is very easy to state that Muslims do not share a homogenous identity. When we move to the question of subjectivity, it should be equally easy to state that a Muslim's subjectivity may be constituted through more than their ascription to a religious identity; there are the considerations of race, nationality, language, culture, political affiliations, etc. Then there are even more subjective factors such as family history, upbringing, and personal experience. The intersection between what Islam 'says' and what Muslims 'do' could be witnessed at the conference as well. This is not surprising as the terms draw upon each other. So, the chapters in this edited volume constitute a collective dialogue on both Islam and Muslims.

This brings us to the topic at hand: Islamic psychoanalysis and psychoanalytic Islam. Is there an Islamic psychoanalysis? Can Islam be understood through a psychoanalytic perspective? Or does modernity keep the two apart, where psychoanalysis is a product of modernity and of European Enlightenment, and Islam is the undying monstrosity from before the dark ages and the beyond of Western civilization? The fabled 'clash of civilizations' that peaked at the turn of the millennium spun thousands of media reports asking the question: Is Islam incompatible with the West? After the violent demolition of the Twin Towers in the United States of America in 2001, followed by the NATO-backed 'War on Terror' conducted within the regions of Afghanistan, Iraq, Yemen, and Pakistan, there have been a slew of events that have invoked the trope of the clash of civilizations, too many to enumerate here, each one feeding the frenzy of imagining an imminent apocalypse. Thus, it would seem that bringing a product of modernity to a fossilized religion should meet with a great deal of resistance. After all, psychoanalysis born at the beginning of the twentieth century in Europe should be far removed from a 1,400-year-old theology originating in the Middle East.

In this book, Islam and psychoanalysis come together ... much too simply if the theories of the great divide between Islam and the West is to be believed. The possibility that modernism has already met with Islam, as it did with Christianity, is not entertained. Perhaps the opposition between Islam and the West may not be of rational science against blind faith but of Western modernity against Islamic modernity. After all, critical theory has only recently begun to venture into the Islamic discursive traditions, a growing body of work in psychoanalysis with contributions from Salman Akhtar, Fethi Benslama, Omnia El Shakry, Andrea Mura, Stefania Pandolfo, Moustapha Safouan, and Slavoj Žižek (by no means an exhaustive list).

The outcome of the encounter is uncanny. The chapters in this book attest to the fact that the encounter throws up interesting and unexpected challenges to psychoanalytic theory and practice. What this book does is start a conversation in order to demystify a subject caught between Islam and psychoanalysis, the strangeness of whom is less shocking than we thought it would be. Our contributors explore if Islam and psychoanalysis have an 'epistemological reso-nance' (El Shakry, 2017) that breathes life into an Islamic psychoanalysis and a psychoanalytic Islam. Perhaps the psychoanalytic subject and the Islamic subject find something familiar, though not the same, in the other.

References

El Shakry, O. (2017). *The Arabic Freud: Psychoanalysis and Islam in Modern Egypt*. Princeton, NJ: Princeton University Press.

Pew Research Center (2012). *The Global Religious Landscape: A Report on the Size and Distribution of the World's Major Religious Groups as of 2010*. Washington, DC: Pew Research Center. Retrieved from www.pewforum.org/2012/12/18/global-religious-landscape-exec/.

1

'THE UNITY IN HUMAN SUFFERINGS'

Cultural translatability in the context of Arab psychoanalytic cultural critique

Eva Tepest

The literature on psychoanalysis and the Arabic-speaking Islamicate,[1] or the Arabo-Islamicate world is marked by the 'assumption of an alleged incommensurability between psychoanalysis and Islam' (El Shakry 2014, 90). Hence, on the one hand, writers such as the scholar of modern Arab politics and intellectual history Joseph Massad (2009) have criticised the neo-colonial nature of psychoanalysis and its incorporation by – mostly French-based – Arab psychoanalysts (2009, 195). On the other hand, Arab psychoanalysts themselves have put forward a *resistance hypothesis*. Accordingly, Arabs (due to Islam, or the patriarchal nature of their communities) are inherently less responsive to the benefits of psychoanalysis than others (El Khayat 1993; Osseiran 2010). Ultimately, both of these arguments represent one side of the same coin: They claim the untranslatability of Islam and psychoanalysis. This assumption, far from being incidental, is based on views according to which modern notions of subjectivity are specifically and uniquely Western (El Shakry 2014, 94). Elsewhere, it has been argued that these views are often bound up with the presupposition of a secular psychoanalytic subject (Toscano 2009, 112) as opposed to the inherently religious non-Western subject in general, and the Muslim subject in particular.

In contrast, this chapter, by looking at the translatability of psychoanalysis and the Arabo-Islamicate in Arab psychoanalytic cultural critique, aligns itself with those endeavours that, presuming the universality of the unconscious (El Shakry 2014, 94–95; Gorelick 2009, 2015; Hartnack 1990, 2001; Homayounpour 2012; Kapila 2007; Khanna 2003), consider cultural translation as a reciprocal, multi-layered process 'through which both psychoanalysis and Islam will be forced to confront the distinct challenges that each poses to the other' (Gorelick 2009, 189). Specifically, I will suggest to what extent the study of Arab psychoanalytic cultural critique through the lens of cultural translatability will not only nuance our understanding of the status of 'culture', 'Islam' and 'psychoanalysis', but also generate knowledge on the distinctions and transgressions between couplets such as psychoanalysis/religion, religion/the secular, religion/culture.

In order to accomplish this, I will begin by tracing the emergence of Arab psychoanalytic cultural critique from within Arab contemporary thought. Second, I will discuss *cultural translatability* from the interdisciplinary perspective of the social sciences, the humanities and psychoanalysis. In the main part of this chapter, I will discuss the reciprocal epistemological resonances of studying Arab psychoanalytic cultural critique through the lens of cultural translatability by considering the multiple ramifications at the conceptual field defined by the conjunction of religion, culture, science and psychoanalysis and pointing towards the crucial importance of considering cultural translation as always embedded in the concrete social reality of power. I will argue that focusing on the collapse of distinctions (identity) as well as the persistence of boundaries (difference) is essential for any study of 'Islamic psychoanalysis/psychoanalytic Islam'. Hence, I will offer some methodological guidelines for studying psychoanalysis in the context of the Arabo-Islamicate.

'All of its culture became Salafist': Arab psychoanalytic cultural critique post-1967

Arab cultural critique, according to Lebanese philosopher Elizabeth Kassab in her seminal work *Contemporary Arab Thought: Cultural Critique in Comparative Perspective* (2010) is deeply marked by the paradigm shift of the 1967 Arab defeat by Israel, in the wake of which she attests to a shift of focus from a united front against colonialism to self-reflexivity and criticism (2010, 73).[2] This shift – brought about by the apparent failure of the pan-Arab nationalistic project and the ensuing demise of the Arab left – led to a focus on questions of cultural identity. According to Kassab, these concepts are often embedded in a nostalgic and essentialising framing of identity, 'eclipsing to a great extent the political aspect of the malaise and privileging identity issues over questions of critique' (2010, 115). Against this authenticist turn of Arab thought in the 1970s and 1980s, which she identifies with the rise of the Islamist movements,[3] Kassab makes a case for those radical thinkers who urge a 'radicalization of critique' (Kassab 2010, 2; see also Ajami 1992) by employing a historicising, contextualising framing of identity. Among them is the Syrian translator and intellectual Georges Tarabishi. His cultural critique, being distinctly psycho-analytic, differs from most of his contemporaries in that it addresses the reactions to 1967 not merely in terms of the evolution of political thought, but rather in terms of its psychological effects. He argues that Gamal 'Abd al-Nassers defeat in 1967 and his death in 1970 inflicted a 'terrible narcissistic wound upon the Arab world' (*blessure narcissique terrible du monde arabe*) (Zoueïn and De Rochegonde 2004, 93). This represented the second stage in the 'neurosis of the Arab world' (*névrose du monde arabe*), the first being the shock of colonialism (2004, 93). As a result, Arabs – particularly male intellectuals – turned to the consolation promised by Islamic ideologies of tradition (*turāt*) and authenticity (Tarabishi 1991).[4] It was like the "'fall of the Father", a symbolic Father. [...] The Arab world, the Arab way, was completely dismantled, and all of its culture became Salafist' (*C'était comme la «chute du Père», d'un Père symbolique [...]. Le monde arabe, la rue arabe, a été totalement défait et toute la culture devint salafiste*) (Zoueïn and De Rochegonde 2004, 93).

According to Tarabishi's diagnosis, regression replaced the work of mourning[5] as the formation of the Arab subject became deeply compromised by neurosis.[6]

Tarabishi and his contemporaries continued the earlier project of Arab secular critique by addressing Islam not as a faith, but as a cultural formation and socio-political project.[7] It is against the backdrop of the history of Arab thought and practice post-1967 that not only Tarabishi's works, but the remainder of the texts that constitute Arab psychoanalytic cultural critique need to be understood. In the following, I identify these by the following characteristics (1) an engagement with Arabo-Islamicate culture *as one's own*, (2) an embeddedness within a psychoanalytic epistemology, (3) an analysis that takes phenomena such as identity or religion as historically, socially and culturally bound.

Houria Abdelouahed is a French-Moroccan psychoanalyst, translator and philosopher. She is currently an associate professor at Université Paris Diderot, and has, in addition to several other works, among them translations of works by the Syrian poet Adonis, published two monographs on questions of femininity in Islam, *Figures du Féminin en Islam* (2012), and *Les Femmes du Prophète* (2016).

Fethi Benslama likewise is a professor at Université Paris Diderot, where he directs the psychoanalytic studies programme. Born and raised in Tunis, he moved to France in 1972 where he has been practising psychoanalysis ever since 1987. He has published extensively on questions of what he termed the 'clinique of the exile', culturalism, Islam, violence and gender. Among his recent monographs are *Psychoanalysis and the Challenge of Islam*, first published in French in 2002, and *Un Furieux Désir de Sacrifice: Le Surmusulman* (2016).

Rafah Nached has spent most of her life in Syria, where she became the first practising psychoanalyst and established a psychoanalytic training programme. After being incarcerated by the Syrian regime in 2011, she emigrated to France shortly after. Nached reads Lacan's *jouissance* against ideas of Sufi mysticism. To the best of my knowledge, only a small collection of her essays have been published in the French volume *La Psychanalyse en Syrie* (2012).

Georges Tarabishi was a Syrian translator and intellectual. He has translated more than 200 books, among them most of the Freudian oeuvre, into Arabic. This is how he spent most of the Lebanese civil war before eventually emigrating to France, where he passed away in 2016. At the end of the 1970s and the beginning of the 1980s, he published a range of Arabic monographs in psycho-analytic literary criticism (e.g. 1981, 1983). Throughout, he investigates the question of masculinity, ideology and the status of the intellectual in Arab cultural life and literary production.

Between identity and difference: conceptualising cultural translatability

In epistemological terms, this research takes the discussion of *cultural translation* as a point of departure. Extensively discussed in fields such as translation studies, the social sciences (particularly migration studies), postcolonial studies, anthropology and the study of culture,[8] cultural scientist and literary scholar Doris Bachmann-Medick (2016) defines *cultural translation* firstly as 'the translation of cultures as well as translation between cultures' (2016, 175). Furthermore, she goes on to demonstrate how scholars have transcended this extension of the object field to inter- and intra-cultural processes by assessing the 'translatory character' of cultural objects themselves (2016, 180): 'Culture is no longer viewed as a special "original" life-world, but as an impure, blended, "hybrid" stratification of meaning and experience' (2016, 182). From this follows

> a non-dichotomous model of translation that no longer assumes fixed poles but stresses the reciprocity of transfers as well as the state of always having been translated [. . .]. Conceived in this way, translation resists the seeming purity of concepts such as culture, identity, tradition and religion and shows all claims of identity to be deceptive because identity is always infused with the other.
>
> *(2016, 181)*

Cultural objects are inherently ambiguous. They are *reciprocally constitutive*, while at the same time remaining *insurmountably distinct*. Through the workings of distinctions, differences between semantically inter-dependent cultural objects are established. Inevitably, these acts of distinction (drawing a boundary) bring miscomprehension (irritation/collision/friction) and conflation (transgression) in its wake (cf. Bachmann-Medick 2016, 181).[9] This understanding of the translatory character of cultural objects is grounded in the paradigm of *cultural translatability*. Developed as a counter-concept to the alleged *untranslatability* of cultures (cf. Samuel Huntington's proverbial 'clash of civilizations' hypothesis), it claims the 'mutuality' governing cross-cultural relations (cf. Iser 1994, 8). According to Bachmann-Medick (2016), this paradigm can be based on the deconstructivist vantage point of the 'differential character of [all] language' (2016, 181) or studied from the action-analytical perspective of 'the practical manner in which interdependencies and reciprocal influences are dealt with' (2016, 181).

I argue that engaging with Arab psychoanalytic cultural critique allows for an important complication of cultural translatability as conceived in the social sciences and humanities. In *Figures du Feminine*, French-Moroccan psychoanalyst Houria Abdelouahed, starting with the question of the *Text* in Muslim culture, that is, the Quran and Hadith and classical interpretations thereof, goes on the meditate upon the question of translation. Briefly speaking, she operates with the idea of a real experience, which, once lived through, is irretrievably lost. Any subsequent act of signification, then, is separated from this brute experience, nevertheless bearing its trace. 'Signification happens in the aftermath that transforms the brute experience into a signifying experience' (*Car ca ce signifie dans ce temps de l'àpres-coup qui transforme l'expérience brute en experience signifiante*) (Abdelouahed 2012, 163). The subject can only address the subconscious in a language that is socially, culturally and historically bound, that is imperfect. Translation, on a subconscious, textual or collective level, manifests the desire to bridge the insurmountable gap between the contingent frame of reference and 'that residue of the human experience that sticks to the margins' (Gorelick 2015, 4). Any translation, while indispensable for semiotic exchange, is bound to fail.

According to Abdelouahed, the translation of finite texts is related to translations within cultural communities and translation as individual, subconscious process: 'No trace, no writing, without the trace of the sexual' (*Nulle trace, nulle écriture sans la trace de sexuel*) (164). These dimensions, in her work, are not mere facets of the same metaphor, but equivalents of a similar structuring momentum, and variously intertwined. Notably, her analysis hinges on psychoanalytic writings as well as Arabic textual tradition. Freud, in *Moses and Monotheism* (1955 (1939)), describes psychic life as dialectically related to the development of the religious community. It is the individual's denial, suppression, renunciation, or repression of the erotic and aggressive instincts – their translation – that shapes the culture at large and vice versa.[10] Similarly, in Arabic, the word *tarǧama*, a loanword from Aramaic, is equally fluid and points out various 'acts of interpretation in which the self, as interpreter, is heavily implicated' (Mehrez 2012, 7). Specifically, *tarǧama* not only signifies translating 'from one language to the other [. . .], but also to write the other (as in biography: *tarjama*), and to write one's self (as in autobiography: *tarjama dhatiya*)' (2012, 7). Abdelouahed's discussion of translation suggests the complication of cultural translation through psychoanalytic cultural critique by indicating not only the translatory character of cultural objects (their always having been translated), but their being bound up with the translatory character of humans and therefore, infused with desire and pain.

As a consequence, cultural translatability, in this chapter, is understood as the analytic focus on the hybridity and complexity of cultural agents, practices, concepts and institutions. What may the discussion of the status of psychoanalysis, culture and religion in psychoanalytic cultural critique tell us about their translatability? Which defining processes of distinction, irritation and conflation are thrown into relief? What methodological implications for the study of psychoanalysis and the Arabo-Islamicate follow?

'The unity in human sufferings': the cultural translatability of psychoanalysis and the Arabo-Islamicate, part 1

The notion of establishing religion as a cultural formation so prevalent among Arab psychoanalytic cultural critique resonates with the central works of psychoanalytic cultural critique, specifically Sigmund Freud's writings on religion (1928 (1927);

1955 (1939); 1962 (1930)).[11] These mirror his ambiguous stance towards religion, which he addresses in its importance for the formation of culture. Charged with 'the task of solving the riddles of the universe and of reconciling us to the sufferings of life' (1928 (1927), 15), religious belief is but a fantasy that is supposed to shelter us from civilisation and its discontents, namely the unpleasure released due to the cultural control of our aggressive and erotic drives (Freud 1962 (1930)). On the other hand, as Freud grew increasingly sceptical towards human nature and modern progress, he stood more and more in awe of the achievements of religion in general and his native Judaism in particular. This is especially at the core of *Moses and Monotheism* (1955 (1939)), Freud's very last monograph before his death in his London exile, and 'his most enigmatic book' (Benslama and Nancy 2009, 76). In this somewhat erratic and meandering collection of essays, his affection for the cultural manifestations and achievements of monotheism is obvious. For instance, he claims that Judaism, for its success in maintaining culture's repressive workings by upholding a rigid mono-theism, has achieved the highest cultural refinement.

As has been demonstrated, according to Freud, religion has always had a psychological function in the cultural formation of human civilisation (1955 (1939)). In an interesting twist, while he acknowledged its importance, he hopes that humanity, with the advance of scientific progress and reasoning, would eventually dispose of religion (Freud 1928 (1927), 22). In hindsight and against the backdrop of the critique of secularisation theories (Asad 2003; Casanova 2011), it seems safe to say, especially in today's world, that religious sentiment still constitutes cultural organisation and allegedly secular public culture remains, structurally speaking, soaked in religious sentiment. In *The Triumph of Religion* (2013), a talk given by Jacques Lacan to Italian journalists in 1974, mirroring Freud's argument, he argues that religion, since it can give meaning to science's introduction of 'all kinds of distressing things into each person's life' (2013, 64) expands in proportion to the growth of science. Historically, 'in spite of appearing to be bound up with atheism, far from secularising the world, the advent of modernity will certainly entail in the future a new triumph of religion' (Chiesa 2015, 59). This is a specific psychoanalytic reading of religion vis-à-vis the secular challenges which tend to relegate religious belief to the private sphere and assume neutrality of the public domain (science, politics, etc.). However, it is in one important regard that Lacan shies away from his own argument: Like Freud, he radically opposed psychoanalysis to religion (Chiesa 2015; Gorelick 2015).[12]

Against the theoretical backdrop of cultural translation developed above, I argue that this distinction, much like any modern distinction, necessarily produces a set of contradictions that are of interest to this present endeavour: If everything has always been translated, this surely must hold true for psychoanalysis vis-à-vis religion, here Islam.[13] In the context of Arabo-Islamicate societies, Islamic knowledge production has been used alongside psychoanalytic concepts and practices to meet individual needs or societal shortcomings (Pandolfo 2009, 2017). In practice, the insistence on the analyst (or patient, for that matter) being neutral (read: secular) not only seems like analytical fraud (since the status of neutrality is never a given, but rather an immensely powerful act) but detrimental to the therapeutic progress. This is exemplified by the professional experiences of a Britain-based therapist who describes herself as unanimously identified as religious because of her headscarf. She explains how, in one case, she was convinced that this identification seemed necessary for gaining the trust of a fellow Muslim patient and thus, the success of the whole therapeutic endeavour. In contrast, in another instant, while she was treating a homosexual man who had been forced to flee from his native Iran, she feared him to be particularly reluctant towards her or even re-traumatised upon being faced with the religious garment. In any case, delegating religious belief to the private realm in the context of psychoanalysis creates a blind spot that obfuscates important elements of the therapeutic condition.

On a more abstract level, Arab psychoanalytic cultural critique aims for a synthesis of psychoanalysis and Islamic knowledge: Syrian psychoanalyst Rafah Nached (2012) insists that Muslim mysticism, irreducible to neither pure ecstasy nor Al-Qaida (2012, 25), was not founded on 'dogmatic law' (*l'ordre du dogme*) (2012, 25) but on a type of 'philosophical reasoning that engulfed the human experience in its pure subjectivity' (*la pensée philosophique que envelope l'experience humaine dans sa pure subjectivité* (2012, 25). Hence, by studying the Sufi poet al-Hallağ, 'the Muslim mystic who was crucified in the name of truth' (*ce mystique musulman crucifié au nom de la verité*) (2012, 34), she demonstrates how both psychoanalysis and Sufism aim at assisting the subject to find her personal, truthful path: 'That is the victory of life over death' (*C'est la victoire de la vie sur la mort*) (2012, 35). Likewise, Abdelouahed, at times in tandem with Nached and others, engages with Sufi mystic Ibn 'Arabī (2012, 34) to counter-balance what Nached describes as a refusal in Arab society to respect any deviation from the law of the collective (2012, 35). In writing, Nached and Abdelouahed question the usefulness of the distinction between psychoanalysis and religion, that is: their untranslatability. In these instances, Arab psychoanalytic cultural critique unsettles the 'dovetailing of psychoanalysis with secular ideologies' (Kabesh 2017) and encourages a rethinking of psychoanalytic practice and thought as inevitably bound up with religious meaning and belief.

It is from the vantage point of Freud's ground-breaking studies of religion as a cultural phenomenon that more important impulses for Arab psychoanalytic cultural critique emanate: this time regarding the translatability of distinct religious formations, with a particular focus on Islam. Psychoanalytically speaking, it seems that a given culture A, or religious formation, may differ considerably from a given culture B in the way that religion – this symptom of the psycho-cultural – is configured. However, at second glance, this difference – leading to the initial incomprehensibility within the translation process – emanates from the same human needs and organising principles.

> There is a unity in human sufferings. What differs from one subject to the
> other is the specific expression of that pain, a language that is marked by

culture according to her geographic situation, historic experience and the heritage of her roots (*Il existe une unité dans les souffrances humaines, et ce qui diffère d'un sujet à l'autre s'incarne à travers l'expression de cette douleur, une langue qui se colore de tons culturels et civilisationnels divers allant de pair avec sa situation géographique, son experience historique et l'héritage de ses racines*).

(Nached 2012, 28)

Ultimately, even belief systems that prominently claim their untranslatability are very similar on a structural level. This is what Jean-Luc Nancy and Fethi Benslama in their exchange on 'Translations of Monotheism' seem to claim when they point to the similarities between the three monotheisms: 'Judeo-Christianity, and then Islam, did not fall from the sky [. . .] but were products, called for or enabled by a general state of the culture' (Benslama and Nancy 2009, 77). This state of the culture, in Nancy's reading of Freud's *Moses and Monotheism* is a melancholic one: 'A great sadness seems to have taken hold of the people of the Mediterranean' (2009, 78).

The discussion of the status of psychoanalysis, culture and religion in contemporary Arab psychoanalytic cultural critique from the perspective of Freud and Lacan's classic psychoanalytic cultural critique, as well as cultural translatability, has demonstrated that psychoanalysis, far from being religion's secular, neutral antagonist, is infused with religion, and vice versa. On this basis, the productive potential of Islamicising (or: de-colonising) psychoanalysis and psychoanalysing religion has been suggested. Furthermore, I have claimed the translatability of Islam vis-à-vis other religions or different symptomatic manifestations of the modern psycho-cultural. In more abstract terms, I have established similarity rather than distinction with regards to the cultural translation in question. Which consequences does this privileging of identity over difference entail? And how can we re-enter difference into our psychoanalysis/Islam equation?

The politics of difference: the cultural translatability of psychoanalysis and the Arabo-Islamicate, part 2

The ethical consequences of vouching for the cultural translatability of psychoanalysis and the Arabo-Islamicate are immense. Indeed, conceiving of a type of Islamicate psychoanalysis counteracts the deeply Islamophobic notion of the incomprehensibility of Islam. By defying disparateness and embracing analogy, looking at the collapse of distinctions is not only analytically but also politically indispensable.

Inversely, the negligence of the differential character of any signifying experience, as argued above, is not only analytically objectionable. Rather, as scholars of translation studies have pointed out, the paradigm of 'transnational translationalism' (Bachmann-Medick 2016, 183) with its 'claims of identity, standardization tendencies and essential determinations' (2016, 184) often fosters the interests of the economically powerful while being to the detriment of those who are already exposed and vulnerable. In contrast, as put forward by Homi Bhaba, '[a]ny transnational cultural study must "translate", each time locally and specifically, what decentres and subverts this transnational globality, so that it does not become enthralled by the new global technologies of ideological transmission and cultural consumption' (Bhabha 1994, 241). In the case of the Islamicate, collapsing the myriad and often disparate signifying experiences that are constitutive into one establishes Islam as a globalised brand (cf. Roy 2006). Thereby nullifying cultural, economic, ethnic and religious differences, 'Islam inc'. not only buys into the necessity of commensurability grounded in the needs of corporate transnational capitalism (Teegen and Teegen 2000), but also obfuscates the ideological project of players such as the Saudi Arabian regime, which pursues its own interest in globally promoting its specific brand of a pure (neutral) but effectively Saudi (and Arabic) Islam.

For these two reasons, any study of cultural translation always needs to acknowledge that which remains untranslatable, unwieldy and impenetrable, 'that residue of the human experience' (Gorelick 2015, 4) *and* the textual: to lay bare the discontinuity of translation, to embrace the politics of difference. Whether to privilege the reciprocally constitutive character of cultural objects, or their status as insurmountably distinct, needs to be aligned with the nexus of power that any translational act is embedded in. Here, again, debates on cultural translation have proven useful. Not the least due to their origin in postcolonial critique, these debates are often concerned with 'remapping and critically recharting the center and the periphery' (Bachmann-Medick 2016, 241) vis-à-vis the 'unequal power relations of world society' (2016, 182). Hence, deliberations that emanate from the postcolonial condition of any act of cultural translation allow me to account for the actualisation of translatability in the modern setting of power and culture. Hence, the methodological specification of cultural translation, in this research, requires 'sustained efforts of contextualisation' (Ramstedt 2017, 50).

By relating the textual level to the structural level – that is, questions of power, social norms, institutionalisation, and subjection – any analysis of psychoanalysis and the Arabo-Islamicate must address the following set of sub-questions: What are the socio-political events prompting the transposition of psychoanalytic practices, institutions and concepts? What are the history and connotations of the terms and practices to which they are transposed? Who authors and controls the translation of psychoanalysis, what socio-political interests are involved? What are the parallel and/or overlapping translation chains – not the least within the Global South – and their possible interaction? What is lost and what is gained in the translation process?[14] How am I myself as a researcher (intellectually, emotionally, socio-economically) implicated in the translation of psychoanalysis?

In this way, an equal and mindful conversation between psychoanalysis and the Arabo-Islamicate may be facilitated, a conversation that will challenge and enrich both, and confound comfortable attributions while being mindful of either one's respective inaccessibility. Here, as elsewhere, enduring contradiction – in this case, the indissoluble tension between identity and difference – this deeply ethical position, will confront the interrogating subject with a trace of her own truth, a glimpse of the other and the commonality of desire and pain, '[t]he unity in human sufferings' (Nached 2012, 28), in the process.

Notes

1 The term *Islamicate*, first introduced by Marshall Hodgson (1974), designates the penetration of regions by the 'social and cultural complex historically associated with Islam and the Muslims, both among Muslims themselves and even when found among non-Muslims' (1974, 59), without necessarily referring to Islam as faith or religious doctrine. Hence, in the following, it designates a distinct cultural formation.

2 Scholars unanimously agree on the paramount significance of the 1967 defeat for Arab societies and its intellectual production. As a consequence, all of the surveys on contemporary Arab thought take 1967 as their starting point. See Abu-Rabi' (2004); Ajami (1992); Binder (1988); Hatina and Schumann (2015); Issa (1990).

3 For a similar perspective, see e.g. Ajami (1992); Binder (1988); Salem (1996).

4 Among Tarabishi's oeuvre, his 1991 study on the relation of Arab intellectuals to *turāṯ* ('heritage') in the wake of 1967 is his most explicit account of the consequences of Arab defeat on Arab culture. However, all of his lifelong intellectual work – concerned with the ideologies that hinder the development of Arab culture, among them patriarchy and Islamism – has been deeply informed by the events of 1967 (Zoueïn and De Rochegonde 2004, 93).

5 In psychoanalysis, mourning is the healthy psychic reaction of the ego to the lost of a loved object during which that object is released and replaced. In contrast, melancholia is a process during which the ego pathologically identifies with the lost object (Freud 1922).

6 Tarabishi's analysis bears a resemblance to what Sadik Al-Azm, in his polemic 1968 monograph *Self-Criticism After the Defeat*, describes as 'the logic of exoneration and the evasion of responsibility and accountability' in reaction to the psychological trauma of 1967 (2011, 40). Notably, Al-Azm tackles the anti-semitic structure and content that characterises 'the exaggeration of [Zionism's] power and influence, to the extent of ascribing it overwhelming mythical powers that make it the mistress of capitalism, socialism, and the course of history at the same time' (61).

7 This modern, secular critique was first developed during the so-called Arab 'renaissance' (*nahḍa*) from the mid-nineteenth century onwards. For the continuities (and discontinuities) between (pre-1930s) Arab 'liberal' thought and the post-1967 period see the contributions in Hanssen (2016) and Hatina and Schumann (2015). See on the problematics of translating *nahḍa* as 'renaissance' specifically Recker's contribution to the latter.

8 For a concise overview, see Ramstedt (2017). Otherwise, Backmann-Medick's work is indispensable (2006, 2009, 2012, 2013, 2016). Notably, paradigms associated with cultural translation are often closely linked with what has been termed the 'translational turn' in the social sciences and the study of culture (Bachmann-Medick 2016, 175).

9 This resonates with what Hussein Agrama (2012), conceptualising the distinctions that are put into place by secularism and their concomitant contradictions, has termed *secular power*.

10 On the one hand, in the Freudian understanding, culture necessitates a suppression of the erotic and aggressive instincts that effects the translation of the individual from the state of the child to that of the adult. This process results in the release of psychic unpleasure. In those cases in which the psyche rejects the release of unpleasure, the 'failure of translation' results in neurosis (Young 2014, 377). It is in much of his clinical work that Freud wanted to release his patients from neurosis and other symptoms resulting from of a repression of the instincts. Psychoanalysis is thus an emancipatory project that tries to re-write the individual's truth and release it from

'civilization and its discontent'. On the other hand, culture, even though causing unpleasure and, in extreme cases, neurosis, seems necessary in order to provide for the stability of human societies, cultural development, and the human psyche. 'Culture is a process [...] for the individual where each one learns to control and/or displace their erotic and aggressive drives'.

11 These works are frequent points of reference for Arab psychoanalytic cultural critique.

12 To be sure, in Lacan's view, psychoanalysis, like religion, is 'a historical product of science, a symptomatic discontent of scientific civilization' (Chiesa 2015, 59). As such, he was aware of this danger of psychoanalysis becoming 'against his will, a form of meaningful religion' (2015, 60). However, by confronting the individual with the truth of her (and the world's) insufficiency ('the real'), in contrast to the neurotic illusion religion has to offer, is religion's antagonist (Lacan 2013, 65–67).

13 Note that likewise, Western scholars have described psychoanalysis' religious connotations. For an example, see Foucault's famous critique of confession, which is central to the first volume of *The History of Sexuality* (1978): Accordingly, psychoanalysis, as *science sexualis* 'caused the rituals of confession to function within the norms of scientific regularity' (65).

14 Cf. Ramstedt (2017).

References

Abdelouahed, Houria. 2012. *Figures du Féminin en Islam*. Paris: PUF.

Abdelouahed, Houria. 2016. *Les Femmes du Prophète*. Paris: Seuil.

Abu-Rabi', Ibrahim M. 2004. *Contemporary Arab Thought: Studies in Post-1967 Arab Intellectual History*. London: Pluto Press.

Agrama, Hussein Ali. 2012. *Questioning Secularism: Islam, Sovereignty: and the Rule of Law in Modern Egypt*. Chicago, IL: University of Chicago Press.

Ajami, Fouad. 1992. *The Arab Predicament: Arab Political Thought and Practice since 1967*. Cambridge: Cambridge University Press.

Al-Azm, Sadik. 2011. *Self-Criticism after the Defeat*, translated by George Stergios. London: Saqi Books.

Asad, Talal. 2003. *Formations of the Secular: Christianity, Islam, Modernity*. Stanford, CA: Stanford University Press.

Bachmann-Medick, Doris. 2006. 'Meanings of Translation in Cultural Anthropology'. In *Translating Others*, edited by Theo Hermans, pp. 33–42. Manchester: St. Jerome.

Bachmann-Medick, Doris. 2009. 'Introduction: The Translational Turn'. *Translation Studies* 2 (1): 2–16.

Bachmann-Medick, Doris. 2012. 'Translation: A Concept and Model for the Study of Culture'. In *Travelling Concepts for the Study of Culture*, edited by Birgit Neumann and Ansgar Nünning, pp. 23–43. Berlin: De Gruyter

Bachmann-Medick, Doris. 2013. 'The Translational Turn'. In *Handbook of Translation Studies*, edited by Yves Gambier and Luc Van Doorslaer. Amsterdam: John Benjamins Publishing.

Bachmann-Medick, Doris. 2016. 'The Translational Turn'. In *Cultural Turns: New Orientations in the Study of Culture*, edited by Doris Bachmann-Medick, pp. 175–209. Berlin: De Gruyter

Benslama, Fethi. 2016. *Un Furieux Désir De Sacrifice: Le Surmusulman*. Paris: Seuil.

Benslama, Fethi, and Jean-Luc Nancy. 2009. 'Translations of Monotheisms'. *S* 2 (1): 74–89.

Bhabha, Homi K. 1994. *The Location of Culture*. London: Routledge.

Binder, Leonard. 1988. *Islamic Liberalism: A Critique of Development Ideologies*, translated by Adam Blauhut. Berlin: University of Chicago Press.

Casanova, José. 2011. 'The Secular, Secularizations, Secularisms'. In *Rethinking Secularism*, edited by Craig Calhoun, Mark Juergensmeyer and Jonathan Van Antwerpen, pp. 54–74. Oxford: Oxford University Press.

Chiesa, Lorenzo. 2015. 'Psychoanalysis, Religion, Love'. *Crisis & Critique* 2 (1): 56–71.

El Khayat, Ghita. 1993. 'Psychanalyse Au Maroc: Résistances Culturelles'. *Revue française de psychanalyse* 57 (3): 879–882.

El Shakry, Omnia. 2014. 'The Arabic Freud: The Unconscious and the Modern Subject'. *Modern Intellectual History* 11 (1): 89–118.

Foucault, Michel. 1978. *The History of Sexuality: Volume 1*. New York: Pantheon.

Freud, Sigmund. 1922. 'Mourning and Melancholia'. *The Journal of Nervous and Mental Disease* 56 (5): 543–545.

Freud, Sigmund. 1928 (1927). *The Future of an Illusion*, translated by Trevor W. D. Robson-Scott. London: Hogarth Press and Institute of Psycho-Analysis.

Freud, Sigmund. 1955 (1939). *Moses and Monotheism*, translated by Katherine Jones. Letchworth: Garden City Press.

Freud, Sigmund. 1962 (1930). *Civilization and Its Discontents*, translated by James Strachey. New York: Norton.

Gorelick, Nathan. 2009. 'Dialogues: Fethi Benslama & the Translation of the Impossible in Islam & Psychoanalysis'. *UMBR(a): Journal for the Unconscious* (Islam): 188–193.

Gorelick, Nathan. 2015. 'Translating the Islamicate Symptom: A Review Essay of Doing Psychoanalysis in Tehran and Lacan and Religion'. *SCTIV Review.* 1–13.

Hanssen, Jens, ed 2016. *Arabic Thought beyond the Liberal Age: Towards an Intellectual History of the Nahda*. Cambridge: Cambridge University Press.

Hartnack, Christiane. 1990. 'Vishnu on Freud's Desk: Psychoanalysis in Colonial India'. *Social Research* 57 (4): 921–949.

Hartnack, Christiane. 2001. *Psychoanalysis in Colonial India*. New Delhi: Oxford University Press.

Hatina, Meir, and Christoph Schumann. 2015. *Arab Liberal Thought after 1967: Old Dilemmas, New Perceptions*. New York: Palgrave Macmillan.

Hodgson, Marshall G.S. 1974. *The Venture of Islam, Vol. 1: The Classical Age of Islam*. Chicago, IL: University of Chicago Press.

Homayounpour, Gohar. 2012. *Doing Psychoanalysis in Tehran*. Cambridge, MA: MIT Press.

Iser, Wolfgang. 1994. 'On Translatability'. *Surfaces* 4: 5–13.

Issa, J. Boullata. 1990. *Trends and Issues in Contemporary Arab Thought*. Albany, NY: State University of New York Press.

Kabesh, Amal Treacher. 2017. 'Itjihad: The Necessity of Thinking Anew'. *Islamic Psychoanalysis/Psychoanalytic Islam*, Manchester: The College of Psychoanalysis, 26 June 2017.

Kapila, Shruti. 2007. 'The "Godless" Freud and His Indian Friends: An Indian Agenda for Psychoanalysis'. In *Psychiatry and Empire*, edited by Sloan Mahone and Megan Vaughan, pp. 124–152. Basingstoke: Palgrave Macmillan.

Kassab, Elizabeth Suzanne. 2010. *Contemporary Arab Thought: Cultural Critique in Comparative Perspective*. New York: Columbia University Press.

Khanna, Ranjana. 2003. *Dark Continents: Psychoanalysis and Colonialism*. Durham, NC: Duke University Press.

Lacan, Jacques. 2013. *The Triumph of Religion Preceded by Discourse to Catholics*, translated by B. Fink. Cambridge: Polity.

Massad, Joseph. 2009. 'Psychoanalysis, Islam, and the Other of Liberalism'. *Psychoanalysis and History* 11 (2): 193–208.

Mehrez, Samia. 2012. 'Translating Revolution: An Open Text'. In *Translating Egypt's Revolution: The Language of Tahrir*, edited by Samia Mehrez, pp. 1–23. Oxford: Oxford University Press.

Nached, Rafah. 2012. *Psychanalyse en Syrie*. Paris: APJL et Érès.

Osseiran, Mouzayan. 2010. 'De Quelques Difficultés de la Pratique Psychanalytique au Liban'. *Topique* 1: 97–103.

Pandolfo, Stefania. 2009. '"Soul Choking": Maladies of the Soul, Islam, and the Ethics of Psychoanalysis'. *UMBR(a): A Journal of Unconscious* 1: 71–103.

Pandolfo, Stefania. 2017. *Knot of the Soul: Madness, Psychiatry, Islam*. Chicago, IL: University of Chicago Press.

Ramstedt, Martin. 2017. 'On the Cultural Translation of Traveling Legal Concepts, Organizational FrameWorks and Procedures: The Case of Indigenous Rights in Indonesia'. *Translation and Translanguaging in Multilingual Contexts* 3 (1): 47–63.

Roy, Olivier. 2006. *Globalized Islam: The Search for a New Ummah*. New York: Columbia University Press.

Salem, Paul. 1996. 'The Rise and Fall of Secularism in the Arab World'. *Middle East Policy* 4 (3): 147–161.

Tarabishi, Georges. 1981. *Ar-Ramzīa al-mar'a fi-r-riwāya al-'arabīya* [Woman's Symbolic in the Arab Novel]. Beirut: Dār aṭ-ṭalaīya li-ṭ-ṭibāʿa wa-n-našr.

Tarabishi, Georges. 1983. *Ar-Ruǧūla wa 'īdūlūǧīya ar-ruǧūla fī-r-riwāya al-'arabīya* [Masculinity and Patriarchal Ideology in the Arab Novel]. Beirut: Dār aṭ-ṭalaīya li-ṭ-ṭibāʿa wa-n-našr.

Tarabishi, Georges. 1991. *Al-Mutaqqafūn Al-'arab Wa-T-Turāt: Tahlīl an-Nafsī Li-'aṣāb Ǧamā 'ī* [Arab Intellectuals and Their Heritage: Analysis of a Collective Paranoia]. London: Riyyad el-Rayyes.

Teegen, Hildy, and Marta Teegen. 2000. 'Globalization's Impact on the Marking/Marketing of Islam'. In *Rethinking Globalization (S)*, edited by Preet S. Aulakh, pp. 218–237. London: Springer.

Toscano, Alberto. 2009. 'Fanaticism as Fantasy: Notes on Islam, Psychoanalysis & Political Philosophy'. *UMBR(a): The Journal of the Unconscious* (Islam): 105–125.

Young, Robert JC. 2014. 'Freud on Cultural Translation'. In *A Concise Companion to Psychoanalysis, Literature, and Culture*, edited by Laura Marcus and Ankhi Mukherjee. Chichester: Wiley Blackwell.

Zoueïn, Josette, and Thierry De Rochegonde. 2004. 'Rencontre Avec un Traducteur en Arabe, Georges Tarabichi'. *Che vuoi?* 21: 93–99. doi: 10.3917/chev.021.0093.

2

ISLAM

A manifest or latent content?

Maryam Aslzaker and Forough Edrissi

Just as a Christian's actions are not necessarily based on Christian principles, a Muslim's actions, similarly, could not be solely judged by Islamic principles. Each religion takes a certain form in each culture. Each country, with its unique culture, modifies particular narrations of religion like Islam in its own specific ways. As a result, a Muslim's way of practicing Islam might be closely related to the specific culture rather than Islam itself. We think of religion and culture in a dialectical fashion, religion transforms culture and culture transforms religion.

There seems to be a general supposition that psychoanalytic concepts cannot go together with the essential ideas of Islam. A glance at the history, however, reveals that Christianity and Judaism had their own struggles with fanaticism. Islam, as a new recurrent religion, seems to be struggling with the same problems which other religions have mostly but not entirely overcome. It seems to us, at the manifest content level, Islam is considered to be a religion that inherently contradicts the psychoanalytic principle, but the latent content is about how the current political culture is transforming Islam. In other words, does Islam function as a simple residue of cultural and political issues or as latent content, Whose associations are important for interpreting the dreams of Islam, Islamophobia and culture of Muslims? In this regard, the present study tries to investigate the interaction and dialogue between psychoanalysis and Islam in Iran as an Islamic country with its various subcultures.

There is a dominant and legitimate view of the hostility between Freudian psychoanalysis and religious thinking, and a longstanding suspicion of psycho-analysis is evident within the Islamic context. Some of this skepticism seems to derive from the common assumption that psychoanalysis propagates secularism, from the writing of Freud on religion, and from the hostility of theologians to Freud and psychoanalysis in particular. Akhtar (2009) stated that 'psychoanalytic thinking ... took Freud's atheism at face value and regarded psychoanalysis and religion (and mysticism and spirituality) as antagonistic' (p. 269). Besides, while religion teaches that humans have souls, 'Freud demolished this conception and denied the existence of God, the soul, the here-after and human free will' (Badri, 2002, cited in Mura, 2014).

Freud and secularization

According to Freud (1933), 'Religion is an illusion and it derives its strength from the fact that it falls in within our instinctual desires.' Freud said that God is nothing other than an idealized father figure from whom is needed faithful anticipation, protection and salvation (Benslama, 2006). Many psychoanalysts such as al-Abdul-Jabbar and al-Issa; Azhar and Varma; Sabry and Vohra; and Rassool (2016) have stated that in non-Western Muslim cultures, psychoanalysis and psychoanalytic approaches are not widely accepted as a form of therapy and counseling because some of the conceptual framework and modalities of the psychoanalytic school have a degree of incongruence with Islamic values and practices.

Freud and early analysts focused on infantile aspects of religion but disregarded the fact that religion is more complex than they allowed for. Although Freud did not refer directly to the cultural, political and ethnic issues closely related to religion, his life is deeply involved with them.

In 1925, when Freud decided to write his autobiography, he began with this: 'my parents were Jews, and I will remain a Jew too.' We should give specific attention to Freud's Jewishness. Throughout his life, Freud expressed his attachment to Jewish culture and religion and at the same time confessed his atheism. He suffered anti-Semitism and his childhood was full of such agonizing memories. Freud introduced himself as an 'atheist Jew,' someone who didn't believe in God but was clearly attached to the individual and collective past of Judaism.

Of all histories, that of the Jewish people is the most refractory to secularization because this history alone, as a national history, is considered by all to be sacred to begin with. This point was made forcefully by Karl Lowith (Olick et al., 2011). There is only one particular history—that of the Jews—which as a political history can be interpreted strictly religiously. Christians are not a historical people. Their solidarity all over the world is merely one of faith. In the Christian view, the history of salvation is no longer bound up with a particular nation but is internationalized because it is individualized. From this, it follows that the historical destiny of the Christian peoples is not a possible subject for a specifically Christian interpretation of political history, while the destiny of the Jews is a possible subject of a specifically Jewish interpretation.

Billig (1997), in the paper 'Freud and Dora: repressing an oppressed identity,' looks again at the relations between Freud and Dora, in order to show how the position of Jews in that society was not irrelevant to their conversations. Freud was not a comfortable member of his society. The description 'educated, bourgeois male' neglects a category which was central to Freud's political and social position.

He was a member of a much-discriminated minority; so was Dora. Ultimately, both Freud and Dora were driven from their society in fear of their lives. The politics of anti-Semitism, nevertheless, did not begin in Vienna with the arrival of the Nazis. When Freud and Dora met at the turn of the century, anti-Semitic parties controlled the city. At the turn of the century in Vienna, the Jewish/Christian division was central, politically, socially and culturally. It fashioned the very conditions of Freud's and Dora's lives (Billig, 1997).

In this case, does being a Jew define a religious identity or a racial and cultural one? When we began writing about this topic, we had to stop several times because we were struggling to find a way to distinguish the Islamic part of our identity from the Iranian (national) part of it. Are religion and culture separable? What are differences between Islamic and Western psychoanalysis? Is there any difference between the clients' problems who we meet in our practice and the ones who receive psychoanalytic services in the United States or Turkey? So the main question is: 'What do we talk about when we talk about Islam?'

Identity is a fundamental aspect of human beings and has been widely discussed within the scope of psychological, social and political studies. When compounded with Islam and Muslims, it becomes a much more complicated subject in the contemporary world where Muslim communities are spread widely around the globe and face xenophobia and Islamophobia. Besides this, Muslims' internal and external transformation through encounters with the West, through migration and through their historical experience of colonization, nationalism and Westernization, has left immense imprints on the diverse Muslim psyche wherever Muslims live—Asia Pacific, the Middle East and Africa—making the Muslim identity-formation question inevitably complicated (Iner and Yucel, 2015).

Edward Said's criticisms of Orientalism demonstrate how the relationship between the scholar and the subject shapes the scholarship. Said states that Orientalism is a body of theory about the 'Orient' and about Islam based on power differentials between the European scholars and their subjects (Said, 1978).

Said (1978) makes the distinction between *manifest* and *latent* Orientalism. *Manifest* Orientalism is that of scholars (for example, the works of Gibb, Lane and Westermarck), which grew and changed, and is perhaps now extinct. *Latent* Orientalism is part of folk theory and, as such, it is more likely to persist 'in the face of formal training' (Kempton, 1987).

According to Edward Said's criticisms of Orientalism, A non-Muslim will always approach the study of Islam with non-Muslim assumptions about the nature of the world, religion, and human nature. The question becomes whether a non-Muslim can study Islam without being subject to the criticism of being an Orientalist. At least to some of the more extreme critics, it seems as if any critical analysis of Islam or an Islamic society is 'Orientalism.'

Our experience in Iran, as an Islamic republic country, is more related to Said's view. Our various accounts of Islam and its similarities and dissimilarities with an Arab account, lead to different images of us as Muslim and our inner experience as a Muslim. Religion should be greatly defined in the political and cultural matrix. When we talk about psychoanalysis of a group of people, we cannot neglect anthropological perspectives.

An influential model for anthropological studies of world religions was proposed by Robert Redfield (1956). He suggested that all world religions and some local religions (i.e., Mayan religion) could be divided into a 'great tradition' and 'little tradition' (Redfield, 1956). The great tradition, the orthodox form of the cultural/religious center, is that of the urban elite. It is the religion of the reflective few and is cultivated in schools and temples and is 'consciously cultivated and handed down' (Redfield, 1956).

Great traditions have also been called 'textual traditions,' 'orthodoxy,' 'philosophical religions,' 'high traditions,' and 'universal traditions.' The little tradition is the heterodox form of the cultural/religious periphery. The little tradition incorporates many elements of local tradition and practice. The little tradition is the religion as it practiced in daily life by ordinary people (in Redfield's assessment, the largely unreflective many). The little tradition is taken for granted and is not subject to a great deal of scrutiny, refinement, or improvement (Redfield, 1956). Little traditions are also referred to by the terms 'local tradition,' 'low tradition,' and 'popular religion.'

This issue is also evident in Muslim communities. In this regard, religion should be approached in two manners in Iran; political religion as 'great tradition' and unorthodox religion fused with Iranian culture. What determines the different manifestations of religion in Iran depends on to what extent tradition is considered as the core of Islam and to what extent religion is influenced by culture.

This has 'lent a normative and cultural priority to the Middle East vis-a-vis the rest of the Muslim world' (Bowen, 1993). Ignaz Goldziher (1981) suggested as early as 1910 that it was a mistake to see Islam as a monolithic whole. Goldziher (1981) demonstrated the dynamics of diversity evident in Islam from early in its history to the time of his writing. The diversity in Islam is far more than the split between Shi'i and Sunni. The worldwide Islamic community, even within each major section, is typified by cultural diversity (Davies, 1988). Neither great nor little traditions are unified wholes. Even the little tradition of a single village is not unified (Antoun, 2014). There is individual interpretation in theology and practice involved at both levels.

If, as much contemporary scholarship suggests, we cannot use the distinction between great and little traditions, we must find some other way to deal with the diversity in Islam. Talal Asad (1986) suggests that there are three common anthropological solutions to this problem. The first suggests that there is 'no such theoretical object as Islam' and therefore there is no need to deal with the diversity between Muslim societies. The second uses Islam as a label for a 'heterogeneous collection of items, each of which has been designated Islamic by informants.' The third holds that Islam is a 'distinctive historical totality which organizes various aspects of social life' (Asad, 1986).

Although Asad (1986) sees too little value in approaches to Islam other than his own, his definition of Islam as a discursive tradition is useful. The approaches which Asad (1986) hastily rejects contribute two important reminders. The first suggests that it is a mistake to study Islam using a monolithic, essentialist conception of Islam; there may be as many forms of Islam as there are Muslims. The second suggests that it is crucial that we accept the self-identification of Muslims. If someone calls himself a Muslim and identifies certain practices as Islamic, as scholars, we must begin by accepting that statement as true and then examine how these practices differ from those of other Muslims. The question to be explored is why there are differences between various groups which identify themselves as Muslims. This is where Asad's notion of Islam as a discursive tradition is most useful. As a discursive tradition, Islam is constantly being reshaped to fit with an ever-changing world.

Here, we can use this view about the inner world. Islam is constantly being reshaped to compromise with our ever-changing mental world and conflicts. So, Islamic rules and concepts could act as day residues in the service of making social and individual dreams. Islam and being Muslim functions in various ways as manifest content by covering the hidden meaning of dreams. As 'condensation' in dreams that involves minimizing the representation of hidden urges during the dream. Multiple elements might be combined into one single image—Islam—that serves to disguise the real meaning.

In Winnicott's (1949) seminal article on the mind, he writes 'do not think that mind really exists as an entity' (p. 243), but that it is no more than a special case of the functioning of psyche-soma (p. 244). He considered the mind as a special function of psyche/soma/culture, therefore, we can say that to speak of culture is to speak of the mind, and to speak of culture is necessarily to speak of a gestalt; there is no culture without different people, and implicit in that, no notion of self except within a particular social context. Just as Winnicott could write, now rather obviously, that there is no such thing as a baby (without a mothering environment), so we can say that the self does not exist in itself. The 'I' is a cultural-imaginative construct. It is a way in which our culture attempts to organize experience into meaningful patterns (Jacobs and Capps, 1997).

So, what about religion? Can we talk about pure religion without considering it as a culturally constructed issue?

Constructing Islam from the standpoint of the West

In the West, Islam is usually associated with the Middle East and Arabs, who constitute only a minority in the global Muslim world. No wonder that most cannot distinguish Islamic religious practices from cultural practices in the context of Muslim-majority countries. There are certain areas of overlap. People's religion influences their culture, and culture influences how they practice their religion. As Richard Martin (1982) has written:

In order to know *what* the Koran means we have to ask *how* it means in Muslim culture. To answer this question we need to identify the various contexts—the textual, ritual, social and cosmological spaces—it occupies in Muslim culture.

(Martin, 1982)

Although a group of people have the same religion, they have different cultures. They eat different types of food and listen to different types of music. Their style of clothing and, of course, their languages would be different. More than likely, they would have certain cultural and traditional practices that are not derived from their religion. In the same way, Muslims from different parts of the world would have varying cultures even though they share the same religion. For many Muslims, as with people of other faiths, their cultures play a strong role in their lives. Modood (2005, 2006) notes that this heterogeneity is further complicated by political, cultural and socioeconomic factors. Modood (2003, 2005) suggests that the category 'Muslim' is as internally diverse as other group categories such as 'British' or 'Christian' (Modood 2003, 2005).

Many of the countries that are commonly called 'Islamic countries'—which in fact are merely 'Muslim-majority countries'—practice an amalgam of Islamic practices and pre-Islamic/non-Islamic practices. More than ten centuries ago, when Islam became the predominant religion of the part of the world that today has a Muslim-majority, those countries already had very distinct and very patriarchal cultures, as many remain patriarchal today. After embracing the religion of Islam, many of these cultures abandoned some of the pre-Islamic cultures and traditions, but they hang on to many others. Some of the practices that are performed by Muslims and are given an Islamic dimension are, in fact, cultural practices.

Institutional teachings of religion and the role of religion in shaping individuals' actions and daily lives may be moderated by culture. Religion may be differentially represented and psychologically experienced according to the cultural context. Culturally-shaped religious practices and values represented in cultural products may be internalized and experienced on an individual level.

In 'Why things matter: Psychoanalysis and Religion,' David Black (2011) refers to some people who make seemingly contradictory choices: to choose to marry, but retain one's lover, to become a Muslim, and yet continue to get drunk several nights of the week. Black believes that it is possible to imagine a society, where a split life can be led with consistency and significant social support. In his book, these types of character are not a 'split personality,' both selves have social support, and have, in some respects, admirable qualities. From his own experience in the consulting room, the capacity to live a radically divided life seems to show up more frequently in men than in women (Black, 2011). Freud ([1930] 1961), in *Civilization and Its Discontents*, noted: 'People become neurotic because they cannot tolerate the frustration which society imposes in the service of its cultural ideals' (Freud [1930] 1961). So, in such cases, which Black refers to, does culture determine ideals or individual religious rules or country laws? When cultural ideals and religion operate in different fields of experience, which of them dominates people's behaviors? People who define themselves as religious are prone to feel guilt (behaving against religious rules) or shame (against social ideals)? We see lots of people included in the category Black described. Is it an intra-psychic conflict or completely ego-syntonic?

A study by Sasaki and Kim (2011) showed that secondary control—an individual's spiritual growth in religion, acceptance of circumstances, and dampening of personal control—is particularly relevant in religion for European Americans, who tend to have a more independent self. On the other hand, the use of social resources may be an important part of religious coping for both collectivistic and individualistic cultures, but the value of social relationships—that is social affiliation and maintaining relationships with others in church or other believers—is especially important for East Asians, who tend to foster the interdependent self. Although religious beliefs and traditions may travel across various communities, people from different cultures may experience the same religion quite differently. For people from individualistic cultures, who are driven by goals of personal agency, the sense of control they gain from religion may help them withstand hardships. Conversely, for those from collectivistic cultures, who are motivated to maintain strong relational ties, religion may be more centered on promoting affiliation with others in the community. For people at an American evangelical outreach and in a Korean mega-church, the roles of religion may indeed differ. However, people from both cultures may use religion in a way that ultimately affirms their culturally construed sense of self (Sasaki and Kim, 2011).

In one culture, religious messages may emphasize spiritual growth in the individual, whereas, in the other, the strength of the community may be the focus. Just as religion has played a role in the development of cultures through traditions and ideologies, culture may act as a frame through which religion is made meaningful.

Therefore, a critical task is to determine how culture may shape individual psychological experiences and collective expressions of religion. Throughout history, there have been many instances of religion being shaped by the cultural context. For example, qualitative research in religious studies has shown that mainstream American values, such as independence and personal choice, have influenced the way Christianity is practiced in the United States today (Wolfe, 2005).

With regard to this close interrelation of cultural, political themes, and religion, how is psychoanalysis in Iran related to social and political changes or Islamic issues? Against this backdrop, we are going to discuss the history of psychoanalysis in Iran and its relation to Islam and Muslimhood in Iran. Although, like many other countries, there is a wide range of religious beliefs in Iran, however, in this country, religion is co-constructed with politics, and it has dominated the laws thus adding more complexity to the issue of Iranian Islam. We will discuss some parallel issues regarding the relationship between Islam and culture, a brief glance on two major social changes (including the Islamic

Revolution and the Iran–Iraq War), as well as a few experiences and observations of some Iranian psychotherapists in which Islam and culture are interacting.

One of the main factors concerning the development of psychoanalysis in Iran is the history of the country, according to Sanati's idea (Javanbakht and Sanati, 2006). The ebb and flow of psychoanalysis in Iran appears to be influenced by revolution, war, and social phenomena. Therefore, the way psychoanalysis develops in Muslim societies varies depending on its historical course and social conditions, as has been the case since the beginning of the history of psychoanalysis.

Psychoanalysis in Iran

Before the revolution in Iran, there was also a series of psychoanalytic discussions for ordinary people on a popular radio program run by non-analysts. This program began in the 1950s and continued for some 20 years. In parallel with the Iranian socio-cultural division between mysticism and Marxism in the 1950s and 1970s, psychoanalytic literature translated into Persian focused on Jung and the post–Freudians, Erich Fromm and Karen Horney. These three have become the most popular in Iran. After the 1979 revolution, there was a common change in the intellectual attitude which turned eastward and rejected the Westernization of Iranian culture which was called 'Gharbzadegi' (Western malady, Western bites). This reflected a renewed emphasis on the native Iranian identity and a quest for its past religious and traditional perspectives. Following the 1979 revolution, there was a widespread negative attitude toward psychoanalysis, particularly the sexual emphasis in Freud's ideas. Another important factor was the engagement of Iran in the war with Iraq. This conflict demanded enormous healthcare resources and saw a return to biological therapies. During the first few years of war, there was no place for psychoanalysis in universities and academic settings. Therefore, psychoanalytic practice was done outside the academic system in the private sector by only a few practitioners.

Following the Second World War, Iranian socio-political life was divided between traditional religion and the secular Marxist ideology. Psychoanalysis was introduced in this context by a series of poor and distorted translations of Freud's abridged texts made by common translators. At the same time the first U.K.-trained Iranian psychoanalyst, Mahmoud Sanaie (1918–1983), a professor and the head of the department of psychology, made some interesting contributions to the understanding of Iranian culture by analyzing mythological figures in Ferdowsi's Shahnama, and then Mohammad Sanati, a U.K.-trained psychoanalytic psychotherapist, began working on psychoanalysis and academic education.

So, what we see in the history of psychoanalysis in Iran is that religion has not been a barrier, but that it was the society in crisis and the political decisions made which were a determinant. Although the government has spoken in the name of religion.

Gohar Homayounpour is a psychoanalyst and an author who lives and works in Tehran. She has published various psychoanalytic articles and has written extensively on psychoanalysis and culture, cinema, femininity, and language. Homayounpour has written a number of papers about her experience as a psychoanalyst in Iran and presented them at international conferences. 'The couch and the chador,' 'Doing psychoanalysis in Tehran' are examples. In the latter, later a book, (Homayounpour, 2012), she states:

> It seems as though religions were socially constructed to fulfill the collective fantasies of these differing cultures. In Iran one can observe a moment of discontinuity from the past, and also from the future, because we have killed our sons, our future. We never properly mourned the loss of our glorious past, before it was taken over by Islam. Our melancholic response was to create Shiism, which is a culture of mourning, as a way of mourning the symbolic past. Through this ever-repetitive mourning we attempt to master the sudden trauma of having suddenly lost our sense of who we are.

At the two-day conference on Geographies of Psychoanalysis/Encounters between Cultures (Preta, 2015), held on October 16th, 2014, in Tehran, Homayounpour (2012) declared:

> There is a strong presence of psychoanalysis in the media, at universities and hospitals in Iran; Freud is a common reference not only in intellectual environments, and people in the street speak using the psychoanalytical jargon—phrases such as 'don't repress yourself' or 'betrayal of the unconscious' can be heard at any table in a café. Psychoanalysis is not a secret or embarrassing practice there and it is not unusual to hear somebody interrupt a conversation to 'go to the analyst'.

The psychoanalytic approach has attracted so many students in Iran despite the fact that mainstream scholars in academia disapprove its credibility. *Psychoanalytic Discourse* is a quarterly international journal published by a psychoanalytic training group in Tehran. It is devoted to cross-disciplinary debate among theoreticians, clinicians, cultural scholars, and literary critics working within the psychoanalytic framework.

Recently there has been an increasing interest in psychoanalysis among therapists and patients in Iran. There is an increasing interest in analysis and training even in Mashhad, one of the religious cities of Iran.

So, the fluctuations of psychoanalytic practice in Iran as an Islamic country appears to be influenced by revolution, war, and social phenomena while the religion of the majority of people has been Islam throughout all these years. Therefore, the development of psychoanalysis in Muslim societies seems to depend on its historical course and social conditions, as this has been the case since the beginning of the history of psychoanalysis.

Analyzing issues related to Islam and Muslims without considering the historical and cultural contexts as latent issues would not seem to be comprehensive. What can often be interpreted as a reflection of religion, is, in fact, a kind of integration of religious beliefs with historical events, collective memories, and traumas. One of the best examples are the attitudes towards Muslim women's clothing. Some narrow perspectives misinterpret Islam and Muslims, culture, and the dynamics of state behavior in different Muslim societies, assuming that they are homogenous and immutable. Given that the meaning of Islam changes historically and cross-culturally, state policies and political movements, at least in modern times, can also vary and be explained through their interactions with gender. Nor do religious ideologies alone shape women's lives and gender relations in Islamic states. Women's position is historically specific and takes different forms in various cultures and societies, particularly those undergoing rapid transformation. Women's experiences are also shaped by their class, ethnicity, and nationality. Islam can be seen 'as an ideological system' that provides 'some unifying concepts that influence women's experiences of subordination,' as Deniz Kandiyoti indicates. She suggests that 'these are vested in the culturally defined modes of control of female sexuality, especially insofar as they influence subjective experiences of womanhood and femininity.' Although religion and culture leave important imprints on women's lives, they must be understood within the broader historical, socio-political, and economic contexts as they may be shaped by trends in the global political economy (Sedghi, 2007).

Of course, doing psychoanalysis in an Islamic context will be different in some aspects from non-Muslim contexts but this difference seems to be cultural. We often come across reports from patients in which one is apparently talking about a religious or symbolic issue regarding Islam but gradually we notice that the main story is interwoven to other issues. Most of the time, religious issues seem to be as day residues for intra-psychic conflicts. For instance, the Islamic Revolution in 1979 in Iran and the Iran–Iraq War were two major social events that link to religious symbols but this religious content may reflect one`s internal conflicts rather than religion itself.

About 28 years have passed since the Iran–Iraq war and sometimes we deal with clients in the therapy room that have been a victim of the war during childhood or have lost their close relatives during the war. In Iran, war is closely associated with religion and Islam because the state organizations have excessively emphasized the sacredness of it and highlighted religious issues. A patient reported that after she lost her father in the war, her mother, who had a different appearance before, suddenly changed her hijab and wore the chador. For her, this new appearance in her mother's chador was associated with the trauma of losing her father. She not only lost her father but was also faced with a sudden change in her mother that she could not mentally digest. In fact, in this case, the chador at a manifest level is related to Islam and religion, but it also reflects a narration of the patient's insecure relationship with her mother.

In Iran, another interesting point is the interactions and differences between Muslims and non-Muslims. The patient might or might not be aware of the therapists' religion. Iranian Christians can often be recognized because of their particular names and therefore the patient would be aware of their therapists' religion from the beginning, but Jews cannot usually be distinguished from Muslims by name. According to an interview performed by the authors of this chapter with two Iranian Christians therapists about their experience with Muslims, both reported their religious differences with their own therapists were not highlighted in their mind. Also, their cultural and national similarities with their patients predominated over their religious differences. Of course, in some cases, the patients have directly referred to the religious differences they have with the therapist, but, according to these two therapists, this issue has occurred at the particular stage of the therapy which reflects transference matters. Even where the therapist and the patient share the same religion, that is that both are Muslims, the degrees of their beliefs are often recognizably different due to external manifestations and the patients might experience different feelings. For instance, when the therapist is a woman, her hijab is observable for the patient and, during Ramadan, any sign of drinking tea or coffee in the therapy room would make some religious patients feel distant, anxious, or sometimes angry. Moreover, sometimes these differences would make the patient feel reluctant to talk about their religious beliefs in the analysis.

Therefore, religion is considered, as with any other materials in analytic situation, as that which should be analyzed by a good enough and neutral therapist. As Kernberg (2000) pointed out in 'Psychoanalytic Perspectives on the Religious Experience':

> The psychoanalyst's function is to free the patient from unconscious conflicts that limit this capability, including the systematic confrontation, exploration, and resolution of unconscious conflicts that preclude the development of concern, guilt, reparation, forgiveness, responsibility and justice as basic aspirations of the individual. Psychoanalysis also has to help certain patients to free themselves from the use of formal religious commitments as a rationalization of hatred and destructiveness directed against self or others.
>
> *(Kernberg, 2000)*

Besides, it seems psychoanalysis is growing up among patients and trainees, as well as the religious and non-religious, so, as noted before, the authors' experience shows that in Iran as an Islamic country, the culture dominates in the treatment room. In recent decades, psychoanalytic thought has been growing increasingly not only in treatment but also in other fields. Iranian director Asghar Farhadi's films are the best examples. They portray humans in crisis and conflict, as those who experience anxiety, shame, and guilt. So, it seems that culture is a more determinant element in practicing psychoanalysis between Muslims and Islamic countries than religion itself. There is no set formulation for everyone with the same religion.

In a case such as Iran, interpreting a latent meaning is complicated by political issues. Joan Copjec (2006) in 'The Object-Gaze: Shame, Hejab, Cinema,' examines the films of the Iranian filmmaker, Abbas Kiarostami, who directs films under the conditions of censorship imposed by a hijab, and an examination of the philosophical and psychoanalytic literature on shame. She stated that Post-revolutionary Iran witnessed the flourishing of a heavily subsidized and officially promoted cinema, though one strictly regulated by the Ministry of Culture and Islamic Guidance, which explicitly forbade the smallest details betraying foreign influence —such as the wearing of ties or bow ties, the smoking of cigarettes, the drinking of alcohol, and so on—and, more globally, any infraction of the Islamic system of hejab (Copjec, 2006). Besides restricting narrative situations and tabooing the most common style of editing, the system of modesty also obliged any filmmaker committed to maintaining a modicum of realism to shoot outdoors. Although in real life Iranian women need not and do not wear headscarves at home, in cinematic interiors they were forced to don them because of the presence, once again, of the extradiegetic look, which exposed them to the view of unrelated men. Incongruous images of headscarves in scenes of family intimacy were more than unrealistic; they were oftentimes risible and thus filmmakers tended to avoid domestic scenes as much as possible. Ultimately, then, interiority was one of the most significant cinematic casualties of hejab. Iranian cinema came to be composed *only* of exterior shots, whether in the form of actual spatial exteriors—the improbable abundance of rural landscapes and city streets, which is a hallmark of Iranian cinema—or in the form of virtual exteriors—interior domestic spaces in which women remained veiled and isolated from desire, outside the reach of any affectionate or passionate caress. The challenge facing all Iranian filmmakers, then, is to make credible and compelling films under these conditions, namely: the censorship of interiority and of intimacy (Copjec, 2006).

Now we have to ask, to what extent this image represents internal images. Does it advocate the idea that one cannot practice psychoanalysis in Iran? Can one work on internal censorship while there is too much outside censorship? Do these movies represent Iranian Muslim women? Does psychoanalysis face the same obstacles as moviemaking in Iran?

As noted, Islamic belief, like other religions, could be considered a manifest content for human psychic conflicts, but it seems this perspective is applicable just for the clinic. It does not apply to the social level. Analysis of Islam at this level could be a latent content in itself. Most of the time, Islam is not merely a religion in comparison to Christianity or other religions, but it is associated with various things. Of course, no one has equated the Jonestown massacre or the destructive frenzy produced at the two concerts in Cincinnati or the devastation of Indochina with Christianity or with Western or American culture at large, that sort of equation has been reserved for 'Islam.'

Labels purporting to name the very large and complex realities are notoriously vague and at the same time unavoidable. If it is true that 'Islam' is an imprecise and ideologically-loaded label, it is also true that 'the West' and 'Christianity' are just as problematic. Yet, there is no easy way of avoiding these labels, since Muslims speak of Islam, Christians of Christianity, Westerners of the West, and all of them about all the others in ways that seem to be both convincing and exact. We must take the labels seriously. To a Muslim who talks about 'the West' or to an American who talks about 'Islam,' these enormous generalizations have behind them a whole history, enabling and disabling at the same time. Ideological and shot through with powerful emotions, the labels have survived many experiences and have been capable of adapting to new events, information, and realities. At present, 'Islam' and 'the West' have taken on a powerful new urgency everywhere. And we must note immediately that it is always the West, and not Christianity, that seems pitted against Islam. Why? Because the assumption is that whereas 'the West' is greater than and has surpassed the stage of Christianity, its principal religion, the world of Islam—its varied societies, histories, and languages notwithstanding—is still primitive and mired in religion and backwardness. Therefore, the West is modern, greater than the sum of its parts, full of enriching contradictions, and yet always 'Western' in its cultural identity; the world of Islam, on the other hand, is no more than 'Islam,' reducible to a small number of unchanging characteristics despite the appearance of contradictions and experiences of variety that seem on the surface to be as plentiful as those of the West.

Some analysts adopted the perspective of the Freudian paradigm to force extreme limitations on the material including Islam and Muslims through seeking a single predetermined meaning. Reading Freud in this way gives the analyst the privileged power of seeing through the illusion to a hidden reality. As Ricoeur (1974) puts it, 'this can be understood as reduction pure and simple.' However, Freud might be read in a different way—for instance, as Ricoeur reads him. Interpretation does not have to return to a single meaning. For if it is accepted that a symbol has one meaning, then all varying meanings at the level of consciousness are distortions hiding the real meaning which is secret, which cannot be grasped by those who actually live these meanings but only through the insight of the analyst. But if the symbol is left open, its real meaning is no longer a secret but an enigma to be restored by continual interpretation. Without these cultural interpretations, the fixed content of the psyche is mute, and the symbolic relations are not yet in existence (Ricoeur, 1970).

A glance at the history reveals that Christianity and Judaism had their own struggles with fanaticism, Islam, as a new recurrent religion, seems to be struggling with the same problems that other religions have mostly but not entirely overcome. It seems to us that in manifest content, Islam is considered to be a religion that inherently contradicts the psychoanalytic principle, but we believe the latent content is about how the current political culture is transforming Islam. So, still, a question remains. In analyzing issues related to Islam and Muslims, whose associations are important for interpretation?

In the conference on Geographies of Psychoanalysis/Encounters between Cultures, Preta (2015) states:

In the West, we are seeing a crisis where the self is disoriented and fragmented and where the request made to psychoanalysis is to recompose this self. Individuals are seeking to engage with their communities once more to find not only individual, but collective meaning. By contrast, in the East, it seems that the goal is a form of emancipation from the group to find more space for individual choice. These are two different experiences that may be useful for each other and should also be integrated. For this reason, the point in question is not to bring psychoanalytical knowledge, with its predetermined and self-completed theories, to countries other than those in which it was born, and thus create an overlap with the culture of the host country, but rather, to look at the exchange between cultures and find new strength and ways that will allow it to evolve.

Conclusions

Perhaps one of the most important and critical issues in the interaction of religion and psychoanalysis is that nowadays, religious issues are repressed in the same way that sexuality was repressed in the nineteenth century. As with Loewald's view, a schism developed within psychoanalytic thinking which mirrored that of Western culture at large and led to an intellectual culture in which 'forms of religious experience ... [and] aspects of unconscious mentation ... are [currently] more deeply repressed than "sexuality" is today' (Jacobs and Capps, 1997, pp. 69–70). So, the last question is: Which religion is repressed the most or does the degree of religious repression vary in different cultures?

Back to the first question, 'Is it psychoanalysis possible between Muslims (regarding cultural and social issues)?' In Iran, our self and mentality are naturally affected by Islam, as well as by oriental culture, our language, the politics, and the shared history of our society. In our view, this question can be asked in a different way. What is the task of psychoanalysis in the context of a transient society, such as Iran, with an Islamic religion that people have intra-psychic and interpersonal conflicts concerning their religion, culture, and identity?

In Freud's view, 'The business of the analysis is to secure the best possible psychological conditions for the functions of the ego; with that, it has discharged its task' (Freud, 1937).

The American psychoanalyst, Jonathan Lear (2009), who is also a philosopher, has suggested that the overarching psychoanalytic goal is 'freedom,' and the different schools of psychoanalysis, which often appear to be in conflict, are in reality aiming at different aspects of freedom: freedom to be different, freedom to love, freedom to think one's own thoughts, and so on (Lear, 2009).

As most religious scholars have tried to avoid psychoanalytic theory, psycho-analysts have avoided religious issues in their practice. In a society like Iran, perhaps one of the most important functions of psychoanalysis at an individual level is helping people to integrate different parts of the self, including religious. Therefore, addressing these issues requires that therapists consider religious beliefs as they do other materials and provide an opportunity for analyzing functions of these beliefs and making new compromise formations. But, the beginning of psychoanalysis needs to look forward to the formation of a democratic society, or we can build on a democratic individual level so that we can see a change at the social level.

As Suchet et al. (2013) beautifully argue, relational psychoanalysis can provide our patients with an experience of democratic relationships that, over time, may become internalized, thus replacing rigidly organized emotional structures with more flexible, relaxed ones, where the patient acquires a stronger sense of his own agency and desire while being less threatened by others. With their emphasis on the therapeutic action taking place within the analytic relationship, that involves two people engaged in a process (Mitchell, 2014) oriented to more critically self-aware and authentic meaning-making that puts the individual patient's needs ahead of the primacy of theory, relational psychoanalysis has much to contribute to the promotion of democratic minds. From this perspective, the enlarged mentality required for democratic social practice appropriate to complex, diverse modern societies cannot exist in the absence of human beings who have a strong sense of personal agency and the imaginative capacity to see the world from the perspective of the foreign other. As the individual gains the experience of becoming 'increasingly self-authorized' in psychoanalysis, she becomes increasingly capable of expanding her desire for an enriched personal life that includes the creation of those social conditions without which a non-alienated, more satisfying life is not possible. Psychoanalysis is inspired by the hope that personal transformation is possible with an individual becoming the most she can become (Freud, 1917). But, the hope in individual transformation is not enough. Analysts must resist the tendency widely present in psychoanalysis to 'insulate subjectivity from social practices and discourses' (Altman, 1995). If psychoanalysis is about any one thing, it is about freedom, freedom for human beings not only to love and to work but to become while feeling reasonably comfortable with becoming of others. Psychoanalysis is a call to the morality, responsibility, and autonomy-in-relationship that is crucial to truly becoming human beings who are open to themselves and to others in all their complexity and diversity. In this respect, psychoanalysis is thoroughly modern as it challenges humanity to critically self-reflect without which tolerance, cooperation, and peaceful living together are impossible. This challenge cannot be limited to the consulting room; it is a political project as well as a project committed to healing mental illness. At its heart, psychoanalysis is both a social theory of democracy as well as a clinical treatment oriented to individual change whose goal is inevitably the cultivation of a democratic mind.

Acknowledgments

We thank Dr Mohammad Mojtahed Shabestari for his comments on the conceptualization of religious concepts in Iranian society, and Dr Sara Mazinani Shariati for her comments according to the sociological approach that greatly improved the structure of our discussion. We are thankful to Dr Babak Roshanaei-Moghaddam and Dr Nahaleh Moshtagh Bidokhti who provided expertise that greatly assisted the research, although they may not agree with all of the interpretations provided in this research.

References

Akhtar, S. 2009. *Comprehensive Dictionary of Psychoanalysis*. London: Karnac.

Altman, N. 1995. *The Analyst in the Inner City*. Hillsdale, NJ: The Analytic Press.

Antoun, R. T. 2014. *Muslim Preacher in the Modern World: A Jordanian Case Study in Comparative Perspective*. Princeton, NJ: Princeton University Press.

Asad, T. 1986. *The Idea of an Anthropology of Islam*. Washington, DC: Georgetown University Center for Contemporary Arab Studies. *Occasional Papers Series*.

Benslama, F. 2006. Islam and psychoanalysis: a tale of mutual ignorance. *Qantara*, https://en.qantara.de/content/islam-and-psychoanalysis-a-tale-of-mutual-ignorance (accessed 10 October 2018).

Billig, M. 1997. Freud and Dora: repressing an oppressed identity. *Theory, Culture and Society*, 14, 29–55.

Black, D. M. 2011. *Why Things Matter: The Place of Values in Science, Psychoanalysis and Religion*. London: Routledge.

Bowen, J. R. 1993. *Muslims through Discourse: Religion and Ritual in Gayo Society*. Princeton, NJ: Princeton University Press.

Copjec, J. 2006. The object-gaze: shame, hejab, cinema. *Gramma*, 14, 163–182

Davies, M. W. 1988. *Knowing One Another: Shaping an Islamic Anthropology*. London and New York: Mansell.

Freud, S. 1917. Transference. In ed. J. Strachey. *Lecture XVII, Introductory Lectures on Psychoanalysis, Standard edition, Vol. 16*. London: Hogarth Press, 431–447.

Freud, S. [1930] 1961. *Civilization and Its Discontents*, 64–145. London: Hogarth Press.

Freud, S. 1933. *Freud – New Introductory Lectures on Psycho-Analysis*. New York: Norton.

Freud, S. 1937. Analysis terminable and interminable. *The International Journal of Psycho-Analysis*, 18, 373.

Goldziher, I. 1981. *Introduction to Islamic Theology and Law*, trans. A. Hamori and R. Hamori. Princeton: Princeton Univerity Press.

Homayounpour, G. 2012. *Doing Psychoanalysis in Tehran*. Cambridge, MA: MIT Press.

Iner, D. & Yucel, S. 2015. *Muslim Identity Formation in Religiously Diverse Societies*. Cambridge: Cambridge Scholars Publishing.

Jacobs, J. L. & Capps, D. 1997. *Religion, Society, and Psychoanalysis: Readings in Contemporary Theory*. New York: Westview Press.

Javanbakht, A. & Sanati, M. 2006. Psychiatry and psychoanalysis in Iran. *Journal of the American Academy of Psychoanalysis and Dynamic Psychiatry*, 34, 405.

Kempton, W. 1987. Two theories of home heat control. In eds. D. Holland and N. Quinn. *Cultural Models in Language and Thought*. Princeton: Princeton University Press, 222–242.

Kernberg, O. F. 2000. Psychoanalytic perspectives on the religious experience. *American Journal of Psychotherapy*, 54, 452–476.

Lear, J. 2009. Technique and final cause in psychoanalysis: four ways of looking at one moment. *The International Journal of Psychoanalysis*, 90, 1299–1317.

Martin, R. C. 1982. Understanding the Qur'an in text and context. *History of Religions*, 21, 361–384.

Mitchell, S. A. 2014. *Influence and Autonomy in Psychoanalysis*. London: Routledge.

Modood, T. 2003. Muslims and the politics of difference. *Political Quarterly*, 74, 100–115.

Modood, T. 2005. A defence of multiculturalism. *Soundings: A Journal of Politics and Culture*, 11, 62–71.

Modood, T. 2006. Ethnicity, Muslims and higher education entry in Britain. *Debate Section, Teaching in Higher Education*, 11, 247–250.

Mura, A. 2014. Islamism revisited: a Lacanian discourse critique. *European Journal of Psychoanalysis*, 1, 107–126.

Olick, J. K., Vinitzky-Seroussi, V. & Levy, D. 2011. *The Collective Memory Reader*. Oxford: Oxford University Press on Demand.

Preta, L. 2015. *Geographies of Psychoanalysis: Encounters Between Cultures in Tehran*. New York: Mimesis.

Rassool, G. H. 2016. *Islamic Counselling: An Introduction to Theory and Practice*. London: Routledge.

Redfield, R. 1956. *Peasant Society and Culture: An Anthropological Approach to Civilization*. Cambridge: Cambridge University Press.

Ricoeur, P. 1970. *Freud and Philosophy: An Essay on Interpretation: An Essay in Interpretation*. New Haven, CT: Yale University Press.

Ricoeur, P. 1974. *The Conflict of Interpretations: Essays in Hermeneutics*. Evanston, IL: Northwestern University Press.

Said, E. W. 1978. *Orientalism*. New York: Random House.

Sasaki, J. Y. & Kim, H. S. 2011. At the intersection of culture and religion: a cultural analysis of religion's implications for secondary control and social affiliation. *Journal of Personality and Social Psychology*, 101, 401–414.

Sedghi, H. 2007. *Women and Politics in Iran: Veiling, Unveiling, and Reveiling*. Cambridge: Cambridge University Press.

Suchet, M., Harris, A. & Aron, L. 2013. *Relational Psychoanalysis, Volume 3: New Voices*. London: Routledge.

Winnicott, D. W. 1949. Mind and its Relation to the Psyche-Soma. In ed. D. W. Winnicott. *Through Paediatrics to Psycho-Analysis*. London: Hogarth Press and The Institute of Psycho-Analysis, 243–254.

Wolfe, A. 2005. *Return to Greatness: How America Lost Its Sense of Purpose and What It Needs to Do to Recover It*. Princeton, NJ: Princeton University Press.

3

REPRESENTATIONS OF THE PSYCHE AND ITS DYNAMICS IN ISLAM

The work of Ibn Qayyim al-Jawziyah

Chiara Sebastiani

Psychoanalysis' approach to Islam has mainly been influenced by the Freudian notion of religion as a collective neurosis (some would say a psychosis), to be explained in the same terms as individual psychopathologies. Yet, in this post-secular era of ours, Jung's concept of religions as symbolic systems or clusters of archetypes exerting their influence both on individuals and societies might be more useful. From such a perspective, Islam might have something to bring to psychoanalysis. Here, I explore this possibility by drawing on the work of Ibn al-Qayyim, a medieval scholar whose persistent popularity is much connected to his subtle understanding of the human 'heart' – a concept which within Islam has surprising affinities with the modern 'psyche.'

Monotheistic religions and the contribution of Islam to psychoanalysis

Historically, the relationship of psychoanalysis to religion is embedded in the nineteenth-century 'great demystification' current of thought whose main representatives are Darwin, who demonstrated the continuity between humans and other animal species; Marx, who theorized that history is not the making of individuals and ideals but of inescapable structures of classes and interests; and Freud, who provided the final stroke by stating that the old Cartesian ego 'is not master in its own house.' Great demystification, supported by positivism and materialism, drove theology and metaphysics out of the realm of scientific activities. Religion became a matter of anthropological, sociological, and eventually of psychological inquiry, with Freud's definition if it as a 'collective neurosis' that will be done with when man, understanding through analysis and making accessible to reason the primordial fear of the father, will not need such illusion any more (Freud 1927).

It is true that in his very last book, *Moses and Monotheism* (1939), Freud changes his viewpoint. In the Torah's account of how Moses imposed the cult of a unique, invisible, and undepictable God, he sees a process of 'subordinating sense perception to an abstract idea' and 'a triumph of spirituality over the senses': two processes amounting to 'an instinctual renunciation accompanied by its psychologically necessary consequences' (Freud 1939: 179). In this way, the primitive projection of the child's experience of the father on an omnipotent God produces a system capable of retroacting on the individual to support the development of instinctual renunciation and the overall process of civilization.

Inquiry into the process of formation of the Jewish religion and its psychological consequences is a means, for Freud, to 'translate the concepts of individual psychology into mass psychology.' This approach is consistent with his methodological individualism. With an implicit, polemical reference to Jung, Freud writes:

> I do not think that much is to be gained by introducing the concept of a 'collective' unconscious – the content of the unconscious is collective anyhow, a general possession of mankind. [...] The processes we study here in the life of a people are very similar to those we know from psychopathology.
>
> *(Freud 1939: 208)*

Otherwise said, the formation of collective religious images, beliefs, and practices can be explained in analogy with individual processes of return of the suppressed and symptom formation.

Introducing the concept of the collective unconscious, Jung (1934/1954) operates a reversal of Freud's perspective. He links basic human experiences – such as birth, death, motherhood – to archetypal patterns that are deposited in the collective unconscious and on which human communities draw to make sense of their existences through the production of shared images, narratives, and practices. Religions can thus be conceived of as a cluster of archetypal images which may exert their influence both on societies and on individuals. As a consequence, instead of something to be explained through individual psychopathological processes, religions (like myths and works of art) are used by Jung to explain both the individual and the collective psyche. He sees them as providers of archetypal images that play an important role in social cohesion and individual adaptation. In human groups, suppressed archetypal contents, finding no symbolic means of expression, are bound to surface at some point in time in a potentially dangerous, destructive way during collective outbursts of violence – social upheavals, wars, revolutions. In individuals, their appearance may have a positive function – indicating some creative need of the individual – but it may also lead to pathological processes such as inflation and psychotic breakdown. In Western post-secular societies, sexual repression having all but disappeared, re-emerging clusters of formerly suppressed contents are offered by religions and mainly by Islam. For psychoanalysts, this means that the contents of Islam is that which is the farthest away from the current collective consciousness and less acceptable to it.

The effort of psychoanalysts up to now has been mainly directed at putting 'Islam on the couch' (Benslama 2014; Chebel 2015; Youssef 2007). For Jungians, this sounds like putting Greek mythology on the couch and holding it responsible for all the pathological expressions of the Oedipus complex, including actual cases of parricide and incest. From a different perspective, concepts are offered by Islam that can provide a better understanding of the human psyche. Such as those found in the work of the great medieval scholar Ibn al-Qayyim – one of 'the scholars of the heart' (Krawietz 2006) – which suggest some interesting alternatives to basic taken-for-granted analytical concepts.

Ibn Qayyim al-Jawziyah

Ibn Qayyim al-Jawziyah (1292–1350) – whose name means 'son of the super-intendent of al-Jawziyah school,' Ibn al-Qayyim for short – the most important student of the more famous Ibn Taymiyyah (1263–1328) of the Hanbali school of Islamic jurisprudence, was himself a scholar in theology, jurisprudence, philosophy, and moral doctrine. On these topics, he produced several books as well as extensive compilations and commentaries. A much-respected teacher, he spent most of his life in Damascus, where he was born and where he died, his only relevant journeys having been numerous pilgrimages to Mecca. Two features of his biography appear of particular interest for those interested in the relevance of Islam to psychoanalysis. The first is his spiritual relationship to his master Ibn Tayyim; the second his intellectual position between Sufism and Salafism.

All Ibn al-Qayyim's biographers, ancient and modern (Krawietz 2006), stress alongside his modesty, kindness, and intense spiritual life, his deep loyalty and devotion to Ibn Taimiyyah. Though he was by no means a mere follower and epigone of his master, he did not embrace all his positions and made original contributions that have been rediscovered and appreciated in modern times; yet, the priority he gave to acquiring extensive knowledge of his work (and that of his predecessors) rather than authoring work of his own have won him the qualification of a 'scholar in the shadow' (Bori and Holtzman 2010). His personality offers a striking contrast with the assertive, impatient temperament of his master. Yet, when it came to supporting some of the latter's more controversial doctrinal positions (particularly on the issue of permissibility of the cult of saints and visits to their graves) Ibn al-Qayyim did so publicly and spectacularly. As a result, he was imprisoned in 1326 together with his master in the citadel of Damascus and only released after the latter's death in 1328.

Ibn al-Qayyim's relationship to Ibn Taimiyyah represents an archetypal embo-diment of the Master-Disciple couple (Deak 2012) and offers a striking contrast with the Father-Son relationship constellated by Freud and Jung. The latter is fully embedded in the Western cultural tradition dominated by the Father-Son archetype and its primordial violence – Kronos devouring his children, Zeus overthrowing Kronos, Oedipus killing Laius – on which Freud's metapsychology is based and which has migrated into Christian religion, albeit softened by the image of a benevolent Father sacrificing an acquiescent Son for the love of humanity. Islam, on the other hand, is in no way a religion of the Father and any analogy of Allah with a Father figure is considered a lapse into polytheism: Allah 'begetteth not, nor is He begotten' (Al-Ikhlas 112: 3). Central in Islam is the Master-Disciple archetypal relationship. Though Western literature focuses mainly on the Master-Disciple relationship within Sufi doctrine and practice, in fact, this archetypal pattern supports the whole transmission of knowledge in Islam which is based on traditions transmitted by Muhammad's companions (*al-sahaba*) and their disciples (*al-tabiun*). As opposed to the Father-Son relationship, which is inescapable and thus can be overcome only by a violent act, the Master-Disciple relationship is based on free choice and loyalty. In regard to his Master, the Disciple is a seeker, a *taleb*, driven by a thirst for knowledge, 'begging' for knowledge and for initiation and maintaining lifelong gratitude and reverence to his master.

This biographical feature, connected to the issue of authority, also sheds light on Ibn al-Qayyim's intellectual and doctrinaire position between Sufism and Salafism. His relationship to these two currents of thought in Islam is highly controversial. On the one hand he is deemed belonging to the 'sober' Sufi current, advocating spirituality and asceticism but refusing exoteric and ecstatic practices, on the other he is considered 'an expert in the doctrine and the creed of the Salaf' – the 'pious predecessors' of the early Muslim society which he depicts as 'a model for his fellow Muslims to emulate.' In the over-simplified Western dichotomic construction, Sufism is the mystic and exoteric dimension of Islam and Salafism is a fundamentalist and strictly literalist movement only. Sufism, for more sympathetic scholars, is allowed compatibility with the development of individual personality whereas Salafism would completely contrast any form of subjectivity. But, in the case of radical critiques, such as that by Benslama, there is hardly any space at all for the development of an autonomous subject within Islam since:

> Two opposite trends develop, that may nevertheless jointly exist in the same individual: on the one hand speculative investment of subjectivity in the quest of spiritual perfection through Sufism, on the other hand subjection to the literalistic legalitarism of Shariah
>
> *(Benslama 2014: 13, my translation)*

This kind of critique underestimates the role of knowledge in Islam and the centrality of the issue of acquisition and transmission of knowledge, the main divide being between experiential and scriptural knowledge and the validity and authority of each. Within Sufism and Salafism, these are not opposed polarities but allow for very diverse combinations and degrees. So, the question of subjectivity in Islam should be understood in its own terms (for instance exploring points of contact with the psychology of Calvinism).

Ibn al-Qayyim's position – 'bridging Sufism and Salafism' (Anjum 2010) – offers this opportunity. An in-depth scholar of Sufi doctrines, he was nevertheless critical of Sufi mysticism pursuing the goal of identification of the worshiper with God, this fusional pursuit being for him a sign of immaturity. On the other hand, though setting the utmost importance on the scriptural sources of Islam and on perfect conformity to their teachings and commands for those engaging in the path to Allah, he rejected formal literalism as feeding arrogant self-complacency. Conformity to the commands of Allah as given through the Quran and the Sunna can only be pursued by in-depth awareness of the individual's self, psychological scrutiny and a refined knowledge of the dynamics of the heart or, as we would say, of the psyche.

The Islamic psyche

The affinity between the Islamic concept of 'heart' and the Freudian concept of 'psyche' is by no means something obvious, all the more since 'psyche' is normally translated in Arabic with the word *nafs*, 'soul.'

In the sources of Islam – the Quran and the Sunna (the verbally transmitted *ahadith*, records of the Prophet's teachings, sayings and deeds) – a rich vocabulary refers to the incorporeal, unsubstantial parts of the human being. This includes the heart, designated with three different words (*qalb, fu'aad, sadr*), the soul (*nafs*), the spirit (*ruh*), and the intellect (*aql*). This representation includes explicit references to the relationship between conscious and unconscious (the things within myself that God 'knows better than myself') and a systematic distinction between actions the human being masters and emotions that are beyond his will and unto God's.

On each one of these terms from an Islamic perspective, we find an abundant literature that is mainly theological and philosophical whereas from a Western perspective literature is still wrestling with the issue of the proper translation of each term, following the principle of synonymy exclusion in the Quran. For the purpose of understanding contributions of Islam to the science of the psyche, this terminology can be divided into two groups, one comprising the spirit (*ruh*), and the soul (*nafs*), as well as reason (*aql*), all of which are either theological or moral entities (or both), the other referring to the heart (*qalb, fu'aad, sadr*), as a psychological entity. Whereas *nafs* and *aql* fall in the domain of the human being's rational and conscious faculties, under the control of will (*irada*) and *ruh* is under the exclusive command of the Lord, the second group of words refers to an area where conscious and unconscious are intertwined, which escapes direct power of man's will but nevertheless involves his responsibility.

According to Quran Allah created the human being (*al-insan*) out of clay and then breathed His spirit (*ruh*) into him. *Ruh* may be understood both as the vital principle which departs from the body at the moment of death and as the spark of the divine element in man. In the Quran, there is an abundance of references to *qalb* and *nafs* but very little is said about *ruh*. The reason thereof is made clear by this *ayah*: 'They ask you about the spirit [*ruh*]. Say: "The spirit is of the command of my Lord. Of knowledge, it is only a little that is communicated to you"' (Al-Isràa 17: 85).

On the contrary, quite a lot about *nafs* is communicated. It refers to the theological notion of an immortal principle in man. On Judgment Day the soul will be called to answer for the good and evil it has done. This accountability of the soul is based on its being subject to reason and to will: 'to no soul is asked more than it can give'(Al-Baqara 2: 286). The Quran speaks of three attitudes of the soul: the evil desire-inclined soul (*nafs al-ammara*), the repentant soul (*nafs al-lawamma*), and the satisfied soul (*nafs al-mutnaimma*). Moral theology also describes these as 'stages.'

Reason (*aql*) corresponds to the function of rational thinking. Allah's revelation addresses man's reason: His 'signs' (*ayatihim*) allow man to believe in God if only he takes pains to use it. Thus, the use of reason is for Islam a moral duty: 'Indeed, the worst of living creatures in the sight of Allah are the deaf and dumb who do not use reason [*allatheena la ya'aqiloona*]' (Al-Anfahl 8: 22).

Discussions on issues such as the difference between *ruh* and *nafs*, and whether *ruh* is increased and whether *nafs* is immortal belong to the domain of theology and discussions on the proper use of reason that God has granted man to that of moral doctrine. These domains allow no unconscious or uncontrollable drives or emotions: they are the realm of matters for which the human being is accountable, and on which on the Last Day he will be questioned and judged.

Things are quite different in the realm of the heart (*qalb*). When Ibn al-Qayyim claims to write for 'those interested in the matters of the heart,' he is writing about something which much resembles the modern psyche and its dynamics. The heart is the source of uncontrollable emotions that yet, insofar as they are consciously experienced, must be examined in order that reason may evaluate them and contrast or follow them. There is a specific word for the heart possessed by violent emotions: *fu'aad*. It means literally the 'enflamed heart' which loses control – like that of Moses' mother when compelled to abandon her baby in a basket on the river: her *fu'aad* almost drives her to disclose her secret had not Allah strengthened her *qalb* with faith (Al-Qasas 28: 10). As is made clear by the use of the two different words in the same ayah *fu'aad* is the heart possessed by passions: a psychic attitude which escapes men's control and of which nevertheless he is morally responsible. *Qalb* must be strengthened against *fu'aad* just like the ego must dominate instinctual drives. Love also belongs to the realm of uncontrollable emotions. Invoking Allah, Prophet Muhammad asked to be judged for what is in his power – namely to treat all his wives with fairness and equally – and not for what is only in Allah's power – his heart's preference for one of them, Aisha (Abu Daawood). We cannot be judged for our heart's inclinations, but we will be judged on how we deal with them. This is because the heart is connected to reason: though reasoning (ta'aqqal) is specifically a function of the intellect, man can also reason with the heart ('have they not hearts to reason with' – quloobun ya'aqiloone) (Al-Hajj 22: 46). This attribution of rational functions both to the mind and the heart is very similar to Jung's model of four psychic functions – thought, feeling, sensation, and intuition – the first two being both rational functions, allowing to understand and to make judgments. We find the same idea in one of Pascal's Pensées: 'The heart has its reasons which reason knows nothing of.'

The heart, as a psychic entity, is connected to the soma as well, through the sadr, the chest which is the physical part of the body in which the heart is placed. In the oft-repeated closing surah of the Quran Allah's protection is invoked against Satan 'the surreptitious whisperer' (alwaswasi alkhannas) 'He who whispers [youwaswisou] in the chests [sudoori] of men' (An-Naas 114: 5). Why do we find the plural of the word sadr and not qalb? Synonymy being excluded in Quranic interpretation, the current explanation offered by takfir is that shaytan has no direct access to the heart of man and so launches his attacks through the body and specifically the part of the body that encloses the heart, that is the chest. This is coherent with Islam's holistic representation of the human being which does not allow a radical separation between the body and the psyche and as consequence does not pathologize all bodily expressions of the heart's disease.

Satanic whispers may bring about all kinds of mischief: loss of concentration during ritual prayer (salat), obsessive reprehensible thoughts (hostility, rancor), compulsive behavior especially connected to ritual purification (wudu). Modern psychotherapy is familiar with what is called the waswas syndrome (Dwairy 2006) but has up to now shown little interest in how Islam deals with it. Attributing responsibility for one's forbidden desires or behavior to shaytan does not automatically amount to projection and denial of individual responsibility and does not exclude active engagement in therapy. Ibn al-Qayyim encourages – as we will see in the next paragraph – in-depth psychological self-knowledge.

The heart is both the venue of unconscious things (a well-known hadith reports that the Prophet used to say in his prayers: 'O Allah, forgive my errors and my ignorance, and my transgression in my affairs, and what you know of me better than I do') and the venue of belief: faith is a matter of the heart no less than passion. Another well-known duà (invocation) says: 'Oh God who upturns hearts strengthen my heart in Thy belief.' Thus, following the prophetic sunnah (tradition), the Muslim asks Allah forgiveness for feelings and assistance for belief both of which are beyond his control and yet involve obligations. This complex relationship between individual responsibility and things which the individual does not master is well what psychoanalysis to a large extent is about. Freud expressed it in terms of 'Wo Es was soll Ich werden' whereas Jung has spoken about a 'task' of individuation. In both cases, individuals are called to take responsibility for their unconscious. In Islam individuals will be judged upon their heart though so much of it is in the hands of God: they may be responsible for 'sickness of the heart' or even – according to Ibn al-Qayyim – for 'death of one's heart.' It is thus not surprising that within Islam knowledge has tended to overlap from the field of moral theology to that of depth psychology – or, as Ibn al-Qayyim defines it, the domain of 'matters of the heart.'

Matters of the heart

We find one of the best specimens of this in his voluminous *Madarij al-salikin bayna manazil iyyaka na'budu wa iyyaka nasta'in* ('Stages of the Travelers between the Stations of "Thee only we adore and to Thee alone we pray for Succor"' – a quote from Quran 1: 5, also translated as 'Ladders of the Believers' or 'Ranks of Divine Seekers'): a commentary on a Sufi manual (*Manazil al-sa'irin* – 'Way Stations of the Wayfarers') by eleventh century Hanbalite saint and mystic Abdullah Ansari. A very popular treaty in moral theology – also thanks to many abridged versions – this work is also considered by scholars 'his finest piece on theological psychology' (Krawietz 2006: 48), appreciated even nowadays for 'its piercing spiritual and psychological insight' (Anjum 2010: 161). Two examples of this, of particular interest not only from a psychological but also from a psychoanalytical point of view, are his dealing with repentance (*tawbah*) and submission (*istislam*).

Ibn al-Qayyim concentrates on the issue of repentance at the beginning of his work because 'The Station of Repentance is the first, the last and the middle of all the stations.' In the Quran we find an invitation to repentance addressed even to the best of Allah's servants: those who emigrated to Medina and engaged in jihad (An-Noor 24: 31) and the Prophet himself (An-Nasr 110: 3). This is because, according to man's nature, men are either repentant or wrong-doers: 'And those who do not make *tawbah* are indeed transgressors [*dhalimoon*]' (An-Nasr 24: 31). The paradoxical consequence of this is that repentance *prevents* sin: it amounts to 'holding fast to Allah' who grants His guidance and protection against the evil inclinations of the soul (*nafs*) and against the demon (*shaytan*). Whereas all these terms may be easily translated from a theological to a psychological level depicting man's inner conflicts, the original aspect of this approach lies precisely in this recommendation of a 'permanent' state of repentance.

This sharply contrasts the Freudian – and more generally the psychoanalytical – notion of guilt. According to this, in the economy of the individual psyche, guilt may both cause psychic unbalance (neurosis) or compensation (sublimation); in human society, it is the driving force of the civilization process including its price of instinctual renunciation. In any case for classical psychoanalysis, guilt is a cause of psychic unease – normal or pathological – to be overcome whereas for Ibn al-Qayyim repentance is the basis of spiritual and psychological well-being and progress. To better understand this one must look at Ibn al-Qayyim's representation of the psychological consequences of sin.

According to Ibn al-Qayyim, the believer who sins, intoxicated by desire, experiences an inner heartache, only momentarily covered by desire, which prevents him getting pleasure from it. But, if this remorseful feeling abandons him, overpowered by 'the joy of sinning,' then he should doubt of his faith and 'cry over the death of his heart' (Anjum 2016). The final state of this catastrophic event is the 'sealed heart,' unable to distinguish good from evil: something very similar to the psychopathic personality.

Heartache corresponds to guilt feelings – it is something passive, unwanted but still a useful symptom of some disorder of the heart. Repentance, by contrast, is described by Ibn al-Qayyim as a 'breaking of the heart' – the repentant is literally 'heartbroken' – and a complete surrender that leaves the sinner 'speechless' in the hands of his Lord. As a consequence of this, he experiences repulsion for what formerly gave him pleasure and only such a radical experience can keep him from yielding again to his inclinations or desires. If this lacks, then one should question the authenticity of one's repentance: there are many possibilities of false repentance which Ibn al-Qayyim carefully enumerates. One may thus repent because he has some interest in it and may find in it a personal benefit or because he is tired of running after his forbidden desires or because he does not desire the forbidden object any more. Or he may repent so as not to lose his reputation and his honor.

False repentance is very near to neurotic conflict: like guilt, it brings about all kinds of psychic disorders. On the contrary, repentance frees the individual from neurotic constraints. Thus 'questioning one's repentance' is very similar to bringing the unconscious to conscience. One of the basic assumptions of psychoanalysis is that the individual is not responsible for her unconscious drives yet must answer for their outcomes: the psychoanalytic setting provides the container where are all transgressive, illegal, shameful, dangerous, destructive feelings and desires may be safely brought to light, unraveled, and negotiated. Ibn al-Qayyim tackles the issue of what one knows and what one does not know about one's transgressions in a similar perspective. He admits unconscious contents, pointing to the fact that what an individual does not know about his sins is often much more than what he knows. He then argues that, nevertheless, his ignorance will not absolve him if he has the capability of knowing. 'Such a person becomes doubly responsible for failing in both knowledge and deeds.' But, whereas psychoanalysis' aim is to overcome guilt by raising to consciousness its origins in forbidden desires, Ibn a-Qayyim's spiritual travelers' aim is to gain repentance as a permanent state. Now, this can only be a benefit for the individual psyche if one correctly understands *tawbah* as a process which does away with all collective constraints and judgments – that are the basis of false repentance – and connects the individual exclusively to Allah. So, framed this process recalls Jung's process of individuation (Jung 1972): it aims at psychic authenticity rather than at formal compliance to norms.

This connection between repentance and authenticity involves a second basic concept in Ibn al-Qayyim's writings: submission. As expressed in one of his more popular quotes: 'A sin causing submission is preferable in the sight of Allah than a good deed that causes pride' to the point that to the righteous unconsciously feeding self-complacency Allah may send lapse into sin 'as a mercy.' One may ask if this understanding of *tawbah* might not lead along the experiential path of mystic annihilation of the individual in the Divine thus baffling the constitution of a psychologically autonomous subject. The question is all the more important since Ibn al-Qayyim is commenting on a Sufi manual. But, Ibn al-Qayyim's dealing with mystic 'annihilation' (*fana*) in the *Madarij* opens a different perspective – from a psychoanalytical point of view – on the often misunderstood notion of 'submission' (*istilam*) whose root is the same as that of 'Islam.'

Ibn al-Qayyim, in fact, is highly critical of the Sufi notion of 'annihilation' (*fana'*) (of the seeker in the divine) as the highest state of perfection, the way it is represented by Al-Ansari. Outside its outright heretical forms, annihilation as *jam* (union) or *istilam* (surrender), though it may be driven by sincere love of God, entails blamable 'loss of distinction and understanding' and the only correct form of annihilation is 'to annihilate any resistance to the prescriptive decree of God' (Anjum 2010). Here, let us remark that though 'surrender' may be in many ways an adequate translation of 'Islam' and its semantic field, yet 'submission' more clearly excludes any fusional hue or temptation.

Annihilation of the servant's will into God's' is something quite different from the seeker's whole being annihilation into God through ecstatic union. Whereas ecstatic annihilation is at best a sign of immaturity annihilation that conforms to the texts of revelation involves *active submission* which is preferable to 'sighs of love and tears of longing for the divine' (Anjum 2010).

As a consequence, Ibn al-Qayyim explicitly states the superiority of the 'socially and politically engaged life of the early community' as opposed to 'the later Sufis' moral passivity and denial of causality' (Anjum 2010).

From a psychoanalytical point of view, this suggests that submission involves a radical experience of Otherness as opposed to ecstatic annihilation in which traces of fusional desire may be detected. We may find an echo of this in a contemporary Lacanian analyst asking whether teaching children to pray isn't a way 'to preserve an evocation of an Other that cannot be reduced to the arrogance of our knowledge' and 'a space of the Other that cannot be reduced to that of the ego'? (Recalcati 2017: 3–4, my translation). If so, then submission would be a condition for the integrity of the human psyche (the 'healthy heart').

From a Jungian perspective, submission may be further connected to an 'archetypal need to venerate and worship' (Gordon 1989). Failure to recognize this need or to find an appropriate object for it, may be the origin of psychopathological behavior like masochism – 'the shadow side of the archetypal need to venerate and worship' or defensive projection, since the figure to whom one surrenders may be the recipient not only of idealized characteristics but also of 'shadow characteristics like envy, rage, fanaticism.' as in the case of 'the terrorist, the demagogue, the self-styled freedom fighter' (Gordon 1989).

This paves the way to resume the question: Can Islam's outlook on the human heart help to understand the pathologies of the Western individual and collective psyche?

Islam and the Western unconscious

The concepts of repentance and submission have hardly any space but negative both in psychoanalytic theory and in Western conscience and culture.

Repentance is often confused with guilt. Whatever the analytic solution to the psychic experience of guilt (assimilation or sublimation of unacceptable contents) it must bring in the end, from a Freudian perspective to an honorable compromise with collective values. On the contrary, the spiritual experience of repentance, as described by Ibn al-Qayyim, involves a break with collective values such as opportunity, reputation, convenience, and success. Knowledge of what is right and wrong – be it in conformity to human laws or to revelation-based *shariah* – is necessary for both processes but whereas overcoming guilt is about bringing to conscience that knowledge so that the individual may decide how to deal with it, experiencing repentance is about undergoing a radical change which may not conform to collectively accepted values.

Repentance can thus be understood as one term of the conceptual couple guilt/repentance, the one which has more or less fallen in the cultural unconscious of Western contemporary society. Psychoanalysis, focusing on guilt, has expelled repentance as a metaphysical content, underestimating its psychological dimension. Yet, the repentance polarity of the couple might prove useful, for instance, when dealing psychological dependencies (drugs, food, gambling, etc.) that usually involve intense guilt (and shame), feelings which are an obstacle rather than a support to any therapy. Moreover, guilt being an objective outcome measured by collective standards, repentance a subjective process validated by an intimate relationship with the Self (in Jungian terms) or with God (in Islam), the consequence of this collective unilateral unbalance on the guilt polarity is difficulty in attaining psychic authenticity. In art expertise, the Italian word '*pentimento*' ('repentance') is used when an artist has 'changed his mind' during his work, and traces of his previous painting can be seen on the canvas (either because the painting has become thin or through specific techniques). For art historians *pentimento* is a proof of authenticity: a *pentimento* can only be found in an original work of art. In a similar way, repentance exists when the individual detaches himself from the collective, its approval, its judgment, the benefits it may yield to take responsibility for his true 'self.' Jung calls this the process of individuation: he considers it a task of maturity, following the youthful process of adaptation.

As for submission, the widespread and almost exclusive association of the concept with violence and perversion in whatever domain it is used – political, social, psychological – may well make us question on the suppressed contents of this basic psychic attitude. The general preference for the first term of the conceptual couple ecstatic annihilation/active submission points to the unilateral dominance, in Western societies, of narcissistic individualism and links to Western readings of Islam that have always shown a marked preference for the experiential current of Sufism, perceived as nearer and more congenial to Western values of individuality and personal achievement. Yet, if there is an 'archetypal need to venerate and worship' then we may speculate that every authentically rebellious nature is seeking for an object worthwhile its submission.

Thus, whereas in current understanding, 'submission' is only a degree less intense than 'annihilation,' but belongs to the same polarity which has on its other end individuation and subjectivity, Ibn al-Qayyim's psychology suggests that the real opposition is between active submission which is constitutive of the individual and ecstatic annihilation which reflects immature fusional desires. This is a perspective of no small relevance for psychoanalysis. It means, for instance, that 'radicalization' might be understood as a failure to find a proper object of submission. Although in Freudian terms the moment the infant exits from omnipotent identification with the mother he cannot but submit to the castrating father who orders separation and in Jungian terms the moment the individual exits from uroboric unity with the mother he cannot but submit to collective norms and expectations that require adaptation, yet in both cases permanence in this condition would be pathological. Nevertheless, the idea of an innate or archetypal need for an object of worship and submission may be detected in the background of Freud's *Moses and Monotheism* and is quite explicit in Jung's concept of individuation as submission to one's personal *daimon* or archetypal image showing the path to the Self.

The connection between submission and individuation can be found, as a psychological content, in most initiation rituals. Having these all but disappeared in contemporary Western societies, it is small wonder that the notion of 'submission' is usually understood negatively. To find a different point of view we may need to go back a long way, for instance to these verses of John Donne (1573–1631):

> Take mee to you, imprison mee, for I
> Except you enthrall mee, never shall be free
> Nor ever chast, except you ravish mee.

To these, the Islamic concept of submission might provide an interesting commentary.

References

Anjum, O. (2010), 'Sufism without mysticism?,' *Oriente Moderno*, XC, 1, pp. 161–188.
Anjum, O. (2016), 'Ibn al-Qayyim's Madarij al-Salikin (Steps of the seekers)/The station of repentance (Tawbah) (Part 1),' *Al-Jumuah*, June 8, http://aljumuah.com/ibn-al-qayyims-madarij-al-salikin-steps-of-the-seekers-the-station-of-repentance-tawbah-part-1/.
Benslama, F. (2014), *La guerre des subjectivités en Islam*, Tunis, Cérès.
Bori, C. and Holtzman, L. (2010), 'A scholar in the shadow,' *Oriente Moderno*, XC, 1, pp. 11–42.
Chebel, M. (2015), *L'inconscient de l'islam*, Paris, CNRS Editions.
Deak, Z.T. (2012), *The Master-Disciple Relationship as a Metaphor for Healing in Jungian Psychoanalysis: Exploring Archetypal Transference between Analyst and Patient*, PhD dissertation, Palo Alto, CA, Institute of Transpersonal Psychology.

Dwairy, M. (2006), *Counselling and Psychotherapy with Arabs and Muslims. A Culturally Sensitive Approach*, New York, Teachers College Press, Columbia University.

Freud, S. (1927), 'The future of an illusion,' in *Complete Works*, vol. XXI, London, The Hogarth Press.

Freud, S. (1939), '*Moses and Monotheism*,' in *Complete Works*, vol. XXIII, London, The Hogarth Press.

Gordon, R. (1989), 'Masochism: The shadow side of the archetypal need to venerate and worship,' in Samuels, A. (ed.), *Psychopathology. Contemporary Jungian Perspectives*, London, Karnac Books.

Jung, C.G. (1952), *Foreword* to White's 'God and the unconscious,' in Jung, C.G. (ed.), *Collected Works of C.G. Jung, Volume 11: Psychology and Religion: West and East* (1969), Princeton, NJ, Princeton University Press.

Jung, C.G. (1934/1954), 'Archetypes of the collective unconscious,' in Jung, C.G. (ed.), *Collected Works of C.G. Jung, Volume 9 (Part 1): Archetypes and the Collective Unconscious*, Princeton, NJ, Princeton University Press, 1969.

Jung, C.G. (1972), 'Two essays in analytical psychology,' in Jung, C.G. (ed.), *Collected Works of C.G Jung, Volume 7*, Princeton, NJ, Princeton University Press.

Krawietz, B. (2006), 'Ibn Qayyim al-Jawziyah: His life and works,' *The Mamluk Studies Review*, 10, 2, pp. 19–64. http://mamluk.uchicago.edu/MamlukStudiesReview_X-2_2006.pdf.

Recalcati, M. (2017), *Cosa resta del padre*, Milano, Cortina.

Youssef, O. (2007), *Le Coran au risque de la psychanalyse*, Paris, Editions Albin Michel.

4

POLITICS OF SECULAR PSYCHOANALYSIS IN INDIA

Hindu-Muslim as religious and political identities in Sudhir Kakar's writing

Zehra Mehdi

Situating Edward Said's Orientalism in the context of modern secular nation states, Gil Anidjar (2006), in his paper *Secularism*, presents a complex argument on how religion as a category was created by the secular state, which itself was Christian. The formation of the modern state was used by Christianity to mask itself as religious and thereby it produced the category of religion, which referred to religions other than Christianity. While religion becomes an Other to secularism, it became an 'other' to Christianity, almost simultaneously. There is little doubt that there exists a model of state and governance in contemporary India, which while continuing to be secular, pursues an active religious agenda. Religion here, functions within the paradigm of the nation-state, and in finding problems with 'other religions' identifies itself to be secular. Hindutva ideology dovetails into the production and functioning of the state. Since the state is defined to be secular, Hindutva identifies other religions and defines them but doesn't invest in outlining itself. These other religions are the religions of minorities, namely Islam in India. In not conforming to the Hindutva ideology and practices, Islam isn't rendered anti-Hindu but anti-state, and it's implied that by being anti-state Islam is anti-Hindu. The 'Hindu state' creates Islam as the problematic religion, 'the religion' which threatens its secular practice as the state. A secular state masking as a Hindu state in evoking the rhetoric of anti-nationalism asks of Muslims in India—are they Indian?

Asking the same question, I try and find answers within the discipline of theoretical psychoanalysis in India through the writing of Sudhir Kakar, the noted 'Indian' psychoanalyst.

Sudhir Kakar's work covers a wide spectrum of psychoanalytic thought on sexuality, childhood, culture, religion in the Indian context, and converges to produce what is called Indian identity or Indian psyche. The category of 'Indian' has always evoked intense reactions on the political stage, eliciting polarizing opinions on what gets defined as Indian and who inhabits that identity. With such contestation one begins to wonder what the psychological correlation to political identity would be. The role that Kakar's writing plays in its conception of Indian identity is to explain for us not only what is consciously recognized as Indian but also what is unconsciously constructed as Indian. This unconscious construction is significant for the role it plays in determining the way existing political identities are constituted. In this chapter, I argue how, in rendering a psychoanalytic explanation of Indian identity, the writings of Sudhir Kakar not only excludes Muslims but also unwittingly identifies Islam as a religion which is incompatible with the secular Indian identity. Such politics of secularism identifies Muslims as only religious (Islamic) and religious as essentially fundamentalist, constructing Muslims, inevitably, as Islamic fundamentalists.

In the first section, I examine the political construction of Indian identity in Kakar's writing.

Indian-ness: primarily majority

Indian identity, for Kakar, is better explained as 'Indian-ness,' which he describes as 'the cultural part of the mind that informs the activities and concerns of daily life for a vast number of Indians as it guides them through the journey of life' (2007, p. 1). This Indian-ness, which he elucidates through several of his writings, becomes the cultural identity which he refers to when he speaks of Indian identity. So, when Kakar writes about Indian identity, he doesn't mean the political category of the Indian. It's important to understand that as a psycho-analyst interested in culture, Kakar's area of interest and investigation is the cultural psyche called 'Indian-ness.' His use of the word 'Indian' is essentially cultural, where Indian for him is a cultural identity.

Explaining the dynamics of this cultural identity, he writes how Indian-ness is about similarities rather than the surface dazzle of differences among the inhabitants of this vast continent, similarities produced by an overarching Indic, pre-eminently Hindu civilization that constitutes the 'cultural gene pool of India's people' (1997, p. 19). Processes of assimilation, transformations, reassertion, and recreation are central to the civilization argument, for what Kakar calls 'Hindu,' is a cultural identity, a civilization which includes Islam as well. He writes how despite 'unleashing of the advent of Islam in medieval times' (p. 20), it was effectively assimilated into Hindu civilization such that Indic civilization becomes the patrimony of all Indians irrespective of faith (p. 20).

In my reading, Kakar presents 'Indian' as what I call a psycho-cultural construction, which rests on the cultural psychology argument, asserting the indispensable role culture plays in forming the psyche.

Psychoanalysts, over the years, have thought of culture and its role in self and identity differently. For Freud (1927), culture was a civilization issue built on the renunciation of instincts; for Karen Horney (1937), the pre-genital or Oedipal position was not biologically given and thus unalterable but culturally viable; for

Otto Fenichel (1945, 1954), the ego mediating between instinct and the cultural part of Freudian personality, the superego, would include early cultural identification; for Heinz Hartman (1944), universal instinctual feelings not only manifest differently across cultures but even attempt at resolution between intrapsychic conflict and are determined by culture. Erik Erikson, Kakar's mentor, saw an adaptive relationship between culture and self where the creation of a community identity was indispensable to individual identity. One can see influences of Erikson's thought in Kakar's writing as he formulates 'Indian' as a cultural identity as well as analyzing it in terms of an individual identity. Even as Kakar talks about Indians as a cultural category, he is talking about Indians as 'people,' as individuals who have something fundamentally 'Indian' about them. He explains this Indian-ness more deliberately in his book, *Indians: Portrait of a People* (Kakar, 2007). The book explores conceptions of family, sexuality, gender, modernity, caste, communal conflict, death, and religion and ends with a chapter on 'Indian Mind,' which brings together different facets of 'Indian life' and delivers the 'building blocks of Indian-ness' in Karma, rebirth, and moksha.

In the opening of the chapter on the 'Indian Mind,' Kakar writes how the book carries the spirit of India:

> Spirit of India is not something elusive or ethereal but is a culturally shared part of the mind, a certain Indian-ness which is reflected in the way the inhabitants of the subcontinent approach daily tasks as well as eternal questions of human existence.
>
> *(p. 180)*

This spirit of Indian-ness underlies and guides the inner world of Indians which determines the way they live life and organize the world around them. What Kakar writes after these lines is confusing. 'Let's begin with the Indian (here, again primarily Hindu) view of the world' (p. 180). This is confusing, and with respect to his explanation of what it is to be 'Indian,' I do not understand his use of the phrase 'primarily Hindu.' Primarily 'Hindu,' is confusing more so because earlier Kakar explained how 'Hindu' is a civilizational category which includes people of all faiths, so what does he mean with the word 'primary'? It implies there are Others, who aren't primarily Hindus. Here, 'Hindu' no longer functions as a civilizational category but becomes a religious identity whose worldview Kakar holds central in the discussion of the 'Indian Mind.' This undoing of cultural into religious identity in the context of 'Indian,' makes one wonder who Kakar (almost unconsciously) writes about when he writes about Indians. He provides the answer in his own admission where he says in the introduction of the book how this book is about 'upper caste and middle caste Hindus' while 'Others at the margins of Hindu society (Dalits, Trials, Christians, and Muslims) will only find fleeting resemblances' (p. 7). It is this category of Others that he draws a comparison to earlier when he says 'Indian, but primarily Hindu.' The evocation of the religious identity of Hindus as primary in the discussion of 'Indian,' suggests the possibility that the word 'Indian' doesn't imply a cultural category but a political one; since the majority is referenced. It is an empirical reality that Hindus are the majority community among the religions in the country, and there is a grave danger in promulgating the Hindu worldview as the Indian worldview. Kakar proposes 'Hindu' as if it is a cultural category.

The civilizational argument falls through, as Kakar doesn't expound on what from the Islamic civilization was assimilated into the Hindu civilization, and the ways in which it produced an Indic civilization from which Indian-ness is analyzed. The way in which 'pre-eminently Hindu civilization' produced an Indian-ness as a result of the Islamic acceleration is neither explained nor demonstrated via cultural practices. This cultural argument also falls through with the non-specification of religious difference in 'Hindu' as a cultural category, which gives away to his use of 'Hindu' in terms of a majority. If religious differences don't hold true, then despite majority and minority political numbers, everyone is a Hindu. If the majority status of Hindus is rendered primary to Others, whom Kakar treats as marginal to Hindu society, there is little doubt in believing that 'Hindu' is a religious political category instead of a cultural one. A keen observer would find evidence in Kakar's discussion of the 'Religious and Spiritual Life' of Indians in the book, where he discusses Hinduism and again cites how 'this chapter is considered with the faith of the majority' (p. 134). The constant reminder of the 'religion of majority' in the discussion of 'Indian' culture or identity is perturbing because by doing so Kakar ends up implying the obvious connections between Hinduism, the majority, and 'Indian.' Webbed across these connections, Indian becomes a political category that concerns itself with majority views. At the heart of this political category lies religious difference for it's the basis of marking the minority and the majority. Hindus are the majority because they are larger in number by comparison to Muslims (or Christians, Sikhs, and Buddhists).

Hindus and Muslims as categorical references are punctuated with religious difference, which manifests in political distinctions between them; in the socio-political discourse, Muslims are referred to as 'the religious minority' in the country. It is true that there are other religious minorities in the country with a history of interaction with the Hindu religious majority. The relationship between Hindus and Muslims requires a special mention in the analysis of 'Indian' across Kakar's writing. In his portrait of 'Indian,' the Hindu-Muslim conflict is given a generous inclusion. Its significance is rooted in the fact that it is the only community or minority which is included in Kakar's category of 'Indian.' There is yet to come to a psychoanalytic study of Hindu-Christian or Hindu-Buddhist relations. It's obvious that Hindu-Muslim relations are crucial to the inner world of, to use Kakar's words, 'Indian' but primarily Hindu. In the next section, I outline the political persuasions of the unconscious mechanisms of Kakar's writing on Hindu-Muslim relations.

Ontology of a riot: Hindu-Muslim relations in psychoanalysis in India

The one thing that stands out resolutely in Kakar's writing on Hindu-Muslim relations is their conflictual nature. Even when the object of his inquiry isn't the violence between them, the communal relations are conceived of as conflictual. Inclusion of the Hindu–Muslim conflict in his description of 'Indians' points not only to the psychic and social significance that communal conflict seemingly occupies in the definition of an Indian, but it is the only time Muslims becomes a part of 'Indian' identity for there remains no mention of Muslims in the analysis of 'being Indian.' In his description of the ways in which both the communities perceive each other, Kakar offers as if psychological reasons for this inevitable conflict.

He writes how Muslims see Hindus as 'cruel and cowardly' (Kakar, 2007, p. 158), while Hindus see Muslims as powerful, animal-like, and manifested with images of 'rampant sexuality and physical ferocity' (p. 157). Two different psychic mechanisms are at play which influences the way both the communities view each other.

'Splitting' becomes dominant in the Hindu imagination of Muslims where 'self-esteem is maintained by projecting the bad, the dirty, the impure to another group, the Muslim, with which one is constantly compared' (Kakar, 1995, p. 206). In the process of splitting, a Hindu grandiose self is formed which is righteous and pure, while the Muslim becomes the container of all persecutory fantasies of Hindus. Persecutory anxiety dominates the Muslim imagination of Hindus where 'it signals a situation of great danger and carries with it, the fear of groups symbolic death, an annihilation of group's collective identity' (p. 230). Propelled by this sense of annihilation and triggered by persecutory anxiety around Hindus, Muslims cling deeper to their religious identity. It ends up creating Muslims grandiose in their religious identity while Hindus are the imaginary persecutors. Psychoanalysis with its splitting and persecution explains how Hindus' and Muslims' perceptions of each other as opposites is crucially tied to their narcissism, and it is, for reasons of both grandiosity as well as self-preservation, that they are less likely to see each other as anything else.

Kakar's conception of the Hindu-Muslim conflict reminds of Freud's writing on the 'narcissism of minor differences' where he explains how groups with little differences between them forge these differences to be larger than they are to preserve the narcissism of their identity. He writes on different occasions how it forms 'the basis of feelings of hostility and strangeness; (Freud, 1917) and 'allows for a convenient and relatively harmless satisfaction of the inclination to aggression, by means of which cohesion between the members of the community is made easier' (Freud, 1930, p. 114). In Freud's definition, difference and narcissism are intricately linked with regard to communities such that it seems that communal existence is possible only through difference. Karl Figlio (2012) revises Freud's argument to state how it's not the difference but 'dread of sameness,' which leads communities to create delusional differences. It's through these delusional differences that they preserve narcissistic identity. In the context of Hindu-Muslim conflictual relations, Figlio's conception resonates more than Freud's.

In Kakar's argument, both the communities see each other through unconscious mechanisms. Both splitting and persecutory anxieties lead to a paranoid psychic structure. Melanie Klein's (1946) paranoid-schizoid position is most useful here. The idealized good object is introjected to produce a grandiose self while the devalued bad object is projected to produce the Other for whom one has persecutory fantasies. For Figlio, this splitting happens because one is unable to tolerate that two communities are actually similar. This similarity is what threatens the narcissism of the communities and they create differences, delusionally. Analyzing this dread underlying Hindu-Muslim 'conflictual relations' would be more promising simply because of its depressive potential. It re-centers the argument on the assumption of a kind of narcissism in which people of a community are insecure about who they are, they institute differences. Its depressive potential, i.e. the value of ambivalence, lies in the thesis that communities aren't premised on differences. Since these differences are created, one can imagine psychically working with communities to realize the underlying similarity between them in a way where differences can be tolerated without necessarily splitting to produce not just a paranoid projection laden version of the Other but also an equally paranoid grandiose version of self.

This potential for coexistence remains crucially missing in Kakar's reading of Hindu-Muslim relations for he only etches them narcissistically surviving through difference.

His thesis of difference is drawn from his work with both the communities during the 1990s communal violence in Hyderabad, where it is owing to the event of the riot, latent fantasies of violence manifest in persecutory views of each other. Using these to determine the general perspective of Hindu-Muslim relations is to identify riots not as epistemic to communal relations but as ontological. Views that Hindus and Muslims have of each other through splitting becomes the evidence of phenomenological experience reduced to the ontology of communal relations.

How does one understand this ontology of communal violence in the making of Indian identity? While being Indian continues to be primarily Hindu, Muslims are introduced to the conception of India as the people who Hindus will hate and people who will hate Hindus. Born, as if in the mind of 'Indian,' primarily Hindu through violence, 'Muslim' becomes a category that is not only created out of projected parts but also ceases to exist in absence of projection. It's not just the making of the Muslim as violent which is the consequence of the ontology of a communal riot between the two communities, but it's the absence of any other image of Muslims in the mind of 'Indian,' primarily Hindu. Kakar's insertion of 'acts of compassion and self-sacrifice' (1995, p. 163), disregarding difference in the face of violence, fails to hold true in the absence of any detail or description of such acts from any community. Muslims, thereby, emerge in the mind of an 'Indian,' primarily Hindu, as the violent Other whose Otherness is essentially lodged in religious difference.

In the next section, I explore how religious difference manifests in Kakar's writing to produce the Muslim as an essentially religious entity.

Muslims: fundamentally religious

Kakar explains how tension around violence in riots builds up, 'when religious identities come to the forefront in a large number of people because of a perceived threat to their particular identities' (2007, p. 163). In his study of the 1990 communal riots in Hyderabad, Kakar theorizes the Muslim identity. Based on ethnographic interviews, Kakar identifies the notion of a perceived threat to be central to the formation of Muslim identity. He writes how Muslims, 'tend to see themselves a helpless victim of historical circumstance, where India irrespective of its formal constitution, has become a Hindu country.' They feel that 'the regime is now of the Hindus and discrimination against Muslims has become a fact of life.' Muslims, thereby, 'withdraw further into the shelter provided by the religious community and hold on to all markers of religious identity – the Quran, the Sharia, the Urdu language, the *madarasa* or 'religious school.' Following their religious leaders, 'Muslims believe that these markers lead them out of their current predicament' (Kakar, 2007, p. 160). For Kakar, clinging on to these markers fosters a religious identity, which he defines as fundamentalist. He explains that fundamentalism is a 'narcissistic enhancement to self-esteem fractured by historical fate' (Kakar, 1995, p. 238). I wonder, what he alludes to when he writes, 'historical circumstance as well as historical fate'? I suppose that in writing about historical fate, he alludes to the coming to end of the privilege – economic, social, political, religious – which Muslims enjoyed under the Mughal rule. Historical circumstance, thereby, becomes the incidence of the Hindu majority, despite Muslim political rule. Kakar reads this feeling of victimhood in Muslims and explains it as a consequence of 'lost privilege.' Since Muslims do not enjoy the political privilege, they misconstrue a nonthreatening historical fact, i.e. 'the formal reality of constitution.' According to Kakar, they read historical persecution in the secularism of the constitution. This sense of persecution drives them toward religion, which serves as a narcissistic identification in the identity of the fundamentalist.

Kakar's conjecturing can be questioned on two accounts. First, by eliding the history of communal relations in the country, which besides being hostile and violent has been determined by the political circumstances that enable Hindus to wield sufficient social and political power over Muslims as a minority. In a book written after the demolition of the Babri Masjid in 1992, where 'anti-Muslim sentiment' was politically touted by the right-wing party BJP and its paramilitary force RSS, Kakar insists how Muslims sense of persecution is essentially psychological and emerges out of their own minority anxiety. He fails to account how the 'secular constitution' could do little as the RSS volunteers broke the mosque solely with bricks and stones triggering communal riots across the country.

Where large numbers of Hindus enjoy the support of a national political party that believes India is the land of the Hindu and engages in rioting at one end and discrimination on the other, helplessness of Muslims is far from being imagined.

For Kakar, however, the Muslim sense of persecution is a historical consequence which finds refuge in religion. Even if one were to believe Kakar's argument of religion as the basis of narcissistic enhancement, which is a reasonable psychoanalytic analysis, what disturbs is his one-sided approach in its study. He is only interested in questions of religion with respect to Islam. His subtle implication of madrassas, Islamic religious institutions, being the breeding ground of fundamental Islam (1995, pp. 282–283), reflects his understanding of Islam as potentially fundamentalist. This potential is actualized when Kakar explicitly draws upon how, in clinging to religion, out of persecutory anxiety, Muslims become fundamentalists.

Religion as fundamentalism is a one-sided argument by Kakar, as it exists only in the context of Islam. Hindu identity, even in its most evident violent evocations remains 'revivalist' at best, where the violence is justified in the search of a 'new Hindu identity.' With respect to this Hindu identity, the Sangh Parivar (umbrella term of right-wing organizations namely RSS and BJP), Kakar writes, 'cannot be faulted for fostering a Hindu pride or even trying to claim a sense of superiority vis-a-vis the Muslim. These are normal aims of group's narcissist economy' (1995, p. 214) While, at the same time he writes about Muslim identity, 'even though the appellation of fundamentalist is a derogatory word stigmatizing Muslims, there is no other word which is a satisfactory substitute. There lies in the nature of phenomena itself, its pious passions, strong beliefs and inflexible values' (p. 281) becomes the way a religious community preserves its identity by selective retrieval of doctrines, beliefs, and practices from the sacred past (p. 281).

Even when he analyzes speeches of nationalist demagogues from both the communities, his description differs. The Hindu speaker Sadhavi Rithambra is introduced as a 'star speaker of Sangh Parivar' (p. 197), while Ubedullah Khan Azmi is identified as a 'moderate fundamentalist' (p. 226). A moderate fundamentalist is someone who like all 'fundamentalists subscribes to the founding myth of the existence of a truly great Islamic society but as a moderate believed in politics that adapted to constantly changing political realities' (Kakar, 1995, p. 227).

While describing Sangh Parivar, Kakar writes how it has provided 'cultural memory' of the common presentation of the past in the times of rapid change to the middle-class Hindus and this is the 'reason of their social resonance and political success' (p. 217). He, however, doesn't underlie how this cultural memory is premised on a persecutory fantasy for Muslims, which is at the core of Hindutva, the ideological persuasion of Sangh Parivar, even when he details its persecutory elements while analyzing Rithambahara's speech.

The success of Sangh Parivar and its belief in Hindu pride is premised on the acrimonious relationship with Muslims. The father of Hindu nationalism, Veer Savarkar wrote, in his famous treatise, *Hindutva* (1932), how Muslims were outsiders and till the time they were Muslims, they could be not be assimilated in Hindusthan (Land of Hindus). His description of Hindus as the autochthon's inhabitants of Hindusthan is what governs Sangh Parivar and its ideology of the Muslim as the outsider – an invader who must be remembered in the discourse of history as a 'temple breaker.' Historians Romila Thapar (2004) and Audrey Truschke explain how premodern Indian history has been written in a way to project Muslims as invaders, whose political action is interpreted through religious difference. Historian and Subaltern scholar Gyanendra Pandey (1993), writes how the nationalistic discourse of history has created the belief in a pre-Islamic era of glorious Hindu rule, which necessarily holds Muslim invasions as the reason of its discontinuity. This belief feeds into the resurgence of the Hindu nationalist identity, which according to the political scientist Christopher Jaffrelot (1998, 2005), targets Muslims in India as a way of undoing what seems to be historical wrongs.

In the face of historical, political and social discourses on Hindu-Muslim relations and questions of nationalism, how does one understand Kakar's refusal to identify 'the revivalist Hindu identity' as Hindu militancy, Hindu fundamentalism, or even Hindu nationalism, instead analyzing it as 'an identity that selects many of its symbols, myths and images from a traditional stock' (1995, p. 196)?

Here Kakar's description of 'Hindu' as a cultural identity is useful for arguing how, in his discussion of Hindus, Kakar doesn't invoke religion. He continues to speak of the Hindu identity as a 'cultural community' (p. 214), which finds the definition of religion invoked in the presence of Muslims.. In doing this, Kakar neatly divides religion and culture between Hindus and Muslims, where 'Hindu' becomes a cultural identity, while 'Muslim' remains a religious identity. In not calling out elements of militancy in Hindu nationalism, Kakar doesn't only deliver a biased view of both the communities but also ends up foregrounding fundamentalism in Muslims. What I call, in the next section, the 'politics of secular psychoanalysis' provides an explanation of how Kakar deems the Muslims as fundamentalists and in doing so redeems the Hindus as cultural, non-religious, nonviolent, and hence, secular Indians.

Politics of secular: Indian identity

Kakar laments how, in the writing of political discourses, the role of fantasies are not acknowledged and hence there exists 'only a partial and thus inadequate understanding for the reasons for the success of political formations based on religious mobilization' (1995, p. 195). Responding to Kakar's explanation of a lack of acceptance of the 'cultures of fantasy' in social discourses, I argue that Kakar, in his writing on Hindu-Muslim relations, rejects the articulation of the 'political acting out of fantasies.'

As Kakar outlines the grandiosity of Hindus and the persecutory anxieties of Muslims, he fails to attend to the psychic fantasies of the two communities with the historical reality of political dominance. Nowhere in his writing is there is an acknowledgment of the historical discrimination and social prejudice that Muslims face as minorities. Equally absent is any mention of the political clout

Hindu nationalist parties enjoy in central government. In absence of history and politics, one struggles to understand the positions of 'Hindu and Muslim' in Kakar's writing. In my reading of his work, I find both these categories defined differently, as 'Hindu' becomes a political category, which he masks as cultural (remember, 'Indian,' primarily Hindu), while 'Muslim' becomes only a religious category. Kakar's writing on Hindu-Muslim relations can be envisioned as a dialogue between politics and religion through the realm of fantasies.

Kakar misses the political potential of his argument when he identifies riots as conditions where the two communities experience persecutory fantasies against each other. The calamity of conflict exacerbated in communal riots is equally present for minorities in the everyday regimes of state action. It is true that in riots an intense sense of persecution is experienced by the conflicting communities, however, this sense is what persistently grips minorities in their everyday exchanges. What happens when one of the communities with political leverage ends up tormenting the other community for fantastical reasons? While historians and political scientists have asserted over the years how the discourse of nationalist history 'produced' Muslims in India as an invader and an outsider (discussed in the previous section), Kakar refuses to acknowledge the role this historical memory would have played in sustaining and even reinforcing Hindu grandiosity. He explains how this grandiosity is premised on identifying Muslims as the Other in a way that it almost 'needs' the Muslim to feel Hindu. However, he doesn't articulate how this self-identification as a Hindu necessarily posits Muslims in opposition to Hindus, ruling out all possibilities of convergence or of having a composite category, which includes both. The ontology of communal violence pits one community against the other and this results in the doing away of any possibility of coexistence. It also means that which is Hindu can never be Muslim.

Does it mean if 'Indian' is Hindu then 'Indian' can never be Muslim? Kakar's scholarship doesn't proclaim 'Muslim' to not be Indian, yet all frames and images that are evoked of Muslims in India are with respect to them being Others, belonging essentially to an entirely different civilization – Islam. 'Indian' is unwittingly identified with the Hindu civilization. My concern, however, is not only the ways in which Kakar renders Muslims in India outside the category of being Indian. But, the ways in which he secularizes Hindu identity while incriminates Muslim identity in religion.

As demonstrated in the paper, Kakar refers to Hindus as a cultural category and in terms of civilization. Nowhere does he invoke Hinduism as a religion. Even if a reference to religion is made, it is explained through spirituality and a 'way of life' instead of a system of behaviors and practices which are organized around Hindu Gods.

He evokes religion only with respect to Muslims as he describes how the response to persecution becomes religion and religion become fundamentalism. In placing it akin to religious identity, Kakar makes 'Muslim' in itself a fundamentalist category inscribed in Islam. Islam doesn't only become a fundamentalist religion but, in being fundamentalist, it becomes 'the' religion itself.

My contention is that by making 'Hindu' cultural and not religious, and being Indian as primarily being Hindu, Kakar creates the Indian identity as a secular category. This Indian identity, in being a cultural identity, does not speak of 'religion' hence argues against the inclusion of Hinduism on religious grounds. Even as one speaks of an Indian identity, Hinduism continues to be its frame of reference. What becomes 'religious,' to this secular Indian identity, i.e. the one it must maintain distance from, is Islam. In explaining how Muslims, driven by a persecutory anxiety, end up being religious, Kakar offers a psychoanalytic reason as to why Muslims aren't Indians; they are religious. He punctuates his argument further to say how religion, i.e. Islam, is a problem because its identity rests on it being fundamentalist. 'Regressed, rigid, concrete and devoid of pleasure,' a fundamentalist is but, of course, a Muslim. Islam becomes a reason why Muslims cannot be Indians. In being Muslims, they are religious and in being religious they are fundamentalists. The consequence of Kakar's foregrounding of Muslims as fundamentalists is more far-reaching than just a prejudiced view. Its political impetus resides in rendering Islam as the 'problem.' This problem (of fundamentalism in Islam), Kakar explains, is through its pathological potential for it's a response born out of the persecutory anxiety Muslims have about Hindus. He fails to elaborate how, even if one were to believe in the existence of this persecutory anxiety, it would be related to the persecutory fantasy Hindus have of Muslims. The fantasy of persecution that guides the political and social interactions that Hindus have with Muslims. 'Fundamentalist,' becomes a pathological response to persecution which is central to Islam thereby central to the Muslim identity in Kakar's writing.

Conclusion

In the present chapter, my use of the word 'political' relates to the unconscious desires which manifest in cultural reproduction. Anthony Elliot writes how the issue in psychoanalysis is 'the interlacing of repressed desire and power relations, unconscious passions and cultural reproduction' (2015, p. 182). In agreement with Herbert Marcuse, I don't think psychoanalysis needs to be 'related' to social and political conditions – 'they themselves are social and political categories' (1966, p. 28). My focus in pursuing the 'politics of secular psychoanalysis in India' is to uncover the unconscious mechanism of power relations that govern the way Hindus and Muslims organize each other as well and themselves. In my argument, these power relations produce cultures of domination in the constitution of identity and repressed desire (which is split, interjected, and projected). Indian identity defines the constituents of Hindu identity but also hides it in the argument of 'secularism.' This secular Indian identity, primarily Hindu, exerts a culture of domination which produces religion. This religion becomes Islam. Psychically pathologized as fundamentalist and politically contested as being national, I wonder if psychoanalysis in India dovetails into the existing contemporary political discourse and finds the Muslim only as an Islamic fundamentalist and not Indian.

References

Anidjar, G. (2006). Secularism. *Critical Inquiry*. 33(1), 52–77.

Elliott, A. (2015). *Psychoanalytic Theory: An Introduction*. New York: Palgrave Macmillan.

Fenichel, O. (1945). *Psychoanalytic Theory of Neuroses*. New York: Norton.

Fenichel, O. (1954). *The Collected Papers of Otto Fenichel*. New York: Norton.

Figlio, K. (2012). The dread of sameness: social hatred and Freud's narcissism of minor differences. In: L. Austead, ed., *Politics and Psychoanalysis: Exclusion and Politics of Representation*. London: Karnac, pp. 7–24.

Freud, S. (1917). *Mourning and Melancholia*. S.E. 14. London: Hogarth.

Freud, S. (1927). *Future of an Illusion*. S.E. 21. London: Hogarth.

Freud, S. (1930). *New Introductory Lectures*. S.E. 22. London: Hogarth.

Hartman, H. (1944). *Psychoanalysis and Sociology in Essays on Ego Psychology*. New York: Norton.

Horney, K. (1937). *The Neurotic Personality of Our Times*. New York: Norton.

Jaffrelot, C. (1998). *The Hindu Nationalist Movement and Indian Politics*. New York: Columbia University Press.

Jeffrelot, C. (2005). *Sangh Parivar: A Reader*. New Delhi, India: Oxford University Press.

Kakar, S. (1995). *Colors of Violence*. New Delhi: Penguin Books.

Kakar, S. (1997). *Culture and Psyche. Selected Essays*. New Delhi, India: Oxford University Press.

Kakar, S. (2007). *Indians: Portrait of a People*. New Delhi: Penguin Books.

Klein, M. (1946). Notes on schizoid mechanisms. *International Journal of Psychoanalysis*. 27, 99–110.

Marcuse, H. (1966). *Eros and Civilization: A Critical Inquiry into Freud*. Boston, MA: Beacon Press.

Pandey, G. (1993). The civilized and the barbarian. In: G. Pandey, ed., *Hindus and the Others: The Question of Identity in India Today*. New Delhi: Vikings, pp. 10–34.

Savarkar, V.D. (1932). *Hindutva: Who Is a Hindu?* Bombay: Veer Savarkar Prakashan.

Thapar, R. (2004). *Somnatha: Many Voices of History*. London: Penguin; Viking.

5

BETWEEN NEUTRALITY AND DISAVOWAL

Being Muslim psychotherapists in India

Shifa Haq and Sabah Siddiqui

This chapter emerged from a clinical encounter between Shifa (the first author) and Dev in a Delhi clinic. Both authors of the chapter are Muslim women and psychoanalytic psychotherapists who have worked to the greater extent with Hindu clients in the urban space of the capital city of India. The high proportion of Hindu clients may only reflect the demographics of India, where over 80% of the population is counted to be Hindu. It is rarer to see Muslims in the other chair: that of the psychotherapist. Sitting in this 'other chair' has been difficult and not so difficult for us as psychotherapists. It has been difficult because before we reach the clinic we are already confronted with psychoanalytic literature in India that posits the Indian Muslim as the Other, the outsider (and we shall come to this later in the chapter). On the other hand, working in the clinic has been simpler; we speak the same language as our clients, we are familiar with the idioms that allow patients to locate their personal experiences in cultural context. We do not look too different either; we have the same racial features as our clients and we dress similarly (or at least in the standard way expected in the formal space of the clinic). Our clinical practice is not very different from our Hindu colleagues, after all, we have studied under the same masters, and our psychoanalysis is not 'Islamicised'. We could pass off as anybody … just not Muslim. Nonetheless, our Muslim identity comes up sometimes. It is, in fact, inescapable in an increasingly partisan society. As the body politic is being crossed by religious and caste lines, issues of religious identity are becoming more visible in clinical work in India.

At the same time, the psychoanalyst and the psychoanalytic psychotherapist is confronted by the maxim to preserve the neutrality of the analyst/therapist's person in the eyes of the analysand/patient. It is theorised that the neutrality of the person of the analyst allows the patient to make use of the analyst as s/he requires it. The analyst must allow herself to become an object that the patient can use imaginatively. In Winnicottian terms, this is called object–usage.[1]

Nonetheless, we would like to think what it means for the analyst to be a neutral object in a political scene where acceptance of difference and diversity are no longer ideals of community-living. In the next part, we will begin with a case analysis of Dev, a Hindu man in conflict with Muslim women who has ended up in the clinic of a Muslim therapist.

Making a mistake: a case illustration

In the summer of 2013, I (the first author, Shifa Haq) met Dev – a male patient, age 52 – twice a week for psychoanalytic psychotherapy. His relationship with Shaila – a young, Muslim woman- had come to an end when she slept with another man. A mental health practitioner himself, he had met Shaila in a community setting and soon discovered that Shaila, a married woman with two children, liked having sex and would enter multiple sexual relations outside her marriage with known and unknown men. Soon into their friendship, Shaila told Dev that she was addicted to sex and felt scared of the ferocity of her yearning that had led her into difficult situations in the past (she had slept with her male cousins, brother-in-law, neighbours, and had even been publicly humiliated by women around her for it). Having worked with addictive behaviour after his own recovery from heroin abuse, Dev felt he could intuitively understand Shaila's helplessness. Excited by her overtures and the fantasy of rescuing her, Dev had made her a pragmatic offer: to have sex with each other to avoid the dangers of her picking up strange men. Soon into their sexual relationship, Dev discovered passionate feelings of love and pain on coming to know of Shaila's childhood stories of being sexually abused, her parental neglect as well as their destitution, out of which soared deep longings in him to shelter and comfort her. It was shattering for Dev to experience Shaila drawing boundaries with him, so she could find new lovers! In what looked like a complicated mourning, Dev sought therapy.

He spoke unapologetically about Shaila's moral inferiority and lustfulness, something common in Muslims he thought. In the first month of our work, Dev spoke not so much of his pain as his lack of judgement to have fallen in love with someone like Shaila. 'Muslims are dirty – they don't have prohibitions on who to fuck! What Shaila did is very common in them', he said with much agitation. I shifted in my chair, with intense feelings regurgitating inside me, as I struggled to think about the hate I felt for him filling up the room. It was becoming clear that the equation of love and hate between Hindus and Muslims was begging to give meaning to his loss in our encounter. As I was reflecting upon my role as a psychotherapist in containing the hate and anger he was experiencing, I was impressed by the lack of inhibition on his part about my role as listener and interlocutor to his hate against Muslim women. Did he want to hurt me, deputised to be Shaila in his fantasy? Was he testing my ability to tolerate his misogyny and hate for the Other so as to find a non-retaliatory space for potential mutuality? Or was the mental gymnastics between us, our enactments, a way to recover something redeemable in a hopelessly unchanging palimpsest of communal hurts?

Two months into therapy, Dev rented one of his houses to a Muslim woman. With her husband away making a living in the Middle-East, the new tenant appealed to Dev's pragmatic self: a lonely woman with a child would not be a hassle as a tenant. The scene, however, was ripe for repetition. The new tenant cheated him of a small amount of money, and this opened a deep depression in him. Full of spite, he yelled, 'It's my fate to be stuck with Muslim women!'

I replied, 'And now, a Muslim therapist . . .' After a pause, he asked, 'Are you Muslim?' Baffled by his question, while I prepared to say something, he said chastising me, 'You should not have told me that!' I continued to pick my brain about this sudden realisation that he was shocked to be confronted with my Muslim identity while feeling puzzled about how he could not know that from my name.[2] Piling one more thought to increase my bewilderment, Dev added, 'You made a mistake! You are not supposed to reveal things about yourself. It interferes with therapy!'

In expressing his disappointment, Dev communicated an odd truth about our interaction. In our dyad, one of us was actively excluded without the other's knowledge. Dev did not want to know that his therapist was a Muslim woman. She had to be a neutral object in his fantasy, which also meant by default unexceptionally Hindu. Is this exclusion, its grief, the area of work between the Hindu-Muslim therapeutic dyad? Is the unveiling of this form of relating through exclusion between a Hindu patient and a Muslim therapist, the mistake that ought to have been avoided? Can 'not revealing' be something other than a question of technique or training? Furthermore, within psychoanalysis, how do we look at the 'object' who speaks back and the 'subject' that does not wish to know (Benjamin 1988)?

Between subject and object

Beginning with Freud, the use of the term 'object' stands as a foundational difficulty in recognising the other. Curiously, the translation of an other, in object relations theories, into an internal representation with the use of the term object, remains widely accepted and least onerous. Benjamin (1990) writes:

> Perhaps the elision between 'real' others and their internal representation is so widely tolerated because the epistemological question of what is reality and what is representation appears to us – in our justifiable humility – too ecumenical and lofty for our parochial craft. Or perhaps, as psychoanalysts, we are not really troubled by the question of reality.
>
> *(p. 184)*

Of course, beyond the inexactitude of language, collapsing the subject into an object exposes the difficulty in the psychoanalytic imagination of the meeting of *two subjects* as a requisite for a radical encounter of the self/selves. It is the crux of epistemic ambivalence: to know or not to know the will of the other, our separateness or relatedness.

One of the outcomes of the epistemic ambivalence – that need to know or the need to not know the other – is its compromise formation – to know the other through the vertex of strangeness. Strangeness of the other, as a defence, does not imply the other's singularity or particularity – a 'pure' signifier or the essence that makes the other who they are. Rather, a fatal disconnection, or an attack on linking, that forfeits contact with true knowledge about the other (Bion 1959). In the Indian context, Islam is seen as a stranger to Hindu culture as well as foreign to its organisation.[3] The present-day rhetoric of the Hindu-Muslim divide preserves, at its core, the imagination of the upper-caste Hindu as the core national subject, in a need to defend its expansionist view in service of pure Hindu identity against the threat of Muslim antagonism. Haunted by the unrepresented violence of the Partition of 1947 that saw the killing of several hundred thousand and the displacement of 10–12 million along religious lines, the Hindu Right retains a deep suspicion of the Muslim citizens of India, as well as of liberal thought, secularism, and inter-religious amity[4] (Bhutalia 2000; Das 1997). In effect, the upper-caste Hindus are the 'organic, original nationals', and Muslims are conceived to be 'enduring strangers or at best minor subjects of the nation' (Kumar 2013). For Muslims, a reference to their foreignness bespeaks of a deep alienation and a doubt of their true inclusion in the Indian ensemble or 'homeland'.

The writings of Sudhir Kakar, an eminent psychoanalyst from India, situate the historical conflict between Hindus-Muslims at the heart of intrapsychic and inter-group dynamics. The hateful and the undesirable aspects of the self are projected on the other, who serves as a container for these hated parts (Akhtar 2005; Kakar 1995; Kakar and Kakar 2007; Varvin 2012). Seen from this lens, for Dev, his Muslim lover Shaila was behaving in ways consistent with the Hindu imagination of deceptive, lustful, and aggressive Muslims, an 'object' or a vessel carrying the parts externalised by the Hindu subject. It feels, however, we are back to square one: the other as an object to an agentic subject! The formulation of the other as a container of devalued, dreaded aspects of the self or the group convincingly articulates the intrapsychic expectation and possible resolution. It, however, assumes that the other, the 'object' does not resist or speak back about what is being introjected into the 'object', the other subject.

Why neutrality? Why not disavowal?

Freud (1927), in the paper 'Fetishism', differentiates sharply between the repression of affect and repression of ideas. Speculating on the theory of sexual difference and its role in fetishism, Freud argues and rejects that the boy scotomises his perception of the woman's lack of a penis as a response to castration anxiety. On the contrary, observes Freud, that the perception persists and 'a very energetic action has been taken to maintain disavowal' (p. 154). Freud makes a distinction between the use of the two terms 'repression' and 'disavowal'. He argues that patients may fail to take cognizance of a piece of reality without developing psychosis when an important 'unwelcomed' aspect of reality is disavowed by the ego (p. 156). For Freud, repression signified a defence against the internal instinctual demands whereas disavowal implied a defence against the claims of external reality (Freud 1940; Zepf 2013). The subject defends against the 'unwelcomed' piece of reality, by keeping two currents of the mental life, as if existing side by side, such as knowing and not-knowing, hope and dread, and so on. The 'mutually incompatible assertions' can continue to co-exist as the aspect of reality are banished from knowledge (Freud 1927, p. 157)

We would like to reflect on 'the welcomed' in the clinical dyad between the Hindu patient and a Muslim therapist. How do the two subjects defend against the 'unwelcomed'? What happens when the banished knowledge returns? In Dev's surprise at the therapist's Muslim identity, we get a glimpse into the process of ex-nomination, both psychical and social, of the Muslim subject from the clinic while the Brahmanical Hindu imagination masquerades as 'the Indian psyche' (Kakar 1980). The Hindu patient experiences a sense of danger – what if the projected hate is followed by the return of projection (of hate) by the therapist? For the Muslim therapist, the danger lies in becoming aware of the disavowed anger, its underground existence, and rules of the performance of one's subjectivity. The insistence on neutrality works as a guard against of the discovery of a true recognition of the other's subjectivity. Equally interesting is how the banished or the disavowed other returns as a fetishised object with 'inherent' distinctness.[5] Could an analysis between the Hindu-Muslim therapeutic couple be free of such dynamics in the transference-countertransference matrix?

In an analytic dyad, principles of anonymity, neutrality, and abstinence enter or work seamlessly when the analyst and the patient share religious, ethnic, class, or gender locations. Unlike race, where the colour of the skin becomes a form of self-disclosure in analytic treatment, the religious identification of Muslim therapists, indiscernible in many ways, within a historical background of communal tensions and violence, is congealed to remain unavowed in the service of neutrality. How surprising that neutrality, and its insistence in psychoanalytic work, should imitate the Brahmanical notion of staying above the muddy waters – the filth of a chaotic interpersonal field.

Given the absence of attention paid to caste and religion in Indian psychoanalytic practice and theorisation, and for many analysts' their own training in the West where the cultural nuances may not have been analysed or engaged with, there is much to be recovered and worked through. Seen from the position of neutrality, it could be said that Dev needed to use therapy to articulate the hate and anger he felt at being betrayed and abandoned, as it relates to the pervasive themes in his life beginning from childhood. This was indeed the case. In one view, the therapist's neutrality and anonymity would be an important vehicle to reach Dev's felt experiences and recreate a possibility for a corrective one. Such a view would suggest that by introducing herself as a Muslim subject, the 'anxious' therapist spoke before the patient could voice his discomfort, that is if he did not rely on the disavowal of the 'unwelcomed' knowledge. In another view, however, the stance of neutrality and anonymity fails to interrogate the dynamic between the Hindu–Muslim therapeutic dyad. It could be said that the neutrality of the therapist in this specific case would reveal an underlying masochistic identification of the therapist to take patient's hateful projections about her group or religious identity without questioning the deeper unconscious dynamics between two people in the consulting room or the cultures or groups they belong to.

Could the stance of neutrality, its exalted status, stifle the therapist's identification with her religious identity and ask to distance, or dissociate herself from such identification? Isn't that what Freud did with his Jewish identity? Can a practice in which one's experiences and politics are kept frustratingly out of the picture become personally meaningful (Bobrow 2007)? It is our contention that this impasse can only be dealt with when we, with our patients, are present to what is going on and able to reflect from such a place, especially when our vulnerabilities spring into the room and converge (Mitchell 1993). What was more difficult than object-relating and object-usage, and more 'irksome' than many environment failures, for Winnicott, was 'the subject's perception of the object as an external phenomenon, not as a projective entity, in fact, recognition of it as an entity in its own right' (Winnicott 1968, p. 120). This irksome work is a potential space, something that remains a place for mutual exploration between Dev and the therapist in the fourth year of their work.

In the psychoanalytic theory and training, the modern dualism between emotional mind and rational mind returns in the notion of neutrality and anonymity. In classical psychoanalytic view, emotions and affects are understood to be drive derivatives with sexuality and aggression at its core to be brought under the reflection of secondary process rational thinking (Roland 1996, 2011). The view that emotions and affect could originate in the social and carry layers of cultural meaning remains disavowed from analytic formulations in practice and in training (Layton 2006). Just as psychoanalysis, with its claim to universality, is known to defend against the recognition of its European perspectivist location,[6] keeping non-European experience at an arm's distance, the Indian psychoanalytic theorisation assumes the Brahmanical Hindu worldview as its epigenesis. The myths, the stories, and the lens used to study Indian analysands, or education of trainees in Indian psychoanalytic groups, point towards an 'energetic' disavowal of cultural plurality for the maintenance of a master narrative. What we see between Dev and Shifa in the clinic is but a snapshot of how psychoanalysis is being thought as well as disseminated in India, which we have been witness to as Muslim psychoanalytic psychotherapists. We wish to consider the possibility of a conversation between two subjects, both wishing to know and to be known.

Who sits in the chair of the analyst?

On the one hand, it is possible that the question of the other is the not main object of investigation in an analysis. The question of the other may not be traditionally linked to symptom-formation and symptom relief. So an analysis can unfold (successfully) for a patient who has entered therapy to resolve internal conflicts impacted by family history and early childhood experiences; it may proceed by delving into childhood history, trauma, and object relations that has led them to make normative choices. Psychoanalysis could be a study of the unconscious processes behind the normal adjustments and adaptations a neurotic subject may be given to make. In the course of analysis, the patient will learn about their unconscious drives and experience the process as having been helpful and supportive. This can be a worthwhile analysis in itself.

On the other hand, the question of the *other* reveals an asymmetry in relations between people, an asymmetry in power, knowledge, desire. Therein can be an analysis where the other is at the forefront of the process, stumbled upon or even declared at the outset as the problems in living by the patient. Psychoanalysis would thus be an analysis of the experience of alienation in relation to the normative; alienation as an experience of difference that cannot be disavowed. It is doubly alienating because the projections from the other do not become an assimilable knowledge. Here the analysis would be called upon to reflect on the inassimilablity of the radical difference in an always-already normative society.

To flip the perspective, on the other side of the clinical room, there is the chair of the analyst. More often than not this chair is occupied by an analyst with all the privileges of race, class, caste, and gender. This analyst is the image of the default figure of the analyst, which is to say unexceptional. As long as this chair was filled by the white man in a private office, the *other* operated as an idea rather than a physical presence in the room of the clinic. However, as the chair is occupied by analysts/therapists situated very differently, the other is no longer a distant figure, but an actual presence in the room. The analyst may be not-White (in the context of Western hegemony) or not-Hindu (in the case of Brahmanical hegemony). When the other has come to the analyst's chair, clinical practice is not only about the personal histories and symptomology of the patient. The knowledge of the other is being developed in situ in the clinical encounter. This other analyst/therapist cannot choose to allow this moment to subside where difference strikes right at the heart of the clinical encounter.

We contend that it is not only the burden of otherness that moves this *other* analyst but the limits of the principle of neutrality in psychoanalysis. On insisting on a stance of neutrality, there is an assumption that we can remain neutral in the face of being confronted by radical difference. It is assumed that it is either not hard to be neutral for a properly trained analyst, or if it is hard it is still therapeutic for the analyst to maintain a stance of neutrality. Here we glimpse what is disavowed in neutrality: the will to be found, the will to be known.

Conclusion

Our object of study in this chapter has been the Hindu-Muslim dynamic in India. In the Indian context, psychoanalytic theory and practice retains almost exclusively the cultural aesthetic of the dominant Hindu culture, indisputably influencing other minority cultures through its myths, philosophy, and language deployed to resonate with the Brahmanical experience of society. Both historically and culturally, its most difficult to find the Islamic aesthetic, history or presence in psychoanalysis in India. This has implications for both the training and practice of psychoanalysis. The expectation of neutrality in psychoanalysis, which we suppose directs us to some assumed default position that the analyst occupies, colludes with the Hindu-Muslim dynamics with an unreflected disavowal of the Muslim from the dyad. It is, as if, there is something like an analytic religion performing in the very least at the unconscious of Indian psychoanalysis, which becomes explicit when Indian Muslim psychotherapists interact with it. Nonetheless, psychoanalysis as a clinical practice must not only work with but also challenge social practice. The radical potential of psychoanalysis is its ability to imagine a narrative of subjectivity that is at odds with the consciously repeated 'truth' of society. Both in theory and practice, psychoanalysis turns conventional wisdom on its head about the relation to the other. This chapter was an attempt to reimagine a psychoanalysis in India that is not Hindu, not Muslim. We propose one way to do it is to interrogate the principle of neutrality that bars an authentic engagement with the other in psychoanalysis. There are many subjects here, and so are we.

Acknowledgements

We would like to show our gratitude to those who have helped shape this chapter: Karuna Chandrashekar, constant companion and co-thinker, Shubhendu Ghosh for editorial support, Zehra Mehdi for academic input, Neil Altman for critical feedback, and members of the audience at the Islamic Psychoanalysis: Psychoanalytic Islam conference in Manchester for hearing us out and giving us invaluable comments.

Notes

1 As Joseph Bobrow summarises it in *Disavowal of the Personal in Psychoanalytic Training* (2007, p. 268), 'In Winnicott's imaginative telling, the infant has the marvelous and crucial experience of creating the nourishment that is provided by virtue of the mother's attunement. He creates the object, magically, a creative omnipotence. There is also a ruthlessness we must pass through where we destroy the object, in fantasy, without concern with its protection and survival. Winnicott called this object usage: all-out, no holes-barred usage through we create the object as objectively perceived and place it outside the sphere of omnipotent generation'.
2 In the Indian context, names (especially surnames) are markers of religious and caste identity for the greater majority of the population.

3 The strangeness of the Muslim is in contrast to the the similarity of the Muslim in appearance and language demonstrates that the uncanny is in operation (Freud 1919).
4 Ghar wapsi, the fantasy of conversion of Muslims to bring them back to the original Hindu fold remains a passionate preoccupation of the Hindu Right.
5 In a case discussion, for instance, a colleague who identifies as an upper caste Hindu woman, spoke wondrously about her work with a Muslim woman patient who, despite her lack of insight and concrete thinking (read criteria of analyzability), taught her therapist the value of faith as a dimension of resilience (read orientalism).
6 See Altman, N. (2015). *Psychoanalysis in an Age of Accelerating Cultural Change: Spiritual Globalization.* Routledge: New York.

References

Akhtar, S. (2005). Hindu-Muslim Relations in India – Past, Present and Future. In S. Akhtar (ed.), *Freud along the Ganges: Psychoanalytic Reflections on the People and Culture of India.* Other Press: New York.

Benjamin, J. (1988). *The Bonds of Love: Psychoanalysis, Feminism and the Problem of Domination.* Pantheon: New York.

Benjamin, J. (1990). Recognition and Destruction: An Outline of Intersubjectivity. In S. Mitchel and L. Aron (eds.), (1999), *Relational Psychoanalysis: The Emergence of a Tradition.* Analytic Press: New York.

Bhutalia, U. (2000). *The Other Side of Silence: Voices from the Partition of India.* Duke University Press: Durham, NC.

Bion, W. R. (1959). Attacks on Liking. *International Journal of Psychoanalysis.* 40, pp. 308–315.

Bobrow, J. (2007). The Disavowal of the Personal in Psychoanalytic Training. *Psychoanalytic Review.* 94 (2), pp. 263–276.

Das, V. (1997) Language and Body: Transaction in the Construction of Pain. In A. Klienman, V. Das, and M. Lock (eds), *Social Suffering.* University of California Press: Berkeley, Los Angeles, and London, pp. 67–93.

Freud, S. (1919). The Uncanny (J. Strachey, Trans.) In *The Complete Psychological Work of Sigmund Freud,* Vol XVII. Hogarth: London, pp. 217–256.

Freud, S. (1927). Fetishism (J. Strachey, Trans.) In *The Complete Psychological Work of Sigmund Freud.* Vol XXI. Hogarth: London, pp.147–157.

Freud, S. (1940). An Outline of Psychoanalysis. *International Journal of Psychoanalysis.* 21, pp. 27–84.

Kakar, S.(1980). *The Inner World.* Oxford University Press: New Delhi.

Kakar, S. (1995). *The Colours of Violence.* Penguin Books: New Delhi.

Kakar, S. and Kakar, K. (2007). *The Indians – Portrait of a People.* Penguin Books: New Delhi.

Kumar, P. (2013). Beyond Tolerance and Hospitality: Muslims as Strangers and Minor Subjects in Hindu Nationalist and Indian Nationalist Discourse. In E. Webber (ed.), *Living Together: Jacques Derrida's Communities of Violence and Peace.* Fordham University Press: New York, pp. 80–103.

Layton, L. (2006). That Place Gives Me the Heebie Jeebies. In L. Layton, N. C. Hollander, and S. Gutwill (eds.), *Psychoanalysis, Class and Politics: Encounters in the Clinical Setting.* Routledge: New York, pp. 51–64.

Mitchell, S. (1993). *Hope and Dread in Psychoanalysis.* HarperCollins: New York.

Roland, A.(1996). *Cultural Pluralism and Psychoanalysis.* Routledge: New York.

Roland, A. (2011). *Journeys to Foreign Selves: Asians and Asian Americans in a Global World.* Oxford University Press: New Delhi.

Varvin, S. (2012). Islamism and Xenophobia. In L. Auestad (ed.), *Psychoanalysis and Politics: Exclusion and the Politics of Representation*. Karnac: London.

Winnicott, D. W. (1968). The Use of an Object and Relating through Identification. In D. W. Winnicott (ed.), *Playing and Reality*. Routledge: London, pp. 86–94.

Zepf, S. (2013). A Note on the Application of the Term 'Disavowal' in Psychoanalysis. *The Scandinavian Psychoanalytic Review*. 36 (1), pp. 35–42.

6

THE REPRESSED EVENT OF (SHI'I) ISLAM

Psychoanalysis, the trauma of Iranian Shi'ism, and feminine revolt

Farshid Kazemi

In his book, *Shi'ism: A Religion of Protest* (2011), Hamid Dabashi provides a Freudian reading of the traumatic event of Shi'i history, namely the martyrdom of Imam Husayn, the prophet Muhammad's grandson. In *Totem and Taboo* (Freud 1913), Freud posits an originary theory whereby familial dynamics and traumatic experiences in which the primordial events of symbolic patricide and the ensuing guilt and repression are condensed into the dynamics of the Oedipal universe. Through a reversal of Freud's theory of the murder of the primal father and its communal remembrance in the totemic meal, Dabashi argues that it is the figure of the son (either 'Ali or Husayn) who is at the heart of the traumatic event of Shi'ism's primal murder. If according to Freud, a sense of obedience developed after the murder of the primal father, Dabashi postulates that in the case of Shi'ism, after the trauma of killing the son in place of the father, a constitutive state of permanent revolutionary defiance developed in Shi'ism.

In this chapter, I will problematize this otherwise interesting psychoanalytic reading of Shi'ism by Dabashi by taking it to its theoretical end by uncovering its intrinsic masculinist structure, which owes itself to Freud's own theory. In doing so, I will theoretically reverse both Freud and Dabashi's position by asserting that the originary trauma of Shi'ism is not only at its beginning but also at its *end*. I will argue that, indeed, the repressed secret history of Islam is feminine (following Fethi Benslama's insight), yet it is not to be sought simply in its originary narrative, but in the disavowed secret history of (Iranian) Shi'ism. So the question to be asked here is: what is the repressed event, the traumatic event in Shi'ism *par excellence* (and Iranian Shi'ism in particular)? This traumatic event is none other than the emergence of the evental revolutionary messianic Babi movement (and later the Baha'i faith) in nineteenth-century Iran. The specific trauma and ensuing guilt that is repressed in relation to the Babi movement is no longer masculine but feminine, and is related to the murder of a woman instead of a father or son, namely the death of the radical Babi female poet, philosopher, theologian, and mystic, Tahirih Qurrat al-'Ayn. Hence at the root of the repressed traumatic event of (Iranian) Shi'i history is Qurrat al-'Ayn's act of unveiling vision and voice, and her eventual death by the state through the collective condemnation of the Shi'i clerical ('ulama) order. This is the hidden underside of the trauma of (Iranian) Shi'ism that has remained repressed in the archives of (Shi'i) Islam.

The originary trauma of Shi'ism: a Freudian reading

In the emerging literature on psychoanalysis and Islam, the general approach has been dominated by a tacit reading of Islam through a largely Sunni (as well as Sufi) lens, with Fethi Benslama's text, *Psychoanalysis and the Challenge of Islam* (2009), as the quintessential example of this approach. Benslama's argument in the text is that the secret repressed history in Islam's archives is its suppression of the feminine (i.e., Hagar the slave concubine of Abraham who is never mentioned in the Qur'anic narrative), which coupled with the absence of the paternal divine big Other, results in the masculinist logic and political extremism operative in Islam. Slavoj Žižek in his essay, 'A Glance into the Archives of Islam,' effectively follows Benslama's argument and considers that the significance of the feminine remains repressed in the originary archives of Islam.[1] Another recent volume following a similar trajectory is Omina El Shakry's recent text, *The Arabic Freud: Psychoanalysis and Islam in Modern Egypt*, is perhaps the most recent example of the encounter between psychoanalysis and Islam, with Sunnism and Sufism as the repressed kernel underpinning the whole interpretative discourse. The only exception to this trend is Joan Copjec's *Umbr(a)* edition on Islam, with a number of articles that deploy a psychoanalytic reading of aspects of Islam, including Shi'ism. A number of articles in the volume, such as the philosopher Christian Jambet's two articles 'the Death of Epiphany,' and 'the Paradoxical One,' engage with Twelver and Isma'ili Shi'ism, especially through their Iranian iteration, and this is of little surprise since Jambet was a student of the French philosopher and Islamo-Iranologist Henry Corbin (d. 1978).[2] Indeed, others such as Copjec herself also engage with Iranian Shi'ism (apropos Iranian Cinema) both in the introduction[3] and in her article, 'The Censorship of Interiority.' But, in this volume it is Fathi Benslama in his article, 'Dying for Justice,' who first provides a psychoanalytic interpretation of the originary sacrifice of Shi'ism that later Dabashi argues for in a sustained reading in his text (without acknowledging Benslama), Benslama writes: 'Hussein's torture constitutes the originary sacrificial scene, the foundation of Shiism' (19).

Amid this burgeoning literature Hamid Dabashi in his text *Shi'ism: A Religion of Protest* (2011), provides a Freudian reading of the traumatic event of Shi'i history, namely the martyrdom of Imam Husayn (d. 680) on the plain of Karbala. In *Totem and Taboo*, Freud provides one of the founding myths of psychoanalysis as Lacan puts it (Lacan 1992, 223), where he proposes the murder of the father of the primal horde by his sons, as a way to access the women. After the murder of the primal father, the murderous act was repressed and condensed into the twin Oedipal laws, namely the law against murder and incest, observed through a communal remembrance in the totemic meal. According to Freud, it was through these laws that 'social organization ... moral obligations, and ... religion' were born (Freud 1939, 141–42). Reversing Freud's theory Dabashi argues that in Shi'ism, it is the figure of the son (either 'Ali or Husayn) rather than the father, that acts as the traumatic event of Shi'ism's primal murder and the partaking of a meal in the Muharam ceremonies commemorating the martyrdom of Imam Husayn, called *Zohr-e Ashura*, function as the counterpart to the totemic meal (2011, 9).

Following Freud's reading of Christianity in *Totem and Taboo*, Dabashi argues that Shi'ism is not a father-religion but like Christianity a son-religion, in which the son (either 'Ali or Husayn) is killed instead of the father. It is also significantly different from Christianity where the figure of the son offered himself as a sacrifice (as Freud argued in relation to Christ), but rather in this instance the son-figure ('Ali or Husayn) is killed by paternal-figures (the Umayyad army). Therefore, for Dabashi, Shi'ism is not a father-religion subconsciously aware of the guilt of patricide theorized by Freud in *Totem and Taboo*, but rather a son-religion subconsciously aware of the guilt of infanticide (1913, 13–14). It is here that Dabashi goes on to draw the theoretical conclusion that underlies the core of his argument, namely that unlike Freud's theory in which after the murder of the father a collective sense of guilt developed among the sons who enacted the patricide, in Shi'ism, after the trauma of killing the son in place of the father, a permanent state of revolutionary defiance developed. As he states, 'In political terms this has amounted to a state of permanent revolutionary defiance' (2011, 23).

One of the critical problematics underlying this reading is the conception of Shi'ism as a son-religion constitutively structured by a permanent state of revolutionary defiance.[4] This reading obfuscates the fact that after the martyrdom of Imam Husayn and most of his family and companions in Karbala, the Imams of what was to become Twelver Shi'ism effectively became a quietist movement, and all the Imams sought a politically quietest policy, which was operative for the majority of the history of Shi'ism.[5] It was only with the rise of the Safavids in Iran in the sixteenth century (with their early radically messianic Sufi, Isma'ili and *ghulat* admixture, the origins of which they later repressed by establishing Twelver Shi'ism as the state religion in 1501)[6] and in the twentieth century with the 1979 revolution in Iran, that a political deployment of Shi'ism occurred. Indeed, it was the Zaydi Shi'is in the early period and later Isma'ili Shi'is rather than the Twelvers that had a longer history of political defiance towards the Sunni caliphate (e.g., Qarmatians, Fatimids and Nizaris). Therefore, to read the whole history of Twelver Shi'ism as one long state of revolutionary defiance is to provide a counter-history of Twelver Shi'ism that cannot be corroborated with historical sources.

For Dabashi, this Freudian reading of Shi'ism as a son-religion that mourns the murder of son-figures ('Ali, Husayn or Husayn's son 'Ali Asghar), perfectly tallies with a similar thematic in Iranian myths exemplified in the Epic of Kings (*Shahnameh*) by the poet Abu'l Qasim Ferdowsi (d. 1020), especially the tales of Seyavash, the son of Kay Kavus, and the tragedy of Sohrab, the Son of the Persian hero (*pahlevan*) Rostam. In Dabashi's reading of these stories in the *Shahnameh*, both Seyavash and Sohrab are son-heroes that are killed by their respective fathers, Kay Kavus and Rostam. In the case of Seyavash, he was falsely accused by his stepmother Sudabeh of trying to rape her, and left his father's kingdom in exile for Turan, and thereafter died a tragic death; on the other hand, Sohrab was killed unknowingly by his father Rostam during battle. Hence for Dabashi, both Seyavash and Sohrab act as figurative counterparts of Imam Husayn, 'son-heroes tragically killed by their father-figures to sustain the dramatic course of the narrative history' (2011, 16).

However, there are several problems with this theory, since it collapses the killing of the son-figures by fathers in the *Shahnameh*, in order to derive a reverse Oedipal theory. In the *Shahnameh*, Rostam's killing of his son Sohrab is the only instance in which the father does *not* know that it is his own son whom he is murdering which may be likened to a reversal of Oedipus, whereas every other father-son-killing in the *Shahnameh* is enacted by the father *consciously*. As Dick Davis states apropos the episode of Rostam and Sohrab:

> The atypicality consists primarily of the fact that Rostam does not know it is his son whom he is killing; in every other case in the poem [Shahnameh] when a father acts violently toward his son he is fully aware of the identity of the person he is dealing with.
>
> *(Davis 1999, 103)*

In this sense, the martyrdom of Seyavash, which is the mythic analogue of Husayn's martyrdom, does not function as a proper reversal of Oedipus. Indeed, the profound similarities of the death of Seyavash with that of Husayn has been noted by many scholars before and Dabashi himself acknowledges this stating:

> To be sure, the older Iranian origins of aspects of the Karbala celebrations have been suggested, and the similarities between the mourning for Imam Hossein and those of Zarer[7] and Seyavash in pre-Islamic and *Shahnameh* sources have been pointed out by a number of scholars.
>
> *(Dabashi 2011, 9–10)*

Nevertheless, what is significant is that from this perspective the Iranian Shi'i Oedipal universe is seen as a reverse Oedipalization of the role of the father and the son, where fathers always sacrifice (murder) the son, and which acts as Shi'ism's traumatic point of entry into history.

The question to be asked here is: where does Dabashi's reversal of Oedipal theory in the Iranian and Shi'i imaginary originate? It is interesting to note that this reverse Oedipal theory has been posited by a number of Iranian psychoanalysts, but as I will demonstrate, all of them are ultimately derived from a single source, namely from Iran's first psychoanalyst Mahmud Sana'i. Before coming back to Dabashi, I will briefly turn to the genealogy (to put it in Nietzschean terms) of this Persian Oedipus.

The Persian Oedipus: an Iranian Oedipal theory

In a recent book by the Iranian psychoanalyst Gohar Homayounpour called, *Doing Psychoanalysis in Tehran*, she reflects on the way that Iranians seem to 'eroticize death, mourning, sadness, and depression,' and in a rhetorical gesture asks: 'I wonder if it could have something to do with our Oedipus, a boy named Sohrab?' (2012, 54). Homayounpour then provides the same logic of reverse Oedipalization as Dabashi by retrieving the story of Rostam and Sohrab from the archives of the Iranian national epic, namely the *Epic of Kings* (*Shahnameh*). For Homayounpour, Greek mythology is filled with myths of fathers being killed, whilst 'it is impossible to escape the common pattern of killing sons all over Iranian mythology' (2012, 54). Although throughout her text Homayounpour seeks to demonstrate that there is nothing special about being 'Iranian,' here she succumbs to the same sense of special pleading for the unique dimension of being 'Iranian' and the Iranian libidinal economy, by positing the theory of reverse Oediplization or the logic of son-killing (*pesar koshi*), in which in Iranian mythology it is 'always' the son that is murdered, rather than the father, using the tragedy of Rostam and Sohrab as the *locus classicus* of this reversal of Oedipal theory. For Homayounpour, the masculinist logic operative in this line of thought does not seem problematic, as throughout her text both the father and son act as the privileged site of subjectivity.[8]

Another example is the Iranian psychoanalyst in France, Nader Barzin, who in his text, *La psychanalyse en Iran*, whilst providing an overview of the development of psychoanalysis in Iran, similarly considers that Ferdowsi's *Shahnameh* and the story of Rostam and Sohrab in particular, play an important role in the Iranian libidinal economy.

Barzin considers the *Epic of Kings* as the most important text for the study of psychoanalysis in Iran since it draws its sources from the Iranian mythological tradition. Barzin similarly observes that the myth of Rostam and Sohrab is the reverse of the myth of Oedipus, in which the father (Rostam) unknowingly kills the son (Sohrab) and considers this to be a difference that is significant (Barzin 2010, 158). For Barzin, this reversal of Oedipus in the myth of Rostam and Sohrab where it is the father who kills the son, raises the question of the different logic operative between Greek and Iranian mythology, where there is a major difference in their conception of being and the mythic imaginary, and asks: 'can we always think that a psycho-analytic approach that emerged in the [Western] philosophical tradition and referring to Greek mythology – even if it is used to describe a universal theme – can be applicable to the Persian/Iranian subject?' (Barzin 168–69). For Barzin, the answer to this rhetorical question would seem to be no.

So, where does this 'Persian Oedipus,' this reversal of the Freudian Oedipal theory originate? It is Mahmud Sana'i (1918–1985), the first Iranian psychoanalyst, who first formulates this reversal of Oedipus in the Iranian psychic apparatus. Sana'i was trained as a psychoanalyst in London and in 1955 on his return to Iran became the chair of the Department of Literature and Humanities at Tehran University.

During this time, Sana'i established the first Institute of Psychology at Tehran University. His most important contributions to psychoanalysis in Iran were his translations of Freud's texts on dreams and the formulation of a new psychoanalytic interpretation of the myths in Ferdowsi's *Epic of Kings* (*Shahnameh*). In an important article called, 'Ferdowsi, Master of Tragedy,' Sana'i (based on a lecture at Tehran University in 1976), first introduced the idea of a 'Rostam complex,' (*'uqdeh-ye Rostam*) or son-killing in the Iranian cultural imaginary (psychology), which was a reversal of the Freudian Oedipus complex (Behrouzan 2016, 50).[9] In his text, Barzin also alludes to Sana'i as the psychoanalyst whose most important contribution to understanding Iranian culture was his analysis of mythological figures in Ferdowsi's *Shahnameh*, but fails to explicitly state that his own reading of the tragedy of Rostam and Sohrab owes itself to Sana'i's formulation.

It is here that this otherwise interesting theory of the reverse Oedipalization that is said to be distinctive of the Iranian psychic imaginary has to be problematized. The first point to be noted at the outset is that it is not true that it is 'always' sons that are killed by their father in the *Shahnameh*. For example, in one of the emblematic episodes in the mythic section of the *Shahnameh*, it is King Mardas who is killed by his son Zahhak, who was convinced by the devil into killing his father in order to possess the throne and his vast kingdom. Indeed, Mahmoud Omidsalar in his text, *Oedipus Complex in the Shahnameh*, considers the story of Zahhak to be an analogue of the myth of Oedipus in the *Shahnameh*. He states, 'the tales of Zahhak's patricide, whether oral or literary, clearly demonstrate the elements of intense love for the mother and jealousy and hatred of the father, both of these elements being the essential building blocks of the male Oedipus complex' (Omidsalar 1984, 196). Therefore, what we have here is a significant instantiation of a son-killing the father in the *Shahnameh*. However, even this story does not perfectly tally with the original myth as narrated by Sophocles (1991) since Zahhak knowingly kills his father, whilst in the original tragedy, Oedipus unknowingly kills his father.

The other crucial *problématique* is that we cannot even say that this Oedipus in reverse is a motif that is peculiar to Iranian mythology. For instance, it has long been established that there are thematic motifs that are common between Celtic (Irish) and Iranian mythology.[10] One of the most famous examples is precisely the uncanny resemblance between the tale of Rostam killing his son Sohrab in the *Epic of Kings* and the story of Cuchulainn killing his son Connla, in the Ulster Cycle.[11] Indeed, this is not surprising as there are many common motifs and elements that run through aspects of Indo-European mythology, as well as early Near Eastern mythology. There are also significant parallels between the myths in the *Shahnameh* and some Chinese myths and legends, the most important in this connection is the parallel between the story of Li Tsing (or Li Jing) killing his son No-Cha (or Nezha) and Rostam killing Sohrab.[12] Such parallels could be multiplied here, but these few examples suffice to indicate that the motif of a reverse Oedipal myth is not unique to Iran, but exists in a number of other mythic imaginaries.

Another crucial point to be noted here is that the development of this psychoanalytic interpretation of an Oedipus in reverse is related to the politics of national identity or more properly nationalist ideology, and the desire for the production and articulation of an Iranian identity (*huwiyat*) in opposition to the West – an identity which by the time of the Islamic Revolution became an 'Islamic-Iranian' identity.[13] Indeed, the context in which this theory emerged is related to a process of opposition to the 'morally corrupting' (*fesad*) influence of the West (US) on the decadent Pahlavi regime (Mohammad Reza Shah) and Iranian society (starting with the famous CIA backed coup in 1953 and the ousting of the democratically elected prime minister, Mohammad Mosaddegh (d. 1967) which leftist intellectuals such as Jalal Al-e Ahmad (1923–1969) (who was an important ideological voice in the rise of the Islamic Revolution) branded as Westoxification (*gharbzadegi*), the title of his eponymous text.

Finally, what we have to do here is to turn this around and read the logic of reverse Oedipus back into the Oedipal narrative itself. The crucial clue to the story lies precisely in the detail where the oracle tells the father of the newborn Oedipus, Laius, that he is doomed to perish by the hand of his own son, and the only way to avert this fate was to kill his son. Unable to kill the infant, Laius tells his wife Jocasta to kill him, but equally unable to kill the child herself she orders their slave to kill him, but he is also incapable of killing him and abandons the infant in the mountaintop. A shepherd finds the boy and eventually gives the child to King Polybus. Therefore Oedipus' unwitting murder of his father is precisely due to his original fathers' meddling with fate/destiny (*moira*), by thwarting the sacrifice of Oedipus. In this sense, the tragedy of Oedipus is precisely because Oedipus was not sacrificed by his father and survived and hence the sacrificial victim was displaced from the child unto the father, who became the sacrifice. In other words, the Oedipus myth is effectively about child/son sacrifice gone awry and its catastrophic consequences.

Be that as it may, despite all these problems with Dabashi's argument, what ultimately has to be problematized lies elsewhere, namely its essentially masculinist logic (following Freud), in which the figure of the (sacrificial) son, always functions as the privileged site of subjectivity and revolutionary defiance. Here, I partially follow Mahdi Tourage's line of thought (in an abstract to an unpublished paper), where he perceptively asks: 'If Dabashi is correct in asserting that the guilt of infanticide structures the unfolding of the Shi'i history of protest, then what is the epistemological status of the feminine/female in Shi'i revolutionary defiance where the sacrificed infant is always male?' As it has been shown above, whether it is the paradigm of Karbala (martyrdom of Husayn) or the Iranian mythic narratives (Sohrab or Seyavash), 'the primal murder of the son marks the privileged subject as always already male.' As Tourage (n.d.) states:

> The male remains the agent of history through whom the originary sentiment of collective guilt gives rise to communal possibilities of defiance. The same sense of guilt-ridden collective normativity overshadows the

female autonomous agency in favour of her obedience and loyalty. In other words, in this masculinist economy of sacrifice structured by the primal (male) infanticide, the same central civilizing function of guilt produces male revolutionary defiance but female conformist obedience. Men may defiantly sacrifice themselves in protest; women must sacrifice themselves in obedience to men.[14]

However, to his credit, Dabashi seems to be searching for the revolutionary feminine/female in the archives of (Iranian) Shi'ism but is only capable of retrieving the figure of Tahirih Qurrat al-'Ayn, to whom he dedicates a substantial portion of his book (2011, 159–202). But, of course (as we shall see below), the problem is that Qurrat al-'Ayn is no longer within the coordinates of (Iranian) Shi'ism proper, as she functions as the traumatic point of rupture between Shi'ism and the new messianic Babi movement. In this precise sense, she announces the 'end' of the Islamic dispensation and the Shi'i religious universe and the inauguration of a new (religious) symbolic order. Therefore, here I go beyond Tourage's line of thought, since the logic of female conformist obedience in Iranian Shi'ism (as he calls it), was subverted by the defiant revolutionary figure of Qurrat al-'Ayn. This is precisely why Tahirih represents a point of trauma in the (Iranian) Shi'i religious imaginary and her voice had to be repressed (silenced) in the archives of Shi'ism.

The feminine revolt: Qurrat al-'Ayn unveiling vision and voice

As stated earlier, it was the revolutionary Iranian Babi[15] female poet, mystic, philosopher, and martyr Fatima Zarrin Taj Baraghani (d. 1852), famously known as Tahirih (the pure) Qurrat al-'Ayn (solace of the eyes), who enacted one of the most radical acts in the history of Iranian Shi'ism through the removal of her veil during a conference of Babi notables in Badasht in 1848. As Annemarie Schimmel states, 'During a Babi conference in Badasht in 1848, the beautiful young woman [Tahirih] is said to have preached without a veil, an action that is taken as the first attempt to win freedom for Persian women' (Schimmel 2005). It is from this dramatic event onwards that she has been fabelized as the first Iranian woman to unveil herself in public as the revolutionary act that signaled the abrogation of Islamic law and dispensation. Now, in the historical narratives foregrounding the traumatic dimension of this event, the accent is always placed on Qurrat al-'Ayn's unveiling of her face or what may be termed the 'unveiling of vision,' (in the Qajar period women would often be fully veiled in public, with their faces covered), but what has virtually gone unnoticed in these accounts is the significance of the unveiling of her voice and speech. This radical gesture of unveiling the female voice in public, which has hitherto remained untheorized, is the other aspect of this traumatic event that has remained repressed in the archives of Iranian Shi'ism and which ultimately resulted in her death.

In order to draw out this repressed kernel in the historical narratives related to the traumatic dimension of Qurrat al-'Ayn's unveiling, not only her face but her voice, I will first mobilize two related concepts, that of the *acousmêtre* or the acousmatic voice, developed by Piere Shcaffer (and later elaborated by Michel Chion in relation to the cinema), and Jacques Lacan's concept of the object-voice; then I will shortly note the proscription on the female voice in Islamic jurisprudence (*fiqh*) in order to foreground the traumatic dimension of the unveiling of the female voice enacted by Qurrat al-'Ayn.

Now, let's turn to the acousmatic voice and the Lacanian object-voice. So what is the acousmatic voice? The acousmatic voice (*acousmêtre*) is simply a voice whose source is concealed or hidden from the visual field – it is a voice without a body or the disembodied voice. Pierre Schaeffer traces the origin of the word 'acousmatic' back to ancient Greece, and the philosopher Pythagoras. The term originally referred to a Pythagorean sect called 'acousmatics,' whose disciples listened to the voice of their Master (Pythagoras), whilst concealed behind a curtain, without being able to see him for five years (Chion 1999, 19; Dolar 2006, 61). Apropos the object-voice, in his Seminar X on *Anxiety*, in the chapter called, 'The Voice of Yahwah [God],' Lacan discusses an ancient instrument in Jewish ritual, a horn called shofar, so as 'to bring out what is new in the level at which there appears the form of the [*objet*] *a* known as the voice' (Lacan 2014, 252). In order to better show his concept of the voice as *objet a* (object small a, the *a* stands for the French '*autre*' or 'other'), Lacan 'supported ... its evocation in a separated form, materialized in an object, the shofar' (2014, 259). This object, the shofar, which was the symbolic materialization of the Voice of Yahwah into a separate object, perfectly exemplifies for Lacan the voice as *objet a* or object-cause of desire. In this sense, a homology can be drawn between Lacan's discussion of the Voice of Yahwah as *objet a*, and the acousmatic voice. Indeed, Chion himself refers to the origins of the acousmatic voice as the interdiction against looking, where the disciples of the Greek philosopher Pythagoras 'would listen to their Master speak from *behind a curtain* ... so that the Sight of the speaker wouldn't distract them from the message.' As Chion points out, 'This interdiction against looking, which transforms the Master, God, or Spirit into an acousmatic voice, permeates a great number of religious traditions, most notably Islam and Judaism' (Chion 1999, 19). In this way, Lacan's formulation of the shofar as the Voice of Yahwah (and hence as *objet a*) is directly related to Chion's conception of the voice of God or Spirit in Judaism[16] and Islam[17] as examples of the acousmatic voice.

According to the Islamic logic of the veil (*hejab*), the female voice must be veiled from men's aural field, due to its power to sexually arouse (heterosexual) male desire. In an Islamic theory of the female voice, the voice of women is thought to be a part of her '*awra* or private bodily part (pudenda) and must be veiled before all nonrelated men (*na-mahram*). In this respect, there are a number of Shi'i traditions (*akhbar*) indicating that women are not allowed to speak to anyone either than their husbands or close relatives, except in a few instances

(Mofid 1413/1992, 55–58). As Abdelwahab Bouhdiba states in his *Sexuality in Islam*, 'the voice of a Muslim woman is also *'aura*. Not only because of the sweet words coming from her mouth must be heard only by her husband and master, but because the voice may create a disturbance and set in train the cycle of *zina* [unlawful sexual relations or adultery]' (Bouhdiba 2012, 39). In her discussion of sexuality in the Muslim framework, Fatima Mernissi has argued that the eye 'is undoubtedly an erogenous zone'; similarly, the ear may be said to function as an erogenous zone as well. According to some compendia of Islamic jurisprudence, "aural adultery' (*zina al-udhuni*) was considered a constant danger even where the veil impeded 'visual adultery' (*zina al-'ayni*)' (Mernissi 1975, 141). Indeed, in Lacanian psychoanalytic theory, the ear also functions as an erogenous zone, which forms part of the invocatory drive that is related to sexual desire (Lacan identifies four partial drives, the oral, anal, scopic, and invocatory) (Kazemi 2018). In the same vein, Benslama states, 'there is an obligation to conceal a woman's body by various means, which makes the veil the central element in a sophisticated system of concealment, which includes muffling the sound of the voice and the tinkling of jewelry' (Benslama 2009, 127).[18] In this sense, the aural field must be veiled so that the female voice is always heard through a screen or curtain (literally *hejab*).

Just as at the origin of the acousmatic voice is the figure of Pythagoras who spoke to his disciples from 'behind a curtain,' so similarly at the dawn of early Iranian modernity, Qurrat al-'Ayn, like an *acousmêtre* would speak to her fellow disciples whilst hidden behind a curtain, 'Her lectures at Kerbela [Karbala] were attended by women as well as men, the former being admitted within a curtain which separated her from the male portion of her audience' (Hamadani 1893, 356). It was only later that Qurrat al-'Ayn enacted the paradigmatic traumatic event in Iranian Shi'i history, when she unveiled herself before a male audience at the convocation of Badasht in 1848. As Negar Mottahedeh has perceptively noted, historiographers fascinated by Qurrat al-'Ayn's act of unveiling in public, either valorized it as the originary event of women's liberation in Iran or excoriated it as the heretical act *par excellence* and the proof of the pernicious and corrupting influence of the Babi movement (Mottahedeh 1998, unpaginated). But, what is seldom noted in the historical narratives is that beyond the unveiling of her face (vision), was the unveiling of her voice and speech. In one such narrative in which the shock of unveiling her face is registered, we immediately get the following description:

> [Qurrat al-'Ayn] rose from her seat and, undeterred by the tumult that she had raised in the hearts of her companions began to address the remnant of the assembly. Without the least premeditation, and in *language that bore striking resemblance to that of the Qu'ran*, she delivered her appeal with matchless eloquence and profound fervor. She concluded her address with this verse from the Qu'ran: 'Verily, amid gardens and rivers shall the pious dwell in the seat of truth, in the presence of the potent King.' ... Immediately after, she declared: *'I am the Word which*

the Qa'im is to utter, the Word which shall put to flight the chiefs and nobles of the earth.'

(Zarandi 1953, 211–213, my emphasis)

It is here that we can discern that Qurrat al-'Ayn herself considered the true traumatic dimension of her act to be the embodiment of the 'Word' that was promised to be uttered by the Qa'im (i.e., the Bab), which would put to flight all the 'chiefs and nobles of the earth.' Indeed, in another narrative the content of her impassioned speech is given:

> Our days are the days of interregnum. Today all [Islamic] religious obligations are abrogated and such acts as prayer, fasting and salutation [to the House of the Prophet] are futile. When the Bab conquers the seven kingdoms and unites different religions; he will bring a new *shari'a* and entrust his Qur'an to the community. Whatever new obligations he ordains would then be compulsory to the people of the earth. Thus burden not yourselves with the worthless.
>
> *(cited in Amanat 2004, 140)*

At the end of her speech Qurrat al-'Ayn exclaimed, 'I am the blast of the trumpet, I am the call of the bugle,' i.e., 'Like Gabriel, I would awaken sleeping souls.' (Cheyne, 101–103 cited in Zarandi 1953, 301). In yet another narrative, the unveiling of her voice and her speech act is again linked to the trumpet/bugle blast that attends the Last Judgment in the Qur'an, 'On that memorable day the "Bugle" mentioned in the Qur'an was sounded [*nuqrih-yi naqur*], the "stunning trumpet blast" was loudly raised [*nafkhih-yi sur*], and the "Catastrophe" [*tammih-yi kubra*] came to pass' (Rabbani 1970, 33). In one of her prose works, Tahirih provides a hermeneutics of the apocalyptic trumpet-blast [*nafkhi-yi sur*] in the Qur'an, and refers to the appearance of the Bab (i.e., Qa'im) as the day of the trumpet-blast (Tahirih, 2000). Herein lies the connection between this apocalyptic bugle/trumpet in the Qur'an and the Biblical shofar that Lacan refers to as the exemplar of the voice as *objet a*, and its identification with the voice and speech act of Qurrat al-'Ayn. It is well here to recall that the shofar had a messianic function, which would be sounded on the Day of Judgment,[19] and as noted, it is similarly correlative with the trumpet/horn (*al-sur*) mentioned in the Qur'an, that would herald the messianic Day of Judgment or the *eschaton*.[20] In this sense, Qurrat al-'Ayn's act is the paradigmatic traumatic event of Iranian Shi'i history, by the radical act of de-acousmatizing the female voice and unveiling herself she enacted a double act of unveiling vision and voice.

It is Theodore Reik's interpretation of the sound emitted by the shofar[21] as specifically signifying the 'Voice of the Father' of the primal horde in Freud's *Totem and Taboo*, which may bring out the unconscious traumatic dimension operative in Qurrat al-'Ayan's voice. Reik writes:

> The imitation of the animal's cry signified both the presence of God among the believers and their identification with him. The horn [shofar], the most

characteristic trait of the totemic god, gave birth in the course of centuries to an instrument that was now used as the means of acoustic imitation.

(Reik 1928, 235–36, cited in Dolar 1996, 25)[22]

In this sense, it may be said that the (unconscious) point of trauma in Qurrat al-'Ayn's voice lies precisely here: where the masculine voice (of the Father) was expected from the shofar/trumpet, the feminine/female voice was heard instead.

In his foreword to Pier Paolo Pasolini's screenplay St. Paul, Alain Badiou states, 'Paul is one of the possible historical names of the tension between fidelity to the founding event of a new cycle of the True' (Badiou cited in Pasolini 2014, 7);[23] so similarly, Tahirih (like Paul) was also one of the names of the tension of the fidelity to the event of a new cycle of the True (i.e., the evental Babi movement), with the difference that in previous cycles this name was a masculine signifier (Paul), whilst in the new cycle it is under the signifier of the feminine (Tahirih). In this sense, both figures functioned in the same way towards the substance of their social-symbolic (religious) life-world (Judaism and Islam), by effectuating a radical break from it.

After Qurrat al-'Ayn was arrested in the wake of mass public executions of her co-religionists, she was brought to Tehran to the court of the Qajar King, Nasir al-Din Shah (d. 1896). It was there that upon setting his eyes on her the King is said to have exclaimed, 'I like her looks: leave her and let her be' (Browne 1891, 313). It is not known what precisely transpired in that private audience, or what exactly the King heard and saw, but it is related that she was asked for her hand in marriage should she desist from expounding her beliefs. Her reply was to quote a part of her own poem as a defiant 'No!' (Mottahedeh 2008, 43):

> *Sikandar's*[24] pomp and display be thine, the *Qalandar's*[25]
> habit and way be mine;
> That, if it please thee, I resign, while this, though bad, is
> enough for me.
>
> *(Browne 1918, 349)*

It was thus that her fate was sealed. This gesture of remaining faithful to her beliefs to the end was the quintessential subversive act and can be read as an instance of the Lacanian ethics of the authentic act at its most radical. In Lacanian ethics, the supreme ethical act or the 'authentic act' is one in which the subject does not cede with respect to his or her desire (Lacan 1992). This final ethical act of Qurrat al-'Ayn's saying 'No!' to Nasir al-Din Shah, the King of Iran, may be read precisely in light of Lacan's interpretation of Antigone's act of the feminine 'No!' and an instantiation of Lacan's formulation of an ethics of desire. It is perhaps poignant that Lacan refers to this question of 'have you acted in conformity with your desire?' in apocalyptic terms as possessing the force of 'a Last Judgment' (Lacan 1992, 314). In the case of Qurrat al-'Ayn (and Antigone), the answer to this question is a resounding YES! This is the logic of the feminine revolt embodied in the figure of Qurrat al-'Ayn. From this perspective Tahirih's radical authentic act of the feminine 'No!' is a subversive act that stands up to the Shi'i clerical order and the state as the lynchpin of the (Islamic) Law (*shari'a*). This is why, as Farzaneh Milani has perceptively noted, Qurrat al-'Ayn had to be literally silenced by the Qajar state and the Shi'ite clerical establishment, which is why she was strangled to death in order to forever silence her voice (as Milani reminds us, *khafeh kardan* in Persian means 'suppressing, stifling and silencing' the voice) (Milani 1992, 49). But, in the final analysis, as Amin Banani says of her, 'This is not a face that could be hidden by a veil, and this is not a voice that could be choked into silence' (Banani 2004, 30). This is the repressed traumatic event that haunts Iranian Shi'ism and its clerical authority to this day.

Conclusion

The foregoing study has argued that the trauma of (Iranian) Shi'ism and its consequent guilt and repression is not located so much (or primarily) in the originary traumatic event of the entry of Shi'ism into history via the sacrifice of a son (i.e., the martyrdom of Imam Husayn) as Dabashi has argued, but rather more properly at its end with the traumatic emergence of the new in the Event of the Babi movement and the apocalyptic (trumpet) call of the 'end' of (Shi'i) Islam, enunciated by the revolutionary Babi leader Tahirih Qurrat al-'Ayn. In this sense, the trauma and guilt that is being repressed in relation to the Babi movement is no longer masculine but feminine, as the murder of a woman instead of a father or son, is at the center of (Iranian) Shi'ism's trauma. In this way, Tahirih signals the end of female conformist obedience in Iranian Shi'ism, and the beginning of feminine/female revolutionary defiance. This is the hidden underside of the trauma of (Iranian) Shi'ism – the displacement and destabilization of masculinist power and authority (exemplified by the Shi'ite clerical order), through the revolutionary unveiling of vision and voice by Qurrat al-'Ayn. From this perspective, one of the theoretical consequences of the reading in this study is that: the point of trauma in the historical unfolding of religions lies more at their *end* rather than in their beginning, at the point of the traumatic emergence of the new. This is perhaps to be expected, as in Iranian apocalyptic imaginary there is a perfect correspondence between the beginning and the end, as Hultgård has observed: 'One cannot understand Persian Apocalypticism without taking into consideration its context within cosmic history. There is an inner coherence between the beginning and the end that is unique to the Iranian world-view' (Hultgård 2000, 44).[26] In this way, within the coordinates of monotheistic religions, it can be said that the point of trauma for Judaism[27] was the traumatic emergence of Christianity, for Christianity it was Islam, and for Islam, the Babi movement (and for the Babi movement, the Baha'i faith, etc.).

Author's note: I am grateful to Farzin Vejdani for his comments on an earlier version of this chapter. I also want to acknowledge my gratitude to Mahdi Tourage, whose abstract to an unpublished paper partly inspired my thinking on these issues.

Notes

1 In this text Žižek makes the strange claim that, 'There is in Islam, effectively, a consistent anti-sacrificial logic . . .' (Žižek 2008, x). However, it is clear from Žižek's text that he has virtually forgotten or ignored (or wasn't aware of) Shi'i Islam. Indeed, Imam Husayn is often identified with Jesus in Shi'ite tradition, as one who willingly 'sacrificed' his life for the nascent Shi'i/Muslim community. Indeed, according to Shi'i religious imaginary, it is due to the 'Passion of Husayn,' who is often termed the 'Savior of Islam,' that a profound mythos of sacrifice pervades Shi'ite consciousness. See Ayoub (1978). In another instance Žižek states, '*There is no place for a Holy Family in Islam*' (emphasis in the original) (2008, viii), but again this is not true with regard to Shi'i Islam, as the prophet Muhammad, Imam 'Ali and all the Imams, as well as the daughter of the Prophet, Fatima, form together the Fourteen Pure Ones or Infallibles (*chahardah ma'sumin*), who are considered together the holy household (*ahl al-bayt*) of the prophet.

2 The two essays by Christian Jambet were chapters from his *La Grande Resurrection d'Alamut* and *Le Cache et l'Apparent*, translated by Joan Copjec for the *Umbr(a)* volume.

3 Copjec in her notes erroneously ascribes the term 'Westoxificatin' to the Marxist Islamist Ali Shariati (11), whilst it was originally coined by the Iranian Islamist philosopher Ahmad Fardid and later redeployed by Jalal Al-e Ahmad who theorized it in a new way in a text of the same name (see below). For Fardid see Mirsepassi (2017).

4 For a critique of Dabashi's book on Shi'ism from a religious studies perspective see, Inloes (2013).

5 See Momen (1985, 220).

6 See Babayan (2002).

7 On the 'Memorial of Zarer' see Boyce (1987).

8 Homayounpour writes, 'In Iran one can observe a moment of discontinuity from the past, and also from the future, because we have killed our sons, our future. Ferdousi's discourse communicates a lot of pain, tragedy, and mourning. We killed our sons, became alienated, and thus became a culture of mourning, for we destroyed and killed the best part of ourselves. We destroyed our future and imprisoned ourselves in the past, eroticizing pain and suffering, and celebrating nothing that is not past. Could we say that Ferdousi's discourse provides a diagnosis of Iranian society? He is trying to warn us, awaken us; his discourse is that of a depressive. We never properly mourned the loss of our glorious past, before it was taken over by Islam. Our melancholic response was to create Shi'ism, which is a culture of mourning, as a way of mourning the symbolic past. Through this ever-repetitive mourning we attempt to master the sudden trauma of having suddenly lost our sense of who we are' (56). Besides the masculinist logic operative in this paragraph where the son is always the privileged subject who is the guarantor of the future, it is simply strange to assert that Iranians 'created' Shi'ism as a way to mourn their symbolic past. Shi'ism was not created by Iranians but was the result of disputes regarding the question of succession among Arab Muslims after the death of prophet Muhammad, which eventually gave rise to the Sunni and Shi'i split. See Madelung (1997).

9 Apropos Sana'i, the prominent Iranian psychiatrist and psychoanalyst Mohammad Sanati in his overview of the history of psychoanalysis in Iran writes: 'Sanaie made some interesting contributions to the understanding of Iranian culture by analyzing mythological figures in Ferdowsi's *Shahnama* (the most important Persian epic). These stories told of filicide and fratricide in Iranian culture as compared to patricide in western cultures. His most important theoretical contribution was to introduce the Rostam (as opposed to the Oedipus) complex, comparing son-killing and brother-killing in Iranian culture with patricide in western culture. (Rostam, an Iranian epic hero, unknowingly kills his own son. He also kills Prince Esfanidar, whose downfall was ordered by his father, King Goshtasb.)' Mohammad Sanati and Arash Javanbakht, 'Psychiatry and Psychoanalysis in Iran' *Journal of The American Academy of Psychoanalysis and Dynamic Psychiatry*, vol. 34, no. 3, 2006: 405–414. Available online: www.mohammadsanati.net/1390/culturepsychoanaly-sisiran/580. Accessed 15 October, 2017.

10 For an early study see Ford, (1974): 67–74; for a number of recent parallels drawn between Celtic and Iranian myths, see H. E. Chehabi (2015).
11 Connel Monette (2004): 61–78.
12 Coyajee (1936): 4–7; 116–123. Coyajee's study has largely been neglected in the scholarly literature, but many of its insightful parallels require further elaboration.
13 For an earlier historical appropriation of myths and folklore in nationalist discourse in Iran, see Vejdani (2012).
14 Mahdi Tourage, Abstract: 'Oedipal Foundations of Male Revolutionary Defiance and Female Conformist Obedience in Shi'ism as a Religion of Protest.' Unpublished paper. Available online: www.academia.edu/2653460/Oedipal_Foundations_of_Male_Revolutionary_Defiance_and_Female_Conformist_Obedience_in_Shi_ism_as_a_Religion_of_-Protest–Abstract. Accessed 9 September, 2017.
15 For a comprehensive bibliography of the Babi movement see, Kazemi and Eschraghi (2016).
16 In the Hebrew Bible the Voice of Yahwah that Moses hears on mount Sinai from the burning bush, is precisely an acousmatic voice (Exodus 3:4–21).
17 In many Islamic traditions (ahadith), at the moment of revelation the prophet Muhammad hears a voice that remains at first acousmatic and says to him, 'Read!' (iqra) This voice later becomes de-acousmatized by being anchored in the figure of angel Gabriel. The revelatory event is also mentioned in the Qur'an (96:1–5).
18 For a more detailed discussion of the Islamic and Shi'i proscription on the female voice, especially in relation to post-revolutionary Iranian cinema, see Kazemi (2018).
19 In the Hebrew Bible, it states that the shofar will signal the appearance of the Day of the Lord at the end of the age (Isaiah 27:13, Joel 2:1). Similarly, in the New Testament, the trumpet (shofar) will be blown at the appearance of the Christ and the kingdom of God (Revelation 11:15).
20 See Qur'an 39:68, 27:87, 18:99, 6:73. In a study on the shofar, Shiloah draws a parallel between the Biblical shofar and the Qur'anic al-sur and notes their similarity and the identical function they have in relation to the End Times.
21 Lacan's discussion of the shofar in the Seminar on Anxiety takes its inspiration from Reik. See Lacan (2014): 244–252.
22 Apropos Yahwah, it is worth recalling here one of the letters of Freud to Fliess (Letter 144 July 14, 1901), where he writes: 'Have you read that the English have excavated an old place in Crete (Knossos) which they declare is an authentic labyrinth of Minos? Zeus seems originally to have been a bull. It seems, too, that our own old God [Yahwah], before the sublimation instigated by the Persians took place, was also worshiped as a bull. That provides food for all sorts of thoughts which it is not yet time to set down on paper' [emphasis added] (Freud 1913 [2001], x–xi). Here Freud is alluding to the contact between Persians and Jews after Cyrus the Great conquered Babylon, whence Judaism came into contact with Iranian religion, namely Zoroastriansim, after which many Jewish ideas in theology, soteriology, demonology, angelology and eschatology underwent a change. For these influences see Zaehner (1959), 134–155.
23 It should be recalled that the catalyst of Paul's dramatic conversion on the road to Damascus was none other than the acousmatic voice of Jesus. See, Acts 9:3–8, 26:12–14.
24 'Alexander the Great.' E. G. Browne's note.
25 'A Qalandar is a kind of darwísh or religious mendicant.' E. G. Browne's note.
26 This correspondence between the 'beginning' and the 'end' also exists in Shi'ism, especially with the concept of 'return' (raj'a), and was likely influenced by Iranian apocalyptic imaginary. See Amir-Moezzi (1994; 2005).
27 It should be pointed out that Judaism (apropos Moses) itself functioned as the originary trauma of Egyptian polytheism, since Judaism as the emergence of the traumatically new was a break, a rupture from the old universe of Egyptian polytheism. This can be gleamed from a close reading of Freud's own text, Moses and Monotheism. In his reading of

Moses, Freud posits the existence of an Egyptian Moses and a Midianite Moses who was later collapsed into a single figure in the Jewish tradition, as a disavowal of the Egyptian (vs. Hebrew) origins of their prophet and patriarch. Weather Moses was literally Egyptian or not is impossible to say (this of course, is another primordial myth of psychoanalysis along with the myth of the primal father), but it is impossible to deny that Moses was religio-culturally Egyptian, (this is corroborated by the text of the Biblical narrative since he was the adopted son of Pharaoh's daughter), which is why his adoption of monotheism would have been so traumatic to the Egyptian religio-political order, and as Freud himself was well aware, monotheism was already a point of trauma for the Egyptians, since it was associated with the heretic Pharaoh, Akhenaten. See Freud (2001); also Assman (1998).

References

Amanat, Abbas. 'Qurrat al-'Ayn: The Remover of the Veil.' In Jan T. Jasion (ed.), *Táhirih in History: Perspectives on Qurratu'l-'Ayn from East and West*, Los Angeles, CA: Kalimát Press, 2004.

Amir-Moezzi, Mohammad Ali. *The Divine Guide in Early Shi'ism*. David Streight (trans.). Albany, NY: State University of New York Press, 1994.

Amir-Moezzi, Mohammad Ali. 'Raj'a.' In *Encyclopaedia Iranica*, 2005. Available online: www.iranicaonline.org/articles/raja (Accessed 15 October, 2017).

Assmann, Jan. *Moses the Egyptian: The Mmemory of Egypt in Western Monotheism*. Cambridge, MA: Harvard University Press, 1998.

Ayoub, Mahmoud. *Redemptive Suffering in Islam: A Study of the Devotional Aspects of Ashura in Twelver Shi'ism*. The Hague: Mouton, 1978.

Babayan, Kathryn. *Mystics, Monarchs, and Messiahs: Cultural Landscapes of Early Modern Iran*. Cambridge, MA: Harvard University Press, 2002.

Banani, Amin (ed.), *Tahirih. A Portrait in Poetry. Selected Poems of Qurratu'l-'Ayn*. Los Angeles, CA: Kalimát Press, 2004.

Barzin, Nader. 'La pscychanalyse en Iran,' *Topique* vol. 1, 2010: 157–171.

Behrouzan, Orkideh. *Prozak Diaries: Psychiatry and Generational Memory in Iran*. Stanford, CA: Stanford University Press, 2016.

Benslama, Fethi. *Psychoanalysis and the Challenge of Islam*. Minneapolis, MN: University of Minnesota Press, 2009.

Bouhdiba, Abdelwahab. *Sexuality in Islam*. Alan Sheridan (trans.). London: Saqi Books, 2012.

Boyce, Mary. 'Ayādgār ī Zarērān.' In *Encyclopaedia Iranica*, 1987. Available online: www.iranicaonline.org/articles/ayadgar-i-zareran (Accessed 15 October, 2017).

Browne, E.G. *A Traveller's Narrative Written to Illustrate the Episode of the Bab, by Abdu'l-Baha*. Cambridge: Cambridge University Press, 1891.

Browne, E.G. *Materials for the Study of the Babi Religion*. Cambridge: Cambridge University Press, 1918.

Chehabi, H. E. and Neville, Grace (ed.), *Erin and Iran: Cultural Encounters between the Irish and the Iranians*. Boston, MA: Ilex Foundation Harvard University Press, 2015.

Chion, Michel. *The Voice in Cinema*, Claudia Gorbman (ed. and trans.). New York: Columbia University Press, 1999.

Copjec, Joan (ed.). *Umbr(a): Islam, A Journal of the Unconscious*. SUNY/Buffalo: The Center for the Study of Psychoanalysis & Culture, 2009.

Coyajee, Jehangir Cooverjee. *Cults & Legends of Ancient Iran & China*. Bombay: J. B. Karani's and Sons, 1936, pp. 4–7; 116–123.

Dabashi, Hamid. *Shi'ism: A Religion of Protest*. Cambridge: London: Belknap Press of Harvard University Press, 2011.

Davis, Dick. *Epic and Sedition: The Case of Ferdowsi's Shahnameh.* Washington, DC: Mage Publishers, 1999.

Dolar, Mladen. (1996) 'The Object Voice.' In Renata Salecl and Slavoj Žižek (eds.), *Gaze and Voice as Love Objects.* Durham and London: Duke University Press, 1996, pp. 7–31.

Dolar, Mladen. *A Voice and Nothing More.* Cambridge, MA: MIT Press, 2006, p. 61.

El Shakry, Omina. *The Arabic Freud: Psychoanalysis and Islam in Modern Egypt.* Princeton, NJ: Princeton University Press, 2017.

Ford, Patrick K. (1974) 'The Well of Nechtan' and 'La Glorie Lumineuse.' In Gerald James Larson (ed.), *Myth in Indo-European Antiquity*, Berkeley, CA: University of California Press, pp. 67–74.

Freud, Sigmund. (1913). *Totem and Taboo.* In J. Strachey (ed.), *The Standard Edition of the Complete Psychological Works of Sigmund Freud, Vol. XIII.* London: The Institute of Psycho-Analysis and the Hogarth Press, pp. 141–142.

Freud, Sigmund. (1939). *Moses and Monotheism.* In J. Strachey (ed.), *The Standard Edition of the Complete Psychological Works of Sigmund Freud, Vol. XIII.* London: The Institute of Psycho-Analysis and the Hogarth Press, pp. 3–139.

Hamadani, Mirza Hosayn. *Tarikh-i jadid.* E.G. Browne (trans.), *The New History of Mīrzá ʿAlí Muḥammed, the Báb.* London: Cambridge University Press, 1893.

Homayounpour, Gohar. *Doing Psychoanalysis in Tehran.* Cambridge, MA: MIT Press, 2012.

Hultgård, Anders. 'Persian Apocalypticism,' In John J. Collins (ed.), *The Encyclopedia of Apocalypticism: The Origins of Apocalypticism in Judaism and Christianity,* London: Continuum Publishing, 2000.

Inloes, Amina. 'Shi'ism: A Religion of Protest by Hamid Dabashi (review),' *Journal of Shi'a Islamic Studies* vol. 6, no. 3, 2013: 347–354.

Kazemi, Farshid. 'The Object-Voice: The Acousmatic Voice in the New Iranian Cinema,' *Camera Obscura: Feminism, Culture, and Media Studies* vol. 33, no. 1, 2018: 97.

Kazemi, Farshid and Eschraghi, Armin. 'The Babi Movement,' In Andrew Rippin Chief (ed.) *Islamic Studies: Oxford Bibliographies Online.* New York: Oxford University Press, 2016.

Lacan, Jacques. *The Ethics of Psychoanalysis, 1959–1960, the Seminar of Jacques Lacan.* Jacques-Alain Miller (ed.), Dennis Porter (trans. with notes). London: Routledge, 1992.

Lacan, Jacques. *Anxiety: The Seminar of Jacques Lacan, Book X.* Cambridge: Polity, 2014.

Madelung, Wilferd. *The Succession to Muhammad: A Study of the Early Caliphate.* Cambridge: Cambridge University Press, 1997.

Mernissi, Fatima. *Beyond the Veil: Male Female Dynamics in Modern Muslim Society.* New York: John Wiley & Sons, 1975.

Milani, Farzaneh. *Veils and Words: The Emerging Voices of Iranian Women Writers.* London; New York: I.B. Tauris, 1992.

Mirsepassi, Ali. *Transnationalism in Iranian Political Thought: The Life and Times of Ahmad Fardid.* Cambridge: Cambridge University Press, 2017.

Mofid, Shaykh. *Ahkam al-nesaʾ.* Shaikh Mahdi Najaf (ed.). Qom, 1413/1992.

Momen, Moojan. *An Introduction to Shiʿi Islam.* New Haven, NY: Yale University Press, 1985.

Monette, Connel. 'Indo-European Elements in Celtic and Indo-Iranian Epic Tradition: the Trial of Champions in the Tain Bo Cuailgne and Shahnameh,' *The Journal of Indo-European Studies* vol. 32, 2004: 61–78.

Mottahedeh, Negar. 'Ruptured Spaces and Effective Histories: The Unveiling of the Babi Poetess Qurrat al-ʿAyn Tahirih in the Gardens of Badasht,' *Occasional Papers in Shaykhi, Babi and Baha'i Studies,* vol. 2, no. 2, February, 1998.

Mottahedeh, Negar. *Representing the Unrepresentable: Historical Images of National Reform from the Qajars to the Islamic Republic of Iran.* New York: Syracuse University Press, 2008.

Omidsalar, Mahmoud. *Oedipus Complex in the Shahnameh: Textual,* Folkloristic, *and* Psycho-analytical Studies on the National Persian Epic. unpublished Ph.D. Dissertation. Berkeley, CA: University of California Press, 1984.

Pasolini, Pier Paolo. *Saint Paul.* London; New York: Verso Books, 2014.

Rabbani, Shoghi Effendi. *God Passes By.* Wilmette, IL: Baha'í Publishing Trust, 1970.

Reik, Theodor. *Das Ritual: Psychoanalytische Studien.* Leipzig: Internationaler Psychoanalytischer Verlag (Imago-Bucher), 1928.

Sanati, Mohammad and Javanbakht, Arash. 'Psychiatry and Psychoanalysis in Iran,' *Journal of the American Academy of Psychoanalysis and Dynamic Psychiatry* vol. 34, no. 3, 2006: 405–414. Available online: www.mohammadsanati.net/1390/culturepsychoanalysisiran/580. Accessed 15 October, 2017.

Schimmel, Annemarie. 'Qurrat al-'Ayn Ṭāhirah.' In Lindsay Jones (ed.) *Encyclopedia of Religion,* 2nd ed., vol. 11. Detroit: Macmillan Reference USA, 2005, pp. 7574–7575.

Sophocles. *Sophocles I: Oedipus the King, Oedipus at Colonus, Antigone.* 2nd ed. David Grene and Richard, Lattimore, (eds.) Chicago, IL: University of Chicago Press, 1991.

Tahirih Qurratu'l-'Ayn, *Ishraq-i Rabbani* (Divine Effulgence). MS in private hands. Digitally published, East Lansing, MI: H-Bahai, 2000, pp. 6 and 9.

Tourage, Mahdi. Abstract: 'Oedipal Foundations of Male Revolutionary Defiance and Female Conformist Obedience in Shi'ism as a Religion of Protest.' Unpublished paper, n.d. Available online: www.academia.edu/2653460/Oedipal_Foundations_of_Male_Revolutionary_Defiance_and_Female_Conformist_Obedience_in_Shi_ism_as_a_Religion_of_Protest–Abstract. Accessed 9 September, 2017.

Vejdani, Farzin. 'Appropriating the Masses: Folklore Studies, Ethnography, and Interwar Iranian Nationalism,' *International Journal of Middle East Studies* vol. 44, no. 3, 2012: 507–526.

Zaehner, R. C. *The Comparison of Religions.* Boston, MA: Beacon Press, 1959.

Zarandi, Nabil. *The Dawn-Breakers: Nabil's Narrative.* Shoghi Effendi (ed. and trans.). Wilmette, IL: Baha'i Publishing Trust, 1953.

Žižek, Slavoj. 'Preface to the New Edition: A Glance at the Archives of Islam.' In *The Fragile Absolute or Why the Christian Legacy Is Worth Saving?* London: Verso, 2008.

7

BECOMING REVOLUTION

From symptom to act in the 2011 Arab revolts

Nathan Gorelick

The following consideration of the Arab Uprisings of 2011 wagers that the political and ethical radicality of these events, as well as their ongoing defiance of the strategies of representational and physical containment which have since attempted to domesticate them within an established colonial and Orientalist imaginary, are deeply resonant with the ethics of psychoanalysis. On this view, the emergent notion of the human, of humanity as such, which animated the uprisings is analogous to the subject of the unconscious. This analogy does not mean to absorb the events of 2011 within a Freudian explanatory frame, but rather to push psychoanalysis beyond its original cultural and ontotheological context and into conversation with Islamicate peoples and practices in order to open the Freudian field to practical considerations of its own revolutionary potential. A psychoanalytic attunement to the limits of representation, moreover, makes clear that the 2011 revolts were a historical rupture – an opening onto another, incalculable future – therefore a collective movement from the repressive logic of the symptom to the realization of a new Idea of the political animated by a notion of the human not as a static being, but as a dynamic process of becoming. The horizon of this analysis is the hypothesis that this inchoate revolutionary subjectivity, the Idea it portends, and the model of social justice it promotes are intimately bound, if finally irreducible, to Islam because of the ways in which the latter defies or complicates the unconscious paternalistic fantasy at the core of the other major monotheisms.

What is to be done?

When Mohammad Bouazizi set himself on fire in Sidi Bouzid on December 17, 2010, neither he nor anyone else could have anticipated the consequences. Less than a month later, the Tunisian people had overthrown the government and after more than two decades of despotic rule its President, Zine El Abidine Ben Ali, was forced to flee for Saudi Arabia. Inspired by these events, protests and popular revolts erupted across almost every member nation of the Arab League. The world watched as hundreds of thousands, perhaps millions, of people flooded Cairo's Tahrir Square to deliver a deceptively simple message to Hosni Mubarak and his decades-old regime: *Arhil!* Leave! Another refrain from the Tunisian Revolution resounded throughout the so-called Arab World: *Al-Sha'b Yurid Isqat al-Nizam*, 'The People Want to Overthrow the Regime.'

The radicalism of such demands – audacious, defiant, furious, unprecedented, unforeseen and, for many within and beyond the revolts, unthinkable – was evidenced not only by the results they accomplished but also by the palpable anxiety among European and American commentators, who guardedly approved of the incitement to democracy but fretted about who or what might come to fill the inevitable power vacuums: namely, 'Islamism.' If Bouazizi's suicide instigated an explosion of popular rage that nobody – at least not the regimes or their Euro-American benefactors – saw coming, the response from the latter, particularly the evocation of the specter of Islamism, was pathetically predictable and, more to the point, predictably pathetic.

What I mean by this is that the events now known as the Arab Spring rapidly transformed the global geopolitical imaginary such that the U.S. and its European allies could no longer assume their centrality within the world order or their positions at the vanguard of democracy. They were embarrassed. What began in Tunisia was undertaken in the name of neither Islam nor liberalism – nor, indeed, neoliberalism – and refused the established categories of intelligibility into which the Arab World and the Arab mind have been inscribed at least for the last two hundred years.[1] Here was a series of direct actions nurtured by a solidarity that defied sectarian divisions, socio-economic disparities, colonial geographies, post-colonial sovereignties, and the social fragmentation that is the primary function of any politics of fear. As images of Egyptian youth standing firm against an encroaching brigade of heavily-armed police streamed from both traditional and social media outlets, it was the American and French and British governments' turn to be afraid. Something clearly momentous was taking place, but the enormity and novelty of these widespread insurrections were largely met with a lazy, tired Orientalism, Thatcherite clichés, or attempts to domesticate the events within a self-serving narrative about the implacable march of free market capitalism, as though this was what the masses truly desired. In short, the colonial center had been rendered suddenly peripheral, let us say dis-Oriented. The Orient – the fictive Other world against which the West defines, therefore constitutes, itself; which stands outside history and thus provides a benchmark against which the West measures its own civilizational progress; where despotism is an organizing principle and freedom is a hopeless abstraction – the Orient had passed the West by, shattering the paradigm of its cultural and political imaginary, leaving it befuddled and nervous and struggling to retain the myth of its own authority and coherence, which is also the myth of the West as such.

The West's struggle to re-Orient itself is evident even in the term 'Arab Spring,' which alludes to the 1848 Spring of Nations and thus folds the 2011 uprisings into a history according to which European peoples are the precedent and 150-year-old example. Joseph Massad has shown how 'Arab Spring' further establishes a surreptitious equivalence to the so-called Prague Spring of 1968, which was a top-down neoliberal reform effort and Cold War strategy orchestrated by NATO, thus entirely at odds with the events of 2011 (Massad, 2012). No doubt, the U.S. would have liked to see a repetition of the Prague Spring since, as Freud taught, repetition is the index of a failed resistance to the order of things. In other words, the dis-Oriented, newly peripheralized West would prefer the 2011 uprisings to be a symptom of the West's own political and moral imagination. Hamid Dabashi, meanwhile, prefers the term 'Arab Spring' because it is poetic and inspirational and redolent of new beginnings, but he problematizes the term 'Arab World' (or worse, 'Arab and Islamic World') because this imposes a simplistic, Orientalist colonial map that hinders the advent of a new 'cosmopolitan worldliness' which for Dabashi is the true and inevitable outcome of the Arab Spring. The Arab World contains many worlds, and 'It is those worlds,' Dabashi argues,

> that we must conceptually and categorically retrieve, as they become manifest in revolutionary praxis across the region [. . .], the worlds that are otherwise buried under two hundred years of colonial and imperial domination by an entity that calls itself (a practice habitually echoed by us) 'the West,' along with all of the civilizational alterities invented by mercenary armies of Orientalist and nativist intellectuals alike.
>
> *(2012)*

Thus, 'Arab World,' as with Massad's account of the 'Arab Spring' and consistent with Edward Said's foundational position in *Orientalism* (1979), is an instance of Western auto-referentiality, while 'the West,' too, is a fiction to which the colonial fiction of the Arab World has habituated us.[2]

Both are powerful arguments, and both demonstrate that the Orientalist resistance to the radical opening 2011 represents is inscribed in the very language with which it is habitually discussed, reproducing the same conceptual conventions, violent misunderstandings, and normative assumptions that the uprisings repudiate. The language is a symptom. So, to echo the question which animated another revolution, what is to be done? How are we to speak about the 2011 uprisings in any unified or unifying way without repeating and retrenching the same dull script?

This question confronts us with an impasse in the discourse of the event, an impasse at the level of the signifier which reveals and challenges the limits of representation, which exposes the insufficiency of the history of representation to domesticate the unprecedented eruption of this resistance within its (post-) colonial lexicon and attendant ideologies. An impasse, in other words, which results from both the revolutionary resistance against the prevailing geopolitical order and its counter-revolutionary complement, a resistance issuing from that order against the erosion of its stale, sedimented frameworks of intelligibility. And where we find this sort of double resistance, where that which defies the order of things can be semantically indexed only by its refusal of symbolic assignation, where such refusal subverts and unworks the systems of thought which want to know nothing about it and sustain themselves through precisely this denial even to the point of their becoming preposterous – here, amid such resistance and revolt, at the site of the crisis of representation it provokes, we recognize the incalculable dynamics of the unconscious.

Let us take care at once, however, not to reproduce the colonial logic of the signifier by merely imposing a Freudian interpretation upon the 2011 revolts, appropriating the revolutionary opening to an explanatory model whose European and Judeo-Christian foundations thus would remain unmoved. If we sense something of the unconscious here and, as the ethics of psychoanalysis demands, wish to retain the radical specificity of this (and every) resistance to the order of the signifier, we instead must ask whether and what psychoanalysis can learn from these events. What, in other words, can the 2011 revolts teach us about the potentially revolutionary dimension of the unconscious?

In what follows, I offer an initial response to this question by showing how the revolutionary wave that began with Bouazizi's suicide was animated by an emergent conception of a human being – of what it means to be human – that defies the reduction of the subject to subjectivity, whether theologically or philosophically or ideologically defined, in ways that resonate with both an Islamicate conception of the divine and a Freudian and Lacanian conception of the subject of the unconscious. This resonance should not imply any collapse of the religious into the psychoanalytic or vice versa. Instead, with psychoanalysis we may see how this novel conception of the subject announces a truly revolutionary opening within the Idea of the political, one which portends a new future that cannot be circumscribed by the terms and conditions of the present or its symptomatic repetitions – a future which, like the unconscious, contains an incalculable potential.

The unconscious is constitutively recalcitrant to linguistic determination. It traces the limit of every external frame of reference, but it therefore shares that limit and thus is implicated by but irreducible to the systems of intelligibility that surround it. The unconscious, therefore, addresses itself to history and politics and, emphatically, religion, but its message is never unambiguous. It is, rather, an energy that seeks to carve a space within these formations for what they exclude, refuse or, finally, repress. In this way and through the work of analysis an ethical fidelity to the unconscious can open these fields to the possibility of radical transformation. The same may be said (and has been said) of the 2011 uprisings. This comparison, moreover, can further widen the scope of psychoanalysis beyond its Judeo-Christian and European foundations without its falling into colonial habits of thought or abdicating its strong skepticism toward any religious doctrine or dogma. The analyst's instrument, after all, is the ear. Let us, therefore, listen to what Bouazizi's self-immolation moved from a murmur to a shout, for in this amplification we may also hear a movement from symptom to act, a movement which opens history to a new sort of revolution.

The revolutionary anti-ideal

The requisite touchstone in the Freudian corpus for the present inquiry is Freud's *Group Psychology* (1955a). Prior studies on the topic, Freud claims, are correct to emphasize that a group is a transient entity which frequently exhibits none of the inhibitions or anxieties that its individual constituents might otherwise suffer, in which impulses toward self-preservation are suspended, actions are not premeditated, and anything seems possible. In this way, the crowd is homologous to the dream, and its actions must be interpreted accordingly. This indeed seems an accurate depiction of the spontaneous collective fervor that gripped the people in 2011 as they stood against decades of despotism and – at least for a time, it seemed – defied all probability both in the audacity of their protest and the results they achieved.

But because the psychology of the crowd occasions Freud's most extensive writing on the phenomenon of identification, Freud's *Group Psychology* also corrects a lacuna in all prior texts on the subject (especially Gustav Le Bon's 1895 *Psychologie des foules*), namely, that they either underestimate or totally ignore the function of the leader within the constitution of a group. A collection of individuals becomes a group through their shared identification not with one another but with the great leader. The 2011 uprisings, however, were generally, remarkably, leaderless. Freud's corrective emphasis, therefore, would seem ill-fitted to the present case were it not for his briefly indicating two exceptions to the rule that there can be no group without a leader to unify them. First, the leader might be substituted with an ideal, which, again recalling the *Interpretation of Dreams* (1955c), Freud also calls a wish; second, and following from this:

> The leader or the leading idea might also, so to speak, be negative; hatred against a particular person or institution might operate in just the same unifying way, and might call up the same kind of emotional ties as positive attachment.
>
> *(1955a)*

We should first consider this latter exception. The rather surprising key to understanding how a group can cohere around a negation is – Beatlemania. Freud imagines a 'troop of women and girls' fawning over some famous musician and who, instead of tearing each other to pieces trying to win his attention, spontaneously identify with one another 'by means of a similar love for the same object' and renounce their individual claims to his love. This, Freud says, is an instance of social justice, of equality, which here means 'that we deny ourselves many things so that others may have to do without them as well' (1955a). In foregrounding renunciation, such a conception of social justice flies in the face of liberalism's foundational assertion, grounded in the Enlightenment, that 'all men are created equal.' Whereas this Jeffersonian doctrine treats equality as a natural fact and a lowest common denominator against which individuals have the right to distinguish themselves, Freud recognized that such rights are in fact imperatives to inequality. As Freud's contrary definition of social justice makes clear, equality is not a fact of nature but a social principle – and, we should add, a psychoanalytic one, which is no less universal than its liberal counterpart. It is axiomatic that the condition of belonging to any social order is a primal renunciation whereby the impossible object of desire is relegated to the field of unconscious fantasy. Thus, every group, no matter how loosely bound, is constituted by the assumption among its constituents not of a common property but of a lack which ensures everyone is equal because nobody is satisfied.[3]

In this regard, we should echo Joseph Massad and others who insist that the root of the uprisings was a concern for the material conditions of everyday life. This, indeed, was what drove Bouazizi to suicidal despair (he was no revolutionary, only a young man suffocated by a cascade of humiliating injustices), and in part what compelled the educated but pauperized youth in Tunisia and elsewhere to take to the streets and demand the end of the regime. At the same time, however, Dabashi reminds us that the revolts were open-ended, which is to say, their outcomes were not and could not be calculated in advance; they largely refused specific political prescriptions. Fethi Benslama further warns that to impose a purely materialist causality is to foster a dangerous 'determinist illusion [...] according to which everything seems programmed,' and that 'deprives human existence of its future' by recoding any such historical rupture within a 'logic machine' that can only reaffirm what it already knows (2011). Again, the facts of the case bear this out. The people did not demand a living wage, or expanded state welfare, or rent control, and, in fact, the regimes were flummoxed when such concessions proved useless against the fearless rage of the masses. Here 'the regime' became a floating signifier for all forms of hierarchy driven by corruption, clientelism, and coercion. The regime was not invited to bargain. The crowd was not negotiating. They were not making requests, but issuing a demand: *Arhil!* Leave!

Against the regime, the people did not assert a facile Jeffersonian conception of equality but instead opposed another signifier: *karamah*, dignity. This instances the first of Freud's exceptions to the rule that no group can be without a leader, wherein an ideal replaces an especially magnetic personality. But this, too, was negatively defined. As Rashid Khalidi notes, this call for dignity has to be understood in the double sense of individual dignity, the constant affront to which drove Bouazizi to his suicide, and the collective dignity of the people, which was insulted by their so-called leaders who parroted their colonial benefactors by proclaiming time and again that the people were not ready for democracy or self-determination (2011). Benslama identifies the mechanism by which these two forms of indignity interpenetrate as, precisely, identification, following Freud's definition of this phenomenon in his *Group Psychology*.

Reporting on his visits to Tunisia just prior to Bouazizi's act, Benslama notes a 'nauseated discontent, when the disapproval of power also becomes a disgust with oneself, with accepting the unacceptable,' so that the revolution was catalyzed by Bouazizi's suicide because the act, which far exceeded the man's personal biography or intentions, became 'a source of identification with his despair and his revolt.' This was not a popular calculation – crowds, Freud reminds us, do not calculate, but act – and as such its effects proved incalculable.

Because dignity, moreover, is recalcitrant to quantification, the sudden eruption of this moral virtue into the political short-circuits any 'logic machine' that would determine the act and its effects in advance. On Benslama's reading, 'dignity' in Tunisia became the popular name for the inestimable – the true essence of the human and of any human being, what cannot be taken away because it cannot be counted among the other objects one possesses, because it is irreducible, because it is not a property one owns but a lack one inhabits.

Lack is inestimable because, unlike debt, it is inadmissible within any framework of exchange, including first and foremost the order of the signifier – language itself. When Freud discovered that castration – renunciation – is the condition of social belonging and the foundation of social justice, he also found that no two lacks are alike, that every renunciation institutes what Lacan calls a logic of fantasy which is singular to each human being, and that this singularity – the heart of the meaning of the subject, the truth which peeks perennially from the vanishing point on the horizon of consciousness, beckoning in its interminable withdrawal – thus defies its neat translation into speech and therefore requires a poetic linguistic sensibility. This is why, for all its scientism, psychoanalysis is finally a poetics of experience at the limits of signification. It is also why the singularity of the logic of fantasy and the truth of the subject of the unconscious afford a far more radical basis for equality than liberalism's flattening of being into an original and base commonality could ever imagine.

Bouazizi's suicidal act is a case in point. By identifying with the charred body of a humiliated fruit vendor, the people of Tunisia inverted the Freudian formula according to which the group coheres around the leader who revitalizes for each of its members the archaic fantasy of the primal father whom they fear and adore because he stands outside the dynamics of desire, beyond the limit imposed by the renunciation requisite to the social bond, where he enjoys the impossible plenitude of a limitless satisfaction. Against such a fantasy, the Tunisian revolutionaries instead identified with the 'anti-ideal' (Benslama's term), the fruit vendor as personification of the abject. In so doing, they instantiated a revolutionary moment in the name not of what they held in common, but of what they could never have in common: their inestimability, their singularity, and their collective right, as humans, to their irreducible uncommonness.

This is where the resonance with the subject of the unconscious is most audible. Psychoanalysis is notoriously suspicious of group thinking (one need only visit the shell of Freud's home at Berggasse 19 to understand why). But, in Tunisia in late 2010 something new seems to have taken place: the revolution was not theocratically authorized or religiously motivated; in such Islamicate contexts, the conspicuous absence of any explicit appeal to Islam which so flummoxed both the regimes and Western commentaries indicates that we were indeed watching the unconscious in action – that is, we saw the passage from symptomatic disgust to revolutionary act. Nor was the uprising the fulfillment of a Marxist prophecy or a neoliberal dream. It did not coalesce around a 'great man' who could channel the crowd's lust for heroic violence. It repudiated all of that. It was an opening, a break with the order of things that also broke the order of things. It suggested the possibility of a new kind of community, a community organized around a hole in being, thus one for which there is as yet no word and for which no word will suffice. If the organizing principle of such a community is not what it has but rather what it lacks, then it is consistent with the ethics of psychoanalysis and its injunction that we dwell with what cannot be named or refuses discursive assignation, for it is into that opening that the subject becomes – as Freud says, interminably. Such a revolution thus would not be a discrete event, a promise fulfilled, or a dream deferred. It would be a mode of being: being as becoming, or what, following Alain Badiou, we might call 'an asymmetrical and egalitarian becoming' (2007).

An opening, an interval

Perhaps this all sounds somewhat romantic, especially in light of the political realities that succeeded the 2011 revolts, the terror of the civil war in Syria or Sisi's military coup in Egypt being just two especially visible examples of the revolutionary dream's interruption. But it does not take a Freud to see that we are at present in the midst of a counter-revolution – a symptomatic response, a reaction-formation against what was opened in 2011.

This does not mean that the 2011 uprisings were all 'failures,' since the essence of these revolutions was a refusal to determine the future according to the anxieties of the present and, in this regard, they succeeded and continue to succeed. Of course, this has not stopped the waves of self-satisfied pundits claiming, 'I told you so,' now that Islamism, despite the early optimism of thinkers like Dabashi, has made significant political gains throughout much of the Arab League and the Arab Spring has turned to what, since at least 2013, many have dubbed the 'Arab Winter.' I told you so, the rewarmed Orientalist discourse goes. The Arab World isn't ready for democracy. They can't handle it! Such discourse, of course, and as always, has little to do with the reality of its purported object; instead, it deploys 'the Arab World' as a privileged signifier within its own auto-referential imaginary in order to elide and disavow the obvious: the so-called West is not exactly a bastion of democratic competence, either internally or with respect to its geopolitical others. The patent xenophobia – fear of strangeness – at the core of the countless reactionary responses to neoliberalism's unsustainable excesses and its recoil into the Western metropoles, the resuscitation of nationalism and nativist populism as viable strategies for electoral success – in short, the democratic endorsement of the worst forms of anti-democratic speech and policy – all this, too, has caught the Western technocratic regimes by surprise.

The repressed always returns. As Freud insists, the repressed is its return, the symptom is its cause, only in a displaced form. This should make clear that both revolution and reactionism lay in the blind spots of the political imaginary, and without some ethically informed strategy of relation to the repressed its return can be catastrophic. We therefore should resist the urge to judge, to define, to assimilate with any logic machine the revolutionary opening that took place in 2011 and, we must insist, remains open still. We should resist this urge not only because we (whoever we are) inhabit our own glass houses but because it is only by way of such resistance that we can withhold or withstand the punctuation mark which would close 2011, installing it within the established syntax of the prevailing order as though this revolutionary moment could be contained alongside all the other sad relics in Orientalism's cabinet of curiosities. Thus contributing to the perpetuation of this opening permits us to recognize it also as a break with the past and the announcement of a politics to come, a politics which would be animated by a conception of the human that refuses its reduction to the paradigm of the liberal subject and attendant flattening of human singularity into a base, naturally determined, thus politically and ethically vacuous equality.

The ethics of psychoanalysis compels the prolongation of the opening in language into which the contours of the fantasy can emerge and the subject of the unconscious can, however poetically, begin to speak. In this regard, ethics assumes a double valence: first, the steadfast commitment, on the part of the one who would know the truth of their own desire, to the traversal of unconscious fantasy, wherever it might lead and with whatever unforeseeable consequences it brings about; and second, the responsibility of the analyst to sustain the opening in the order of the signifier into which the subject may come forth.

Following this ethics, to sustain the revolutionary opening of 2011 in the name of a future which has yet to be determined by the traumatic weight of the past is to understand our tortured present as what Badiou calls an 'intervallic period,' a moment at which a rupture with history introduces the possibility of a new Idea of the political,

> a pivotal hypothesis, so that the energy [these revolts] release and the individuals they engage can give rise, in and beyond the mass movement and the reawakening of History it signals, to a new figure of organization and hence of politics.
>
> *(Badiou, 2012)*

This pivotal hypothesis does not spring fully formed out of a historical revolt for the same reason the revolt makes such a hypothesis possible: because, breaking with the order of things and its reflection in the order of the signifier, history does not yet have a way to articulate it. 'It is during such periods [as this],' Badiou reminds us, 'that the reactionaries can say, precisely because the revolutionary road is faint, even illegible, that things have resumed their natural course' (2012). The misidentification of the historical and contingent as the natural and necessary is ideology's principle means for reproducing the dominant order within a field of hegemonic struggle. Against this ideological maneuver, psychoanalysis demands that we attend to the logic of fantasy and the dynamics of desire, and that in so doing we de-naturalize the apparent or the given by exposing the libidinal investments which sustain both individual and collective ideological commitments.

Within and against Islam: a negative affirmation

What remains to be thought in this regard is, precisely, Islam. To begin, we must remember – against the Orientalist insistence to the contrary – that 'Islamism,' like the uprisings' deployment of 'the regime,' is a floating signifier that is not identical with Islam, which is vast and variegated and, more to the point, the ontotheological backdrop against which the 2011 opening took place. As I have argued elsewhere, Islam, like any religion, is a symptom (Gorelick, 2015). It therefore is a displaced expression of the repressed, a return of the repressed. It is also an immensely powerful organizing force within the symbolic order which here concerns us – whence the emergence of the term 'Islamicate,' a correlate of the adjectival 'Judeo-Christian' that characterizes the theological structure and metaphysical habits of the West in which Freud saw the return of a repressed infantile fantasy of paternal omnipotence and protection.

Islamicate thought and theology, however, begins with a repudiation of the doctrine of divine parentage. Allah, in other words, is not a father. In this way, Islam defies the brief treatment Freud affords it in his last work, *Moses and Monotheism*, where he speculates that its origin is a mere 'abbreviated repetition' and 'imitation' of the origins of Judaic monotheism or its Christian permutation (1955b). The symbolic order – what I have otherwise been calling the order of the signifier – both permits and prohibits. It affords the language which is the structure of the social link (always in a given historical and cultural context) and, at the same time and for the same reason, relegates those instances of the human experience that cannot find a place within that structure to the domain of the unsayable, to an-other scene where they work upon and unwork the limits of the symbolic: the field of unconscious fantasy. This is a fact of human being insofar as the human is a linguistic being. Islam, then, would seem to align with the ethics of psychoanalysis at precisely the point of its articulation of the divine as the absence of any adequate articulation.

The first *shahada*, the most ubiquitously repeated testimony of faith among believers, bears this out: *la ilaha illa'llah*, there is no Allah but Allah. The invocation begins with a negation and then supplements it with an affirmation. As Bruce B. Lawrence has argued, the *shahada* makes clear that,

Allah can be affirmed but never exhausted. Every saying produces an unsaying. Allah must be said before Allah can be unsaid; yet it is the unsaid, the unspoken, and the unspeakable 'surplus' of the Thing, the Absolute, the One that is presumed to be the larger platform of reality.

(2015)[4]

In other words, Allah is both more and less than the signifier of an excess of meaning over speech: rather it names the absence in the symbolic order of the order's ownmost cause and object of adoration. Allah names an unspeakable excess, a constitutive hole in the symbolic, because it names both the origin and the destination of desire.

This does indeed draw Islam closer to Freud's construction of the origins of Judaism, but not because it is a repetitive imitation. Prior commentaries on *Moses and Monotheism*, most notably Edward Said's *Freud and the Non-European*, have emphasized Freud's startling claim that Moses, the father of the faith, was an Egyptian (2014). As Said makes clear, this claim that a people originates from the position of the Other is a profound rebuke of the epistemological foundations of anti-Semitism or, indeed, all forms of racism and ethnocentrism, and need not be confined to considerations of the archaic past. But, this displacement of the Exodus narrative is not *Moses and Monotheism*'s most radical insight. What this Egyptian Moses gave to the people that even Akhenaton, the founder of the monotheistic sun cult from whom Moses took his cue, could not provide, and what therefore places their religion at the origin of modern civilization, was a strict interdiction against any representation of the divine. History, in other words, begins with a prohibition which is also a negation: the installation of a hole at the center of the cosmos, a gap in the order of the signifier that marks the absolute, unknowable truth of the universe, a source and final meaning of all things which is present only as an absence. History is a narrative which is animated by what it does not and can never narrate, a symbolic struggle against the internal limit of symbolization itself.

Following the persistent emphasis throughout Islamic scripture upon both the paradoxical unsayability of the divine and the repudiation of the father at the foundation of the faith, we therefore find that Islam fully assumes this gap in the symbolic. Yet, unlike the Mosaic prohibition, which establishes a structural homology between paternal and divine authority, Islam explicitly refuses any such homology and, by extension, any association with the logical position of the father within the Oedipal structure of desire. Like 'Yahweh,' then, but by pushing this internal limit of representation to its logical extreme, 'Allah' is the always insufficient name for the inestimable, the incalculable, that which exceeds the limits of knowing and which pervades and infuses being with an immense but indescribable significance.

This is why the new Idea of the political, which the 2011 revolts announced but which has yet to find or create its symbolic assignation, erupted within Islamicate societies but not in the name of Islam – and why, moreover, its effects could be felt in entirely different social and economic contexts throughout the world. Recall that what Benslama discovers in the demand for dignity at the base of the people's resolve against the regime is the lack in the symbolic which marks the radical irreducibility of the subject of the unconscious: the inestimable which is also the core of the human as such. The demand for dignity does not so much mirror as refract the invocation of the inestimable in the *shahada*. It thus articulates the inarticulable in its very inarticulability, and for this reason will not be appeased through greater access to global markets, obsolete appeals to economic nationalism, Islamist ideologies, or any other established mode of political or geopolitical calculation. *Karamah* is the affirmation of an incalculable humanity only because it is also, and primarily, the negation of the limits of the present in the name of what might be – without any final destination.

We need only note the radicalism of the people's demand and the volume of the reaction against the 2011 revolts to see the truth of Badiou's claim that we are now living in the interval between the eruption of an Idea and its realization. We are indeed at the precipice of a new history, the organizing principle of which can never assume the status of a Great Leader or, much the same thing, a disembodied Ideal. This new history cannot yet and may never speak this principle's name. For it can be approached and affirmed only negatively and by way of negation. It is the unsayable inestimability of the human, which results not from a juridical interdiction against its symbolization but from the insufficiency of all symbolization to exhaust the truth it designates, not from a closure upon the limits of language but an opening within those very limits.

The events of 2011, whatever we may call them, proclaim above all an emergent conception of the human subject as a revolutionary subject, thus of politics as a domain not of administration but of revolution – and finally, an emergent, dynamic ontology according to which being, all being, is becoming. If we wish to accept the dual responsibility of the ethics of psychoanalysis, if we accept the injunction to both venture into the unknown and sustain the possibility of that adventure, then our first task is not to explain revolution to the revolutionaries but to join them, which here means to assume the attunement of the analyst: to listen for the murmuring of the unconscious within and beyond Islamicate societies, to follow the trail of the symptom in order to discover the humanity at its core, to hear its address to a humanity that is also a becoming revolution.

Notes

1 The most notorious text in this regard (which despite or because of its patent ethnocentrism and cultural essentialism remains current especially among soldiers and military strategists) is Raphael Patai's 1978 book, *The Arab Mind*. Curiously, perhaps symptomatically, the revised edition of Patai's book inadvertently signals the imaginary arena of Orientalism in which it operates by including in its front matter a typical 'All persons fictitious' disclaimer: 'This is a work of fiction. Names, characters, places, and incidents either are the product of the author's imagination or are used fictitiously. Any

resemblance to actual events or persons, living or dead, is entirely coincidental.' We can only assume adherents to Patai's position overlook this disclaimer, which here functions as a return of the repressed. For a salient, psychoanalytically informed critique of Patai's book, see Copjec (2009).

2 Dabashi further argues that the Arab Spring, transnational and 'open-ended,' has finally rendered both colonialism and its post-colonial reactions politically obsolete and epistemically bankrupt; we therefore cannot recoil to a nationalist semantics, as though Tunisia's 'Jasmine Revolution,' Egypt's 'January 25 Revolution,' or even Iran's earlier 'Green Movement' are unrelated. But nor can we ignore locally specific grievances, strategies, and tactics through exhausted homogenizing appellations like 'The Arab and Islamic World.' The problem is exacerbated by the various instances of solidarity or strategic resonance that suggest other democratizing movements against unfettered capitalist authoritarianism also could be considered blooms of the Arab Spring – Occupy Wall Street, for instance.

3 Here we should recall Jacques-Alain Miller's assertion that racism springs from the illusion that one person or group lacks less, thus enjoys more, has less restricted access to *jouissance*, than you do (1994). This is a fine explanation for the unconscious fantasmatic origins of racial hatred, but it raises the question: how does the envy at the root of such hatred become institutionalized in the form of systemic racism? How does envy move from personal prejudice to the level of a world-historical discourse like Orientalism?

4 For a more extensive discussion of Allah and the limits of language see Sells (1994). Although I borrow from Lawrence's characterization of Allah as the negation of the speakable, I am grateful to Batool Batalvi for first drawing my attention to this aspect of the *shahada*.

References

Badiou, A. (2007). *The Century*. A. Toscano, trans. Cambridge: Polity.
Badiou, A. (2012). *The Rebirth of History: Times of Riots and Uprisings*. G. Elliott, trans. New York: Verso.
Benslama, F. (2011). *Soudain la révolution! De la Tunisie au monde arabe: la signification d'un soulévement*. Paris: Denoël; my translation.
Copjec, J. (2009). The Censorship of Interiority. *Umbr(a): A Journal of the Unconscious*, 'Islam' Issue, pp. 165–188.
Dabashi, H. (2012). *The Arab Spring: The End of Postcolonialism*. London: Zed Books.
Freud, S. (1955a). *Group Psychology and the Analysis of the Ego*. In: J. Strachey, ed., *The Standard Edition of the Complete Psychological Works of Sigmund Freud*, Volume XVIII. London: Hogarth, pp. 67–143.
Freud, S. (1955b). *Moses and Monotheism*. In: J. Strachey, ed., *The Standard Edition of the Complete Psychological Works of Sigmund Freud*, Volume XXIII. London: Hogarth, pp. 3–137.
Freud, S. (1955c). *The Interpretation of Dreams*. In: J. Strachey, ed., *The Standard Edition of the Complete Psychological Works of Sigmund Freud*, Volumes IV and V. London: Hogarth.
Gorelick, N. (2015). Translating the Islamicate Symptom. *SCTIW Review: Journal of the Society for Contemporary Thought and the Islamicate World*, pp. 1–13. Available at: http://sctiw.org/sctiwreviewarchives/archives/610 [Accessed October 2017].
Khalidi, R. (2011). Preliminary Historical Observations on the Arab Revolutions of 2011. *Jadaliyya*. Available at: www.jadaliyya.com/pages/index/970/preliminary-historical-observations-on-the-arab-re [Accessed October 2017].
Lawrence, B. (2015). *Who Is Allah?* Chapel Hill, NC: University of North Carolina Press.

Massad, J. (2012). The 'Arab Spring' and Other American Seasons. *Al Jazeera*. Available at: www.aljazeera.com/indepth/opinion/2012/08/201282972539153865.html [Accessed October 2017].

Miller, J.-A. (1994). Extimité. In: M. Bracher, ed., *Lacanian Theory of Discourse: Subject, Structure, and Society*, New York: New York University Press, pp. 74–87.

Patai, R. (1978). *The Arab Mind*. Revised ed. New York: Macmillan Publishing.

Said, E. (1979). *Orientalism*. New York: Vintage.

Said, E. (2014). *Freud and the Non-European*. Reprinted. New York: Verso.

Sells, M. (1994). *Mystical Languages of Unsaying*. Chicago, IL: University of Chicago Press.

8

DECOLONIZING PSYCHOANALYSIS/ PSYCHOANALYZING ISLAMOPHOBIA

Robert K. Beshara

In this chapter, I attempt to do two things: (1) theorize what I call 'decolonial psychoanalysis,' and (2) apply my theory to an analysis of Islamophobia. I start by problematizing the Euro-American call for an 'Islamic reformation' à la the Protestant Reformation. I do so by looking at the modern history of Islam from the perspective of border thinkers. Then I briefly tackle the problem of the one (universal) and the many (particulars) before thinking about the dialectical relationship between psychoanalysis and Islam. I follow by arguing for a radical psychoanalysis and an Islamic humanism. After that, I perform a Lacanian discourse critique of political Islam. Next, I use Jacques Lacan's theory of the ~~four~~ five discourses to challenge the hegemonic discourses of counterterrorism and Islamophobia. I proceed to sketch the Discourse of the Analyst in particular as a revolutionary model for radical psychoanalysis and Islamic humanism, while drawing on transmodern/decolonial tools such as delinking and secular criticism. I end the chapter with a critique of Slavoj Žižek's under-theorization of Islamophobia in order to show how decolonial psychoanalysis improves upon Lacanian social theory with its emphasis on liberation.

Islamic reformation

Some Muslims find the phrase 'Islamic reformation' problematic, particularly when the debates take place in Euro-America by means of 'the rhetoric of modernity' (Mignolo 2007). In response, Mehdi Hasan (2015) writes, 'The truth is that Islam has already had its own reformation of sorts, in the sense of a stripping of cultural accretions and a process of supposed "purification." And ... it produced ... the kingdom of Saudi Arabia.' Similarly, Hamza Yusuf (Rethinking Islamic Reform 2010) in his debate with Tariq Ramadan at Oxford University also argues against the 'Reformation analogy' (Hasan 2015) and makes a case instead for the 'renovation' or 'renewal' (*tajdeed*)[1] of the Islamic Tradition. Neither Hasan's nor Yusuf's defense of Traditional Islam should be quickly dismissed as a conservative regressive move; in fact, they both present us with a counterintuitive, and I may add critical, reading of 'Islamic reformation' as perhaps a disguised wish for violence. As Hasan (2015) adds:

> It is Isis [Islamic State of Iraq and Syria] leader Abu Bakr al-Baghdadi, who claims to rape and pillage in the name of a 'purer form' of Islam ... Those who cry so simplistically ... for an Islamic reformation, should be careful what they wish for.

In defense of Traditional Islam, Ziauddin Sardar (2004) makes a very pertinent point when he writes, 'non-western traditional communities do not think of *tradition* as something that will take them to pre-modern times; on the contrary, tradition will take them forward, with their identity intact, to a *transmodern* future' (emphasis added). In other words, transmodern Islam is Traditional Islam because it is *exterior* to modernity's *Totality* in the world-system.

Bracketing the question of political violence for the time being, since the eighteenth-century, *border thinkers* (Mignolo 2007) have debated the place of Islam in modernity. According to Nasr Abu Zayd (2006), two general answers have been put forth: revivalism (*ihya*) in the eighteenth century and reformation (*islah*) in the nineteenth century. By the early twentieth century, however—particularly after the collapse of the Ottoman Empire—the meaning of reformation (*islah*) shifted from a 'rethinking tradition' (Zayd 2004a, p. 8) to 'orthodox fundamentalism' (Zayd 2004a, p. 60), which splintered into two main movements: Islamism (*al-Islam al-siyasi*) and Salafism (*salafiyya*). In this essay, I will argue for the reestablishment of *Islamic humanism* as a *liberation* project from the perspective of *transmodernity* and *decoloniality* (Mignolo 2007).

Certainly, the debate regarding reform will continue for the foreseeable future because, as Zayd (2004b) writes, 'it is not possible to speak about the Qur'an as an absolute that transcends space, time, and place. Human beings understand text through some sort of prism that varies depending on experience—both individual and cultural experience' (p. 60). In other words, the name of both the problem and the solution is 'radical Otherness.' Accounting for difference, or alterity, is essential in any liberation struggle—this is what Walter Mignolo (2007) calls '*identity based on politics* (and not a *politics based on identity*)' (p. 492, emphasis in original). '*[P]luriversality as a universal project*' (Mignolo 2007, pp. 452–453, emphasis in original) then is *an-other* way of describing this *delinking* project. Identity politics as strategic essentialism may be of practical value for the subaltern, but the question of difference from within the Totality of modernity is not an innocent one as Enrique Dussel (2002) instructs us, for that question is often coupled with Eurocentered 'power differentials,' namely 'racial classification' and 'ranking the planet' (Mignolo 2007, p. 497)—or what Anibal Quijano (2000) dubs 'the coloniality of power.' Coloniality, of course, is the repressed truth of modernity; hence, Mignolo's (2007) formula: 'modernity/coloniality.'

Given what I will say later on in the essay about 'terrorism studies,' it is worth adding that Zayd (2004b) believes 'the positive gains by the Islamic Reformation Movement of the nineteenth century came to a grinding halt in 1948 [with the establishment of the State of Israel]' (Zayd 2004b, p. 187). In other words, for Zayd, Islamic reformation (*islah*) depends on a socially just resolution for both sides of the 'conflict' without overlooking the evident power asymmetry: that 'there is no "conflict," only the omnipresent power of the Israeli government and those who resist it' (Sheppard 2014).

The one and the many

My intuition is that even though this book is titled *Islamic Psychoanalysis/Psychoanalytic Islam*, the unconscious (hence, repressed) subtitle goes something like this: *(Muslim) Analysands/(Muslim) Analysts*. In the words of Ahmed Fayek (2004), 'Does the analyst's religion play a part in his [or her] practice, and what would the analyst do with his [or her] patient's religious beliefs?' (p. 456). To answer these two questions, Fayek (2004) distinguishes between Islam 'as an ethnic identity' and Islam 'as a personal belief'; the latter for him is a question of personal choice therefore uncomplicated, while the former he finds problematic since it 'involves aspects of narcissism' (p. 457). A different answer to this dialectic involves a synthesis of Islam and psychoanalysis, such as Yusuf Murad's 'integrative psychology' (El Shakry 2014). This concrete clinical question, however, about the relationship between Muslims and non-Muslims touches on a much deeper theoretical problem that can be traced back to ancient philosophy: *the One and the Many*. Even though both Islam and psychoanalysis have one founder—Muhammad and Freud, respectively—, there are as many Islams and psychoanalyses as there are Muslims and psychoanalysts in the world today.

Radical psychoanalysis/Islamic humanism

Additionally, if we hermeneutically read not only Islam as a religion but also psychoanalysis as a theology (Davis, Pound and Crockett 2014) then, following Marx (1843/1978, p. 54), the criticism of Islam becomes a criticism of (Shari'a) Law and the criticism of psychoanalysis becomes a criticism of (liberal) politics. Of the many psychoanalyses and Islams out there, I will focus specifically on 'radical psychoanalysis' (Fox 2011) and 'Islamic humanism' (Tibi 2012). This will necessitate my reclaiming of the controversial term 'radical' and the passé term 'humanism' in order to decolonize psychoanalysis and psychoanalyze Islamophobia. As Laura U. Marks (2012) argues, 'To decolonise European philosophy [and by extension, psychoanalysis] we need to rediscover its Islamic (and many *other*) origins' (p. 52, emphasis added). Radicalizing psychoanalysis is a critical step in the direction of 'epistemic decolonization' (Mignolo 2007).

Radicalism, an example of 'antisystemic movements,' is one of the 'trinity of ideologies that emerged in the wake of the French Revolution'—the other two being: conservatism and liberalism (Wallerstein 2004, p. 52). Radicalism, an outcome of the 'world revolution' of 1848 (p. 63), is a leftist alternative to the center-right paradigm plaguing most politico-economic systems in the world today.

Antisystemic movements, like radicalism, are about 'progressive social change . . . promoted by those who would benefit by it' (Wallerstein 2004, pp. 96–97). In the words of Karl Marx (1843/1978), '*Theory* [as a *material* force] is capable of seizing the masses . . . as soon as it becomes *radical*. To be *radical* is to grasp things by the root. But for man [sic] the root is man [sic] himself' (p. 60, emphasis added). Marx's critique of capitalism is concerned with the *emancipation* of the European working class men of his time. According to Mignolo (2007), Marx's critique of capitalism is valuable, but is from within 'the rhetoric of modernity,' and hence, is not delinked from 'the logic of coloniality,' which explains Marx's limitations on questions of gender and race, for example. The transmodern and decolonial corrective to emancipation then, according to Mignolo (2007), is *liberation*, which 'provides a larger frame that includes the racialized class that the European bourgeoisie . . . colonized beyond Europe . . . and, thus, subsumes "emancipation"' (p. 455).

The phrase 'radical Islam,' which is popular in the United States among conservatives, denigrates both radicalism and Islam, and so—beyond the liberal-conservative hysteria against what is dubbed by some 'Islamo-leftism'—I am inviting us, 'the Lacanian left' (Stavrakakis 2007), to position the signifiers ('radical' and 'Islam') vis-à-vis psychoanalysis, not in relation to liberalism or conservatism, but in relation to critical and delinking projects like 'radical democracy' (Laclau and Mouffe 1985/2014) and 'radical reform' (Ramadan 2009), respectively. With the dialectic radical psychoanalysis-Islamic humanism, I hope then to enact a 'decolonial shift' by (1) theorizing *decolonial psychoanalysis* in order to (2) analyze Islamophobia using 'critical border thinking' (Mignolo 2007).

Three substitutional metaphors

Drawing on Andrea Mura's (2014) Lacanian discourse critique, I hypothesize that *Salafism as alienation* involves a pre-modern fantasy or '*a stylisation of the Past*,' while *Islamism as separation* involves a postmodern fantasy or '*a utopian visualisation of the Future*' (p. 117, emphasis in original). In the case of Salafism, the traditions of the 'pious predecessors' or the first three generations of Muslims function as the *big Other* dominating the Muslim subject ($) with its literalism. In the case of Islamism, the pan-Islamic caliphate functions as the *objet petit a*, or the Other's desire, subjugating the Muslim subject ($) with its legalism (i.e., Shari'a Law). In terms of the 'trinity of ideologies' (Wallerstein 2004), Salafism may be comparable to conservatism, and Islamism to liberalism. While this comparison works from within the rhetoric of modernity, it does not really work according to the logic of coloniality. For example, Adam Curtis (*The power of nightmares* 2004) argues that neoconservatism and Islamism are dialectically related.

On the other hand, *Islamic humanism as traversing of fantasy* involves 'a *trans*modern *pluriversality*' (Dussel 2012, p. 50, emphasis in original), which can manifest as the transmodern Muslim's subjectification of 'the *cause* of his or her existence (the Other's desire: object *a*)' (Fink 1995, p. 69, emphasis in original). In other words, truly radical Muslims ($), according to both the rhetoric of transmodernity and the logic of decoloniality, are not violent jihadists but are rather what Slavoj Žižek (2014) dubs 'authentic fundamentalists' because they do not resent, envy, or even care about how non-Muslims enjoy. Said differently, transmodern/decolonial Muslim subjects are 'characterized by a kind of pure desiring without an object: desirousness' (Fink 1995, p. 69).

This reading of *Islamic humanism* from the perspective of transmodernity/ decoloniality, goes beyond Tariq Ramadan's (2009) transformative project of 'radical reform' and is more in alignment with what Bassam Tibi (2012) calls 'the grammar of humanism in Islam' (p. 235) or what Zayd (2004a) describes as a 'humanistic hermeneutics of the Qur'an' (p. 13). Islamic humanism as a delinking project is a rationalist tradition within Islamic philosophy associated with the *Mu'tazila* School, classical theorists like al-Farabi, Ibn Sina, and Ibn Rushd, and contemporary theorists like Mohammed Arkoun, Abdullahi Ahmed An-Nai'm, Riffat Hassan, and Mohamed Abed al-Jabri. Tibi (2012) argues, rightly I should add, for the reestablishment of this inconspicuous philosophical tradition in Islam as a contender for the more popular jurisprudential approach championed by both literalists and legalists.

The ~~four~~ five discourses

If we apply Jacques Lacan's (2007) theory of the four—I should say five— discourses (i.e., University, Master, Capitalist, Hysteric, and Analyst) to the twin industries of 'terrorism experts' (Greenwald 2012) and Islamophobia we can name five subject-positions and note the impossible communication on the conscious level between *agent* and *other* as well as the impotence on the unconscious level resulting from the *agent*'s repressed *truth* and the surplus *product* of failed communication (see Figure 8.1). For the sake of brevity, I will only focus on the Discourse of the Analyst.

The discourse of the analyst

With the Discourse of the Analyst, Islam (*a*) is the *agent* in communication with an *other*, transmodern/decolonial subject ($). The *product* is war (S_1) and the *truth* is terror (S_2). The Discourse of the Analyst can be equated in this context with what I am calling *decolonial psychoanalysis*, or a decolonized Lacanian social theory. In other words, I am proposing 'a violent event' (p. 1) and 'an agenda for total disorder' (p. 2) to use Frantz Fanon's (1961/2004) descriptions of decolonization

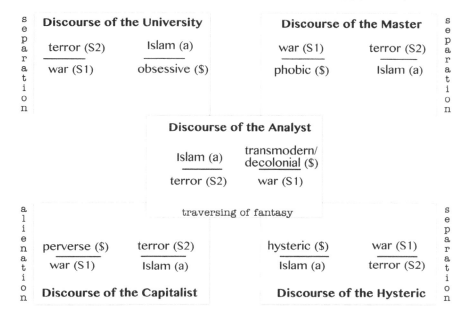

FIGURE 8.1 My application of Lacan's five discourses vis-à-vis the 'war on terror.'

in *The Wretched of the Earth*. My proposal is inspired by Derek Hook's (2008) *postcolonial psychoanalysis*, which according to him has 'the ability to appreciate the paradoxes of the *sociality* of private desires, [and] the *intrapersonal* quality of public wants and fears' (p. 273, emphasis in original) and which is principally committed 'to the political scrutiny of colonial desire, and the multiple roles it plays [in] the psychic life of colonial power' (p. 278). Although postcoloniality and decoloniality share many features, Mignolo (2007) argues that 'the de-colonial shift … is a project of de-linking while postcolonial criticism and theory is a project of scholarly transformation within the academy' (p. 452). In simple terms, decoloniality is not restricted to the academy.

Delinking

Mignolo's (2007) '*critical border thinking*' (p. 485, emphasis in original) is a method that is part of the liberation project of delinking 'the rhetoric of modernity' from 'the logic of coloniality.' Delinking replaces the theo- and ego-politics of knowledge and being with a geo- and body-politics based on 'epistemologies of the *exteriority* and of the *borders*' (Mignolo 2007, p. 462, emphasis in original). Liberation involves marrying *the rhetoric of transmodernity* with *the logic of decoloniality*. Transmodernity (Dussel 2002, 2012) is the epistemology, while decoloniality is the ontology. Transmodernity is what Mignolo (2007) calls for when he writes about 'a different epistemic grounding' (p. 462) or 'epistemic de-colonization' (p. 453).

Ramadan's (2009) decolonial notion of 'radical reform' in Islam is an example of both delinking and transmodernity in action. The *2015 Black Solidarity Statement with Palestine* and the Network Against Islamophobia—a project of Jewish Voice for Peace—are great illustrations of what Dussel (2012) calls 'transversality' (p. 41) —the type of solidarity, which entails 'movement from the periphery to the periphery' (p. 54).

The project of delinking is crucial if we are to decolonize Lacanian social theory and other critical fields in modernity. In other words, as *critical border thinkers*, we cannot afford to be neutral, and so we must morally/politically speak truth to power and stand on the right side of history—this is our social responsibility as intellectuals (Chomsky 1967; Gramsci 1971; Said 1994/1996).

Secular criticism

In addition to the project of delinking, Edward Said's (1983) practice of 'secular criticism'—cf. Marx's (1843/1978) 'irreligious criticism' (p. 53)—is another decolonial tool, which we can use to challenge all forms of oppression, be they Islamic or psychoanalytic. For Said (1983), 'secular criticism deals with local and worldly situations, and . . . is constitutively opposed to the production of massive, hermetic systems,' which is why the *essay* for him 'is the principal way in which to write criticism' (p. 26).

In other words, secular criticism 'must think of itself as life-enhancing and constitutively opposed to every form of tyranny, domination, and abuse; its social goals are noncoercive knowledge produced in the interests of human freedom' (Said 1983, p. 29). This essay is a practice in secular criticism, psychoanalytic cultural criticism, and critical border thinking.

Secular criticism is related to critical humanism—of which Islamic humanism is a type. Critical humanism (Said 1978/2003, 2004) may sound like a contradiction in terms, particularly to the ears of poststructuralists who think of themselves as antihumanists; rather critical humanism is a dialectical practice, which Said (1993), inspired by music theory, develops in *Culture and Imperialism* as an original method called 'contrapuntal reading' (p. 66). In Said's (1978/2003) magnum opus one can see an applied *bricolage* of a poststructural methodology (inspired by Foucault (1980)) from the perspective of a humanist epistemology (inspired by Vico); this critical humanism is foundational for transmodern/decolonial subjectivity.

Secular criticism and critical humanism are 'counter-hegemonic strategies for contesting ideology' (Pannian 2016, p. 165), and as such, they are transmodern and decolonial correctives to the Eurocentrism of Žižek's transcendental materialist theory of subjectivity, as outlined brilliantly by Adrian Johnston (2008).

Decolonizing Žižek

I see a parallel here between Jacques Derrida's (1998) deconstruction of the International Psycho-Analytic Association's (IPA) proposed Constitution of 1977 and Hamid Dabashi's (2013) criticism of an article by Santiago Zabala (2012) published on *Al Jazeera*'s website, wherein Zabala praises Žižek as the exemplar Saidian intellectual. By juxtaposing these two controversial essays, I hope to decolonize the transcendental materialist project as opposed to throwing the baby (Žižek) out with the bathwater (Eurocentrism).

The heated back-and-forth exchanges on *Al Jazeera* and elsewhere online between Zabala/Žižek/Marder on the one hand and Dabashi/Mignolo on the other divided up the critical theory world into two camps: the Emancipators v. the Liberators. Years later, Žižek was charged with Islamophobia for a number of controversial articles, which he wrote for *In These Times* about the Syrian refugee crisis.

I want to make the case for decolonial psychoanalysis by showing that Žižek, though a self-avowed Eurocentrist (Žižek 1998a) who is extremely critical of multiculturalism (Žižek 1997), is not an Islamophobe; however, his recent analysis of Islamophobia leaves much to be desired, which is surprising given his careful analysis of anti-Semitism in *The Plague of Fantasies*. In other words, by using the old Žižek against the new Žižek, I am attempting to salvage a decolonial Žižek without being blind to the traps of neo-Orientalism. Interestingly, S. Sayyid (1997/2015) writes, 'The possibility of an alternative to the anti-orientalist [structural Marxist?] view is provided by the work of Slavoj Žižek' (p. 40).

In *Geopsychoanalysis: '. . . and the rest of the world'*, Derrida (1998) deconstructs the following statement by the IPA from its 1977 Constitution, 'The Association's main geographical areas are defined at this time as America north of the United States–Mexican border; all America south of that border; *and the rest of the world*' (p. 87, emphasis added). This implicitly colonial statement does not explicitly name two of 'four types of territory' (p. 87) according to Derrida (1998). Europe—'the cradle of psychoanalysis' (p. 87)—is not named because it does not need to be named (i.e., it is present through its absence). How about Africa and Asia? According to Derrida (1998), these 'virgin' (p. 65) territories have not undergone 'worldification' (p. 66), so they remain nameless because they have not yet been colonized by psychoanalysis, so they are 'dark continents' (Khanna 2003) where '*Homo psychoanalyticus* is unknown or outlawed' (Derrida 1998, p. 87, emphasis in original).

In *Can non-Europeans think?*, Dabashi (2013), in a decolonial gesture similar to that of Derrida's (1998) in *Geopsychoanalysis*, deconstructs the following statement by Zabala (2012):

> There are many important and active philosophers today: Judith Butler in the United States, Simon Critchley in England, Victoria Camps in Spain, Jean-Luc Nancy in France, Chantal Mouffe in Belgium, Gianni Vattimo in Italy, Peter Sloterdijk in Germany and in Slovenia, Slavoj Žižek, not to mention others working in Brazil, Australia and China.

Dabashi (2013) takes issue with the Eurocentric practice of naming/worldification exhibited in the last sentence of that statement. He writes:

China and Brazil (and Australia, which is also a European extension) are
cited as the location of *other* philosophers worthy of the designation, but
none of them evidently merits a specific name to be sitting next to these
eminent European philosophers.

(Dabashi 2013, emphasis added)

The debate escalated from there to eventually turn into defensive posturing and
name-calling, particularly after Dabashi (2016) published a blog post titled 'Fuck
you Žižek!' as a reply to Žižek supposedly saying, 'Fuck you, Walter Mignolo!' in
a public lecture.

Putting narcissistic identifications aside, this heated exchange exposes a traumatic
kernel of truth, which must be addressed. Without getting lost in the affective
details of that exchange and other controversies like the one at the Left Forum in
2016, I would like to turn now to the accusations against Žižek that he is a bigot.
Even though I believe Žižek can be more careful with his provocations,
particularly when it comes to his 'ruthless' habit of telling 'politically incorrect'
or 'obscene' jokes about women and 'Blacks,' I generally agree with Jamil
Khader's (2016) assessment of Žižek as 'an ally in the struggle and surely not a
racist Islamophobe.' My agreement stems from my reading of some of Žižek's
writings and my viewing of many videos of his lectures. Incidentally, I was
criticized last year at a conference for citing Žižek in my essay on terrorism and
Islamophobia. In one of Žižek's (2016) more recent books, *Against The Double
Blackmail*, he writes:

> And yet another leftist taboo that needs to be abandoned is that of
> prohibiting any critique of Islam as a case of 'Islamophobia.' This taboo is
> a true mirror-image of the anti-immigrant populist demonization of Islam,
> so we should get rid of the pathological fear of many Western liberal
> Leftists that they might be guilty of Islamophobia.
>
> *(p. 20)*

Žižek (2016) mistakenly conflates 'critique of Islam' with Islamophobia without
the slightest effort to theorize the material *othering* of 'conceptual Muslims,'
Muslims and 'Muslim-looking' (Cashin 2010) subjects, in Euro-America. I find
this to be a major flaw on his part as a critical thinker, particularly given his
sustained analysis of anti-Semitism as a fascist 'fundamental fantasy' ($\$\Diamond a$). Even
among secular humanists (not to be confused with 'new atheists')—who are often
credited with the meme that Islamophobia is 'a word created by fascists, and used
by cowards, to manipulate morons'—there is a distinction between 'critique of
Islam' and anti-Muslim bigotry (Cerami 2015). Here, I agree with David Tyrer
(2013) that reducing Islamophobia to a 'critique of Islam' is a form of denial.

In addition to being defensive, Žižek (2016) uses the controversial term
'Islamo-Fascism' (p. 88, 110) a few times throughout his book in reference to
religious terrorism. I believe that Žižek has a moral responsibility as a public

intellectual to improve upon and complexify his theorization of Islamophobia. Again, I reiterate that Žižek is not a racist Islamophobe, but, as a card-carrying Eurocentric philosopher, he does not seem to care about understanding Islamophobia as 'postmodern racism' (Myers 2003, p. 104).

To understand Islamophobia as postmodern racism means that it has nothing to do with Islam or even Muslims, but everything to do with the 'conceptual Muslim.' In the end, I am convinced that if the current Žižek revisits the Žižek (1997/2008) of *The Plague of Fantasies*, he may be able to deconstruct (via decolonial psychoanalysis) the Islamophobic figure of the 'conceptual Muslim' (p. 10), who is the Imaginary other of the Euro-American neoliberal self. As an Imaginary other, the 'conceptual Muslim' is often ideologically represented in the politico-media complex as 'the terrorist.' This is, of course, the classic formulation of the Master-Slave dialectic, wherein the desire for recognition is the engine for aggressiveness or what Georg Hegel (1977) calls the 'life-and-death struggle' (p. 114).

On the other hand, the 'conceptual Muslim' is also the *big Other* standing in for the Unconscious of the Symbolic order. Said differently, the 'radical Otherness' of the Islamophobic figure of the 'conceptual Muslim' covers up the Real trauma at the heart of the 'war on terror' itself. The barred Other signifies this lack through its politics of fear and its aestheticization of violence. In other words, the barred Other capitalizes on the *objet petit a* of fear (the 'conceptual Muslim') in order to legitimize its *jouissance*, namely violence.

Islamophobia, understood as postmodern racism, is then not the result of a clash of 'civilizations' (Huntington 1993), 'ignorance' (Said 2001), 'fundamentalisms' (Ali 2006), 'definitions' (Said 2005), or 'barbarisms' (Achcar 2006), but the result of a 'clash of fantasies' (Myers 2003, p. 109) masking the inconsistency in the *big Other*.

Hassan Hanafi (1998) identifies the *big Other* as Global Capitalism when he writes, 'the clash of civilizations was a cover-up for the real socio-political and economic hegemony [of the West].' This is true of international relations, but more often than not, the *big Other* is the Nation because 'racism is the prop needed to maintain an illusory nationalist subjectivity' (Mertz 1995, p. 87). Today, we see a dialectical relationship between nationalism and neoliberalism, embodied in the presidency of Donald Trump and, to some extent, in the premiership of Theresa May. This paradox or contradiction is channeled through a fantasy called the 'war on terror.' Neil Davidson (2008) writes, 'Nationalism is the necessary ideological corollary of capitalism'; that explains nationalism's production of the 'enemy within' and neoliberalism's production of the 'enemy without.'

On the distinction between racism and anti-Semitism, Sean Homer (2004) writes, 'Whereas classical racism propounds an ideology of national superiority, whereby so-called "inferior" races were enslaved, anti-Semitism involves the systematic and organized annihilation of the Jewish people' (p. 60). In some ways, I see that Islamophobia looks a lot like displaced anti-Semitism except 'politically correct' since anti-Muslim othering is legitimated and (hyper)normalized by the 'war on terror' discourse; while keeping differences in mind (cf. Bunzl 2005), let us not forget that '[t]he "Muslim" [*Muselmann*] is the key figure of the Nazi extermination camp universe' (2001/2011, p. 157). According to this reading, *terrorism is excessive enjoyment*, which involves pushing 'conceptual Muslims' beyond the pleasure principle via legal (e.g., Guantanamo Bay) or extra-legal (e.g., Abu Ghraib) means—for example, 'enhanced interrogation techniques' or torture, indefinite detention, mass surveillance, etc.

In other ways, I see the similarities between Islamophobia and racism, wherein cultural markers of difference (e.g., language, accent, clothing, etc.) become the pretext for racialization, but I also see Islamophobia as a specific form of *othering*. Again, it is important to consider intersectionality (Crenshaw 1991) here, such as 'gendered Islamophobia' (Perry 2014). A lot has been written on the *hijab* vis-à-vis Islamophobia, for example, but Barbara Perry's (2014) remarks are worth highlighting; she writes, 'It is, perhaps, no surprise then that so many attacks on Muslim women involve ripping off her hijab. To satisfy the male *fantasy*, she must be at least *metaphorically* stripped, *unveiled* and thus exposed' (p. 82, emphasis added). Incidentally, did we not see this same fantasy structure at work last year in regards to the controversial but short-lived 'burkini ban' in 15 French towns? After all, as Žižek (2006) argues in *A Glance Into the Archives of Islam*, the prohibition of prohibitions 'is the most oppressive of them all' because it is 'a prohibition of all actual otherness.' Perry (2014) adds that the hijab as '*the central identifier* of the female Muslim body' is 'the sign of *seductive*, yet *reviled* difference' (p. 82, emphasis added).

Interestingly, this is an example of one of the seven 'veils' of fantasy, according to Žižek (1998b); namely, that fantasy has two dimensions: a *stabilizing* dimension (fantasy$_1$) and a *destabilizing* dimension (fantasy$_2$). Žižek (1998b) writes, 'the effectiveness of fantasy$_2$ is the condition for fantasy$_1$ to maintain its hold' (p. 192). Consequently, the Islamophobe 'has to disavow its inherent impossibility, the antagonism in its very heart' and this is where the Islamophobic figure of the 'conceptual Muslim' fits in; its function 'is precisely to render this gap [between thinking and being] invisible' (Žižek 1998b, p. 192). Related to this, we can recognize that nationalism and neoliberalism are two sides of the same coin, or two dimensions of the same fantasy of the Nation or the Market 'as an organic Whole' (Žižek 1998b, p. 190), which ultimately masks intersectional or pluriversal struggles. The dangerous marriage between nationalism and neoliberalism that we are seeing in the world today signifies the hypernormalization of violence.

In the Discourse of the Analyst, the transmodern/decolonial subject now assumes its own alienation and desire, and hence, can produce its own new master signifiers. Let us say these new master signifiers are 'decolonial psychoanalysis.' In terms of transmodern subjectivity, decolonial psychoanalysis is both nonreductionist (i.e., terrorist ≠ Muslim) and nondualist (i.e., terrorist, counterterrorist, not-terrorist, and not-counterterrorist); in other words, the transmodern subject of decolonial psychoanalysis is 'complex' as opposed to 'blank' or 'uncomplicated' (Parker 1997).

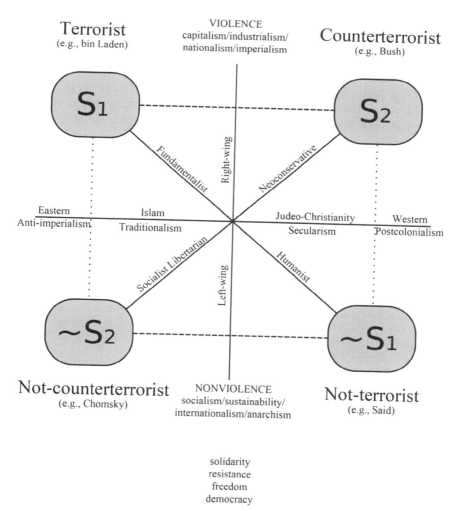

FIGURE 8.2 My application of Greimas's semiotic square vis-à-vis the 'war on terror.'

Conversely, the (post)modern subject of neoliberalism may be an Islamo-phobe or, more generally, a terrorized object of violence; in either case, he or she is more than likely to identify with the 'counterterrorist' subject-position against all other positions given the hegemonic power of the 'war on terror' *dispositif*. The transmodern subject, on the other hand, can identify with one of the two 'antiterrorist' (read: nonviolent) subject-positions, that is, 'not-terrorist' or 'not-counterterrorist' (see Figure 8.2).

Liberation

To conclude, decolonizing psychoanalysis means radically delinking its conscious *modern* rhetoric from its unconscious *colonial* logic. Reclaiming the humanistic foundations of Traditional (i.e., transmodern) Islam entails 'rethinking' Tradition (Zayd 2004a) or rejecting 'abstract universals' (Mignolo 2007). As *critical border thinkers*, we have a moral/political obligation to decolonize knowledge and being from the perspective of transmodernity. Delinking entails, for example, resisting Islamophobia and other forms of violence through our research, activism, and/or by any (nonviolent) means necessary because recognizing the pluriversality of our struggles is the condition for actualizing the universal project of liberation.

Note

1 My use of Arabic, my native tongue, throughout this essay is a decolonial strategy and not a hegemonic representation of 'true' Islam.

References

Achcar, G., 2006. *The clash of barbarisms: the making of the new world disorder*. Boulder, CO: Paradigm Publishers.

Ali, T., 2006. *The clash of fundamentalisms: crusades, jihads and modernity*. New York: Verso.

Bunzl, M., 2005. Between anti-Semitism and Islamophobia: some thoughts on the new Europe. *American Ethnologist*, 32(4), 499–508.

Cashin, S., 2010. To be Muslim or Muslim-looking in America: a comparative exploration of racial and religious prejudice in the 21st century. *Duke FL & Soc. Change*, 2, 125.

Cerami, M., 2015. Fascists, cowards, and morons: combating anti-Muslim bigotry while maintaining free speech. *The Humanist*, 28 July. Available from: https://thehumanist.com/commentary/fascists-cowards-and-morons-combating-anti-muslim-bigotry-while-maintaining-free-speech.

Chomsky, N., 1967. The responsibility of intellectuals. *The New York Review of Books*, 23 February. Available from: https://chomsky.info/19670223/.

Crenshaw, K., 1991. Mapping the margins: intersectionality, identity politics, and violence against women of color. *Stanford Law Review*, 43(6), 1241–1299.

Dabashi, H., 2013. Can non-Europeans think? *Al Jazeera*, 15 January. Available from: www.aljazeera.com/indepth/opinion/2013/01/2013114142638797542.html.

Dabashi, H., 2016. Fuck you Žižek! *ZED Books*, 26 July. Available from: www.zedbooks.net/blog/posts/fuck-you-zizek/.

Davidson, N., 2008. Nationalism and neoliberalism. *Variant*, 32. Available from: www.variant.org.uk/32texts/davidson32.html.

Davis, C., Pound, M., and Crockett, C., eds., 2014. *Theology after Lacan: the passion for the real*. Eugene, OR: Wipf and Stock Publishers.

Derrida, J., 1998. Lane, C., ed., *The psychoanalysis of race*. New York: Columbia University Press.

Dussel, E.D., 2002. World-system and 'trans'-modernity. *Nepantla: Views from South*, 3(2), 221–244.

Dussel, E.D., 2012. Transmodernity and interculturality: an interpretation from the perspective of philosophy of liberation. *Transmodernity: Journal of Peripheral Cultural Production of the Luso-Hispanic World*, 1(3), 28–59.

El Shakry, O., 2014. The Arabic Freud: the unconscious and the modern subject. *Modern Intellectual History*, 11(01), 89–118.

Fanon, F., 1961/2004. *The Wretched of the Earth*. New York: Grove.

Fayek, A., 2004. Islam and its effect on my practice of psychoanalysis. *Psychoanalytic Psychology*, 21(3), 452–457.

Fink, B., 1995. *The Lacanian subject: between language and jouissance*. Princeton, NJ: Princeton University Press.

Foucault, M., 1980. *Power/knowledge: selected interviews and other writings, 1972–1977*. New York: Pantheon Books.

Fox, D., 2011. Anarchism and psychology. *Theory in Action*, 4(4), 31–48.

Gramsci, A., 1971. *Selections from the prison notebooks*. New York: International Publishers.

Greenwald, G., 2012. The sham 'terrorism expert' industry. *Salon*, 15 August. Available from: www.salon.com/2012/08/15/the_sham_terrorism_expert_industry/.

Hanafi, H. (1998). The middle east, in whose world? *The Fourth Nordic Conference on Middle Eastern Studies: The Middle East in Globalizing World*. Available from: www.org.uib.no/smi/pao/hanafi.html.

Hasan, M., 2015. Why Islam doesn't need a reformation. *The Guardian*, 17 May. Available from: www.theguardian.com/commentisfree/2015/may/17/islam-reformation-extremism-muslim-martin-luther-europe.

Hegel, G.W.F., 1977. *Phenomenology of spirit*. A.V. Miller, trans. Oxford, UK: Oxford University Press.

Homer, S., 2004. *Jacques Lacan*. Abingdon, UK: Routledge.

Hook, D., 2008. Postcolonial psychoanalysis. *Theory & Psychology*, 18(2), 269–283.

Huntington, S.P., 1993. The clash of civilizations? *Foreign Affairs*, 72(3), 22–49.

Johnston, A., 2008. *Žižek's ontology: a transcendental materialist theory of subjectivity*. Evanston, IL: Northwestern University Press.

Khader, J., 2016. Žižek is not a racist Islamophobia. *Muftah*, 23 May. Available from: https://muftah.org/zizek-is-not-a-racist-islamophobe/#.WSzSJBPyuuU.

Khanna, R., 2003. *Dark continents: psychoanalysis and colonialism*. Durham, NC: Duke University Press.

Lacan, J., 2007. *The other side of psychoanalysis*. R. Grigg, trans. New York: WW Norton.

Laclau, E. and Mouffe, C., 1985/2014. *Hegemony and socialist strategy: towards a radical democratic politics*. New York: Verso.

Marks, L.U., 2012. A Deleuzian ijtihad: unfolding Deleuze's Islamic sources occulted in the ethnic cleansing of Spain. In A. Saldanha and J.M. Adams, eds., *Deleuze and Race*. Edinburgh, UK: Edinburgh University Press, 51–72.

Marx, K., 1843/1978. Contribution to the critique of Hegel's philosophy of right. In R.C. Tucker, ed., *The Marx-Engels reader*. 2nd ed. New York: WW Norton.

Mertz, D., 1995. The racial other in nationalist subjectivations: a Lacanian analysis. *Rethinking Marxism: A Journal of Economics, Culture & Society*, 8(2), 77–88.

Mignolo, W.D., 2007. Delinking: the rhetoric of modernity, the logic of coloniality and the grammar of de-coloniality. *Cultural Studies*, 21(2–3), 449–514.

Mura, A., 2014. Islamism revisited: a Lacanian discourse critique. *European Journal of Psychoanalysis*, 1, 107–126.

Myers, T., 2003. *Slavoj Zizek*. Abingdon, UK: Routledge.

Pannian, P., 2016. *Edward Said and the question of subjectivity*. Berlin, Germany: Springer.

Parker, I., 1997. Discourse analysis and psychoanalysis. *British Journal of Social Psychology*, 36(4), 479–495.

Perry, B., 2014. Gendered Islamophobia: hate crime against Muslim women. *Social Identities*, 20(1), 74–89.

Quijano, A., 2000. Coloniality of power and Eurocentrism in Latin America. *Nepantla: Views from South*, 1(3), 533–580.

Ramadan, T., 2009. *Radical reform: Islamic ethics and liberation*. Oxford, UK: Oxford University Press.

Rethinking Islamic reform, 2010. Video. Oxford University Islamic Society. Available from: https://vimeo.com/13738819.

Said, E.W., 1978/2003. *Orientalism*. New York: Vintage.

Said, E.W., 1983. *The world, the text, and the critic*. Cambridge, MA: Harvard University Press.

Said, E.W., 1993. *Culture and imperialism*. New York: Vintage.

Said, E.W., 1994/1996. *Representations of the intellectual: the 1993 Reith lectures*. New York: Vintage Books.

Said, E.W., 2001. The clash of ignorance. *The Nation*, 4 October. Available from: https://www.thenation.com/article/clash-ignorance/.

Said, E.W., 2004. *Humanism and democratic criticism*. New York: Columbia University Press.

Said, E.W., 2005. The essential terrorist. In E.W. Said and C. Hitchens, eds., *Blaming the victims*. New York: Verso.

Sardar, Z., 2004. Islam and the west in a transmodern world. *Islam Online Archive*, 18 August. Available from: https://archive.islamonline.net/?p=14902.

Sayyid, S., 1997/2015. *A fundamental fear: Eurocentrism and the emergence of Islamism*. London, UK: ZED Books.

Sheppard, F., 2014. I traveled to Palestine-Israel and discovered there is no 'Palestinian-Israeli conflict.' *The Huffington Post*, 23 July. Available from: www.huffingtonpost.com/ferrari-sheppard/i-traveled-to-palestine_b_4761896.html

Stavrakakis, Y., 2007. *The Lacanian left*. Edinburgh, UK: Edinburgh University Press.

The power of nightmares: the rise of the politics of fear, 2004. Film. Directed by Adam Curtis. UK: BBC.

Tibi, B., 2012. Islamic humanism vs. Islamism: cross-civilizational bridging. *Soundings: An Interdisciplinary Journal*, 95(3), 230–254.

Tyrer, D., 2013. *The politics of Islamophobia: race, power and fantasy*. London, UK: Pluto Press.

Wallerstein, I.M., 2004. *World-systems analysis: an introduction*. Durham, NC: Duke University Press.

Zabala, S., 2012. Slavoj Žižek and the role of the philosopher. *Al Jazeera*, 25 December. Available from: www.aljazeera.com/indepth/opinion/2012/12/20121224122215406939.html.

Zayd, N.H.A., 2004a. *Rethinking the Qur'ân: towards a humanistic hermeneutics*. Utrecht, The Netherlands: Humanistics University Press.

Zayd, N.H.A., 2004b. *Voice of an exile: reflections on Islam*. Westport, CT: Greenwood Publishing Group.

Zayd, N.H.A., 2006. *Reformation of Islamic thought: a critical historical analysis*. Amsterdam, The Netherlands: Amsterdam University Press.

Žižek, S., 1997. Multiculturalism, or, the cultural logic of multinational capitalism. *New Left Review*, (225), 28–51.

Žižek, S., 1997/2008. *The plague of fantasies*. New York: Verso.

Žižek, S., 1998a. A leftist plea for 'Eurocentrism.' *Critical Inquiry*, 24(4), 988–1009.

Žižek, S., 1998b. The seven veils of fantasy. In D. Nobus, ed., *Key concepts of Lacanian psychoanalysis*. New York: Other Press.

Žižek, S., 2001/2011. *Did somebody say totalitarianism?* New York: Verso.

Žižek, S., 2006. A glance into the archives of Islam. Available from: www.lacan.com/zizarchives.htm.

Žižek, S., 2014. ISIS is a disgrace to true fundamentalism. *The New York Times*. Available from: https://opinionator.blogs.nytimes.com/2014/09/03/isis-is-a-disgrace-to-true-fundamentalism/.

Žižek, S., 2016. *Against the double blackmail: refugees, terror and other troubles with the neighbours*. London, UK: Penguin.

9

CONNECTEDNESS AND DREAMS

Exploring the possibilities of communication across interpretive traditions

Julia Borossa

From the outset, it is the question of psychoanalysis' extensibility as a practice and institution beyond its western roots, beyond its historical and current institutional geographies, that needs to be posed; one which obliges us to examine the flexibility of its theoretical foundations, and its potentiality as a discourse for addressing human suffering in non-Eurocentric ways. The term 'extensibility' should be understood here as an explicit challenge to psychoanalysis, which would find itself decentred by its introduction. What is at stake for me and perhaps for several authors in this collection, is an interrelated inquiry: 'where psychoanalysis?' as inextricable from 'how psychoanalysis?' Whereas the universal is often pitted against the local, in the manner of the West and its others, might not practices of cross-cultural dialogue displace this epistemic topography through comparative methodologies alert to the challenges of translation and open to experiments in communication?

Extensions of psychoanalysis

Derrida opened up the question of what may be a 'foreign body' to institutional psychoanalysis in 'Geopsychoanalysis and the rest of the world', whereby the referent 'rest of the world' functioned as a 'dark continent' open to colonisation by its discourse (Derrida, 1991; Khanna, 2003). The IPA's statutes still contentiously divide the territory into three main geographical areas, the phrasing slightly different, Europe (plus Australia, Israel, and India), Latin America (the Western hemisphere, excluding the United States and Canada), and North America (the United States, Canada, and Japan). This makes for a very strange rearrangement of the map of the world, revealing and occluding so much. It is possible to argue that the disavowals of psychoanalysis have much to do with the inability of its theories to adequately account for the material conditions within which our psychic selves evolve. One may even say, in the light of the above, it is blind to the very shape of the world, but also to the multiple histories of colonisation, conquest, trade, oppression, and violence that nevertheless insist on escaping their occlusion.

This, therefore, is the broader context of the essay that follows, a thematic concern that has long preoccupied me as a researcher concerned with the histories and politics of psychoanalysis (Borossa, 1997, 2012). It has also, albeit differently, informed my eventual choice to train as a group analyst and to pursue a development of psychoanalysis whose very premise is to take for granted 'man's social nature' and the importance of the community in which the lives of individuals unfold (Foulkes, 1964, 109). This can be taken to mean that attention is paid to the materiality of 'facts' (and here I deliberately echo Fanon's insistence on the 'fact' of blackness)—while of course this is far from being a given, as the political and social can and do often function as a space of disavowal for the many forms that psychoanalysis takes as practice, let alone institution. However, it is important to clarify that paying attention to this materiality need not displace the unconscious, along with its productive mysteries, but that it may lead us to consider it differently, as we are invited in a spirit of more expansive relations to render our understanding of the psyche more flexible and inclusive. My contention is simply that connection, communication, free association, the varied possibilities of talking, and being heard in profound, effective and transformative ways upon which psychoanalysis as a form of treatment is predicated, are achievable in as yet unrealised ways. The third section of this chapter will provide an illustration of the surprising ways in which this can be worked towards, through a story of how it became possible to share dreams in contemporary Cairo whereby psychoanalytic and Sufi traditions of interpretation co-existed side by side for a while.

Islam/psychoanalysis; side by side

Although there has been a historical (and actual) psychoanalytic presence (much of it para-institutional) in Morocco, Egypt, Lebanon, and Iran, for example, so-called Islamic countries are of course subject to the blind-spots, geographical occlusions, and colonising moves referred to above. It is beyond the remit of this chapter to review the recent literature that has addressed the impasses and/or points of contact between 'psychoanalysis' and 'Islam'. However, in order to frame the account of our encounters in Cairo, I will refer to the writings of three authors, Joseph Massad, Omnia El Shakry and Stefania Pandolfo, whose work emphasises three different aspects of this theme, which can be respectively characterised as primarily political, historical, and clinical.

Massad specifically engages with the question of the limitations of the psychoanalytic project in a core chapter in his latest book *Islam in Liberalism* (2015).[1] The book itself forms part of a wider intellectual project, an avowedly political one, in the lineage of Edward Said's work, one that seeks to uncover the discursive strategies through which the West universalises itself and its values, occluding or assimilating that which stands as other to it, an epistemic violence that is the necessary ally to colonial conquest both in its historic forms and its more recent variations. Here, Massad is intent on uncovering the ways in which 'liberalism' and 'Islam' emerge as interrelated oppositional constructs, through a careful examination of a range of discursive and institutional contexts. The goal is to show how 'the emergence of "Europe" was predicated on a series of projections, disavowals, displacements, and expulsions in order to produce a coherent self cleansed of others to which this self was opposed in its very constitution' (Massad, 11).

It is within this perspective that Massad addresses the recent body of work produced by psychoanalysts from North Africa and the Middle East, for the most part trained and subsequently based in France, with special attention given to the writings of Fehti Benslama whose book *Psychoanalysis and the Challenge of Islam* (2002) is subject to a particularly careful reading. In line with the overall structure of his argumentation, Massad's intention is to show how such texts ultimately depend on a reading of psychoanalysis whose implicit allegiance is to a liberal and Eurocentric view of human universality, privileging notions such as individualism, scientific rationalism, freedom and tolerance. According to Massad's reading, in the work of Benslama, standing as exemplary, 'psychoanalysis becomes a handmaiden of European liberalism and demonstrates neither internal ambivalence nor ambivalence toward its projected other' (Massad, 2015, 307).

While such a critique, harsh as it is, may well be valid to a large extent, the very oppositional terms in which it is set, an oppositionality which structures the book as a whole, makes insufficient allowance for the ways in which psychoanalysis is multiple in its permutations as theory, practice, and institution. It may certainly be the case that the function of psychoanalysis as an institution often indeed serves to reify both its theories and its practice, delimiting and policing what may be said and written in its name, as well as the identity of the psychoanalyst. However, it is important to be reminded that at a very fundamental level, the unknowable, the 'foreign body', the 'other scene' (all terms used to define the unconscious) is a sine qua non of the conceptualisation of psychoanalysis, whereby a very limit to what can be grasped and possessed is part of the very fabric of the work. If this limit to (self) knowledge is accepted, and granted there is no guarantee that it is, it can serve as a bulwark against its reification. It is here that its liberating, as opposed to liberal, the potential may lie, that is, in its possibility of positing the freedom of association which its clinical demands, as freedom of spirit. What remains unclear within the terms of Massad's argument is the way to move beyond the structural position in which psychoanalysis remains trapped through its Eurocentric origins.

What has been unaddressed so far, is the highly complex question as to whether a secular worldview is ontologically necessary for psychoanalysis, and to what extent could certain conceptions of psychoanalysis and religion co-exist. This forms one of the lines of enquiry in El Shakry's *The Arabic Freud* (2017). While recognising the dangers of a potential colonising move which psycho-analysis has often been guilty of, what she calls its 'civilising mission', that is to say, the ways in which it can and has been used to interpret and recuperate the systems of thought within the geographies which lie beyond its European Enlightenment origins, she nevertheless is explicitly interested in the conditions of possibility of its implantation and deployment in Egypt in the twentieth century, within a context that is never entirely secular. Her stated aim is to

> explore specific intellectuals who theorised the self by drawing on both Islamic and psychoanalytic idioms, and reconstruct historical interactions, such as an interlude between Sufism and psychoanalysis in mid-20th century Egypt, in which thinkers read classical Sufi philosophers [...] alongside, in concurrence with and in distinction with Freud.
>
> *(El Shakry, 2017, 10)*

The value of such a work of intellectual history lies precisely in its patient search for a space which is not oppositional but rather one where discourses that may appear incompatible at manifest level, can be seen to enter into a productive dialogue. While such a dialogue may have its limits in terms of the reciprocity that it allows, bounded as it is by a wider socio-political situatedness, one that may well stand at the present moment as oppositional, El Shakry's work appears nevertheless to be crucial in the way it allows for points of potential connection and thus for an extensibility of psychoanalysis. In this respect, it may be argued that the value of such a project lies less in producing consensual doxa but in creating a platform for comparative debate that tests the limits of psychoanalysis itself. The thinkers that El Shakry considers, for example, the Egyptian psychologist Yusuf Murad one of the central figure in her account, drew on multiple sources, mystical, philosophical, and scientific. Murad maintained a conception of 'the porousness of the self to the other', reading Freud alongside Henri Wallon and *Gestalttheorie* (El Shakry, 2017, 38), pointing towards a situated practice that considers both the individual and the community in which he or she is part.

In her chapter in the 2008 special issue of the journal *Umbra* dedicated to Islam, Pandolfo turns specifically to the possibilities of clinical work, writing, however, in her capacity as an anthropologist with a long history of working on the question of subjectivity in the context of contemporary Morocco, rather than as a psychoanalyst. Drawing on her interaction with and observations of an Imam whose healing practice is positioned not in Sufism but in a local version of the Islamic Revival, she juxtaposes his reflections on the paralysing deadliness of a certain kind suffering that precludes any possibility of a continuing struggle (or in other words, connection to the community, connection to life), a suffering which the Imam evocatively terms 'soul-choking', with her reading of Lacan's seminar on *Ethics*, specifically with its elaborations of the death drive. What Pandolfo opens up is the possibility of a common ground between very different traditions and contexts, recording the traces of a dialogue which at times halters on the impossibility of translation, but where cohesion can be found in an ethical project, 'that intimate struggle, with a heterogeneity that can never be resolved, and with a violence that is forever lurking' (Pandolfo, 2009, 86). If psychoanalysis is, indeed, at its most basic level, a response to human suffering, Pandolfo, via her dialogue with the Imam informant as well as with Moroccan psychoanalysts practising in Rabat, presents it as a situated ethical discourse, which is capacious enough to accommodate the theological. What she highlights is a practice which takes the risk of taking the unbearable seriously, sharing an ethics with psycho-analysis, an ethics based on bearing witness through listening.

In this spirit of expansiveness, in the next section of this chapter, I will offer an example (limited and circumscribed to be sure) of possibilities for communication across divisions. Here, the work of Caroline Rooney with respect to what she terms a 'wider universality' is significant, where Rooney argues that liberation struggles often serve to contest the foreclosures of capitalist and imperialist formations of the global in favour of a synchronous, non-dualist understanding of the common ground. Suggesting that the Egyptian Revolution may be seen as a Sufi Spring (drawing on Egyptian perceptions of such), Rooney maintains that what came to the fore in Egypt in 2011 was a collective spirit that managed, at least for a while, to overturn the prevailing hegemonic forms of interpellation in establishing festive solidarities and resonances of mutual attunement across the divides of generation, gender, class, religious sectarianism, the secular and the sacred (Rooney, 2015).

Dreams and connections in Cairo

Dreams, their language, their subjective and social meanings and the politics of their interpretation will provide one of the main prisms through which these wider interrogations on the question of connection and common ground will now be pursued. I was recently involved in an experiment, which was an element of a larger collaborative research project on 'Egypt's Living Heritage' (a project supported by the Newton Mosharafa Fund) in which I participated during 2016/2017 together with British and Egyptian colleagues. The aim of the project as a whole was to enable community engagement and to extend the meanings and potentialities of what had been termed 'heritage'. It was centred on the neighbour-hood surrounding EL Moez Street in Islamic Cairo, whereby traditional and historic forms of craft and art practices were re-evaluated in terms of the living presence of the past. Here the notion of the intangible, tacit transmission of heritage formed a key and innovative aspect of the project. An interdisciplinary approach lay at its core, as it brought together in its inception and implementation, colleagues from the Arts and Cultural Studies (Caroline Rooney), Archaeology (Fekri Hassan), Folklore Studies and Ethnography (Mostafa Gad and Ahlam Rizk), and Psychoanalysis (myself). A series of workshops on photography, film, literature and storytelling, painting, and music were held between September 2016 and April 2017 in Cairo. Memorabilia was collected from the inhabitants in the El Moez neighbourhood, as well as their accounts of their reasons for choosing a particular object. This formed the basis of an exhibition that further served to de-centre the meanings of heritage. I am indebted to Caroline Rooney and Ahlam Rizk for their astute attention to the potential significance of dreams and dream-telling as not only a means of tapping into the tacit transmission of heritage but as an opening towards a different kind of cross-cultural communication. The dreamscapes of El Moez street thus became one of the strands of the project. I originally had in mind, the idea of conducting a series of social dreaming workshops in the community. Ahlam Rizk's work as a folklorist had involved collecting and categorising dreams for a number of years, and she was my main conduit into Islamic traditions of dream interpretation, introducing me to Shayk Mostafa, a traditional dream interpreter based at the shrine of Ibn Sirin, the seventh century scholar who is widely considered to be if not the originator, then certainly the most prominent proponent of a Muslim tradition of dream interpretation.[2]

It is important to be reminded here, that despite the early interest in Freud shown by Egyptian intellectuals such as Murad, but also more centrally by Mustafa Zewar and Moustapha Safouan, psychoanalysis never gained an institutional foothold in Egypt. Safouan, Freud's first translator into Arabic, would later achieve considerable prominence in France as a Lacanian psychoanalyst and theorist. Zewar stayed on in Cairo and founded the Psychology department at Aim Shams University, where his teaching of psychoanalysis became increasingly subsumed by experimental psychology and quantitative methodologies (Abdelkader, 2004; Ben Slama, 2010/2011). Zewar's trajectory is symptomatic, for in Egypt today, psychoanalysis as a form of therapy has a minuscule presence (Zewar's daughter is one of the very few analysts practising in Cairo), whereby the space it may have occupied in response to neurotic suffering has been taken up either by a medicalised discourse modelled on recent cognitive behaviourist methodologies, variants of group therapy that owe more to gestalt or psychodrama than psychoanalysis (Taha et al., 2008) or by the proliferation of helplines and internet sites underwritten by religious cosmographies (Ben Slama, 2010/2011, 89).

Dreams and their interpretation, however, have a long history and continue to have a contested but lively place in contemporary Egypt, as Amira Mittermaier has shown in her brilliant ethnography *Dreams that Matter* (2011). Her book is a result of the fieldwork she conducted in Cairo in the mid-2000s amongst communities who attached a definite significance to dreams and engaged with dream-telling practices in particular ways. She had four key informants in her research, Shayks who all had more or less close connections with the Sufi tradition of Islam. One of these was the predecessor at the Cairo shrine to Ibn Sirin of the Shayk whom I and my colleagues got to know and, as I will go on to tell you, to collaborate with.

A key connecting term in Mittermaier's account is that of *barzakh*, which for her interlocuters functions mainly as a 'space where the Spirits of the dead dwell', but whose meaning she extends and uses throughout the book to refer to an in-between space, a space occupied by both imagination *and* the unknowable. The immediate context of her research is, however, narratives and practices of Islamic dream interpretation which give a specific space to the sacred. For example, she discusses dreams which are to be taken literally as communications from the divine, visitation dreams, and can serve as guidance in life, and such dreams are in fact Mittermaier's main focus in the book. While there are definite traditional accepted meanings to oniric images recorded in the many manuals that popularised Ibn Sirin's teaching, this idea of an in-between is shown to trouble certainties as deployed in an actual practice of dream-telling and dream-hearing, a practice which in Mittermaier's account is shown to be crucially bound up with lived lives, a space of interlocution that is outward looking and reaches towards the future. 'By-passing the laws of a linear temporality and causality, dream-visions are divine messages that can foreshadow or pre-enact the future. They are not only predictive but also evocative. Besides revealing emergent possibilities, dream-visions contribute to their actualisation', she writes (Mittermaier, 2011, 238).

Freud famously warns his readers that every dream, no matter how fully examined, will always retain a navel, a point of contact with the unknown (Freud, 1953 [1900], 525). But, does this 'unknown' extend beyond the confines of the individual subject? The term navel itself is, of course, striking, invoking a literal inwardness, stretching into the unknown of the body, of the drives. Intriguingly, Freud ends his vast opus with these characteristically paradoxical sentences:

> For dreams are derived from the past in every sense. Nevertheless the ancient belief that dreams foretell the future is not wholly devoid of truth. By picturing our wishes as fulfilled, dreams are after all leading us into the future. But this future, which the dreamer pictures as the present, has been moulded by his indestructible wish into a perfect likeness of the past.
>
> *(Freud, 1953 [1900], 621)*

Freud's dream book is a strange tome deeply intimate yet setting out a transmissible means of investigating unconscious processes, ambitious yet self-defeating (the implication being that the object of inquiry is by its nature infinitely receding or renewable), and finally, collapsing the logic of time itself through the power of wish-fulfilment.

But, is there already a social dimension to the wish? Can dreaming the future be extended psychoanalytically to more political meanings? The implication of Mittermaier's work is that individual dreams serve to channel not only individual desires but also the desires of others that continue to affect us even when those others have died, in a system of dialogical ethics. 'Frequently, in visitational dreams' she writes, 'those appearing to the dreamer not only make requests, but also give—and what the dreamer receives, beside the vision, is knowledge. The dream then becomes a site of exchanges' (Mittermaier, 2011, 151).

I mentioned that what I had originally intended to set up as part of the dream-telling stream of our Cairo project was something akin to a Social Dreaming Group. Gordon Lawrence developed this method while working at the Tavistock Institute in London. Simply put, it is a forum in which a group comes together for a set period of time, to share dreams. Lawrence's premise (derived from Charlotte Beradt's work on the dreams of Jewish doctors which she collected in Germany in the lead up to the Second World War) was that dreams tap into social, collective anxieties yet unprocessed, and which can best be collectively drawn out. In discussing the psychoanalytic foundations of his work, Lawrence refers to the usefulness of Bion's theories in allowing for a distinction between the ego-centric and the socio-centric, between the narcissistic and the social. Bion had argued in the preface to his *Experiences in Groups* (1961) that the analyst could approach a group through two vertices, the pair, related to the Oedipal situation and the other, which he terms the sphinx, related to the scientific method, and it is this, according to Lawrence which allows for a way towards a wider way of knowing (Lawrence and Biran, 2002). Social dreaming as a method directs attention away from the inward turning and narcissistic towards wider cultural preoccupations. Dreams shared in a group would 'capture the political and institutional aspects of the dreamer's social context and how these are laced into their struggle for creativity, meaning and ordinariness' (Lawrence, 2005, 14). The best response (including interpretative response) to a dream, Lawrence argues, is another dream.

Strikingly, while social dreaming as developed by Lawrence has had multiple interdisciplinary applications (used in work contexts, or in conference settings, or more intriguingly to work with traumatised groups in a one-off way) it is not a form of treatment, but a form of group enquiry. Group analysis, on the other hand, as I already mentioned, developed as a form of clinical work as an extension of psychoanalysis whereby a free-flowing interaction between the group's members functions as a form of free association. Sharing of dreams plays a part in this, but surprisingly little has been written on their specific function. Foulkes suggests that by the very fact of being shared in the group they lose their individual dimension. Dreams become dynamically significant, that is to say, they function in freeing up the interaction in the group, and in so doing become shared between all group members, a 'group dream' their collective creation (Foulkes, 1964, 126). Ultimately, what I was aiming to achieve with my colleagues was a space where communication could be freed up via sharing dreams, yes, but did we have enough of a common ground?

In the planning phases for the dream workshops, I soon had to put aside any practical guidelines I may have wanted to rely on from social dreaming or group analysis, as well as be prepared to be challenged in any theoretical preconceptions I might have had about the use of dreams as a royal road to the unconscious, through the very different contextual differences in the use and significance accorded to dreams in Egypt and the UK. My more traditional idea of having a series of group meetings with the same participants including members of the community and the people involved in convening the various workshops of the project in a set room soon proved unworkable. One thing I hadn't taken into account is just how contested and even controversial dream-telling may be in a context such as contemporary Cairo in the aftermath of its revolutions. But, what proved possible was something potentially much more radical.

We held two meetings, facilitated by Ahlam Rizk. The first was held in an open space, a café next to Ibn Sirin's shrine. The participants were mainly students from an MA on Heritage Management convened by Fekri Hassan, and following a visit to the shrine, we sat together in the open café mentioned, where we were soon joined by Shayk Mostafa. We offered each other dreams and associations, moving between English and Arabic, between Shayk Mostafa's interpretations and my responses and associations. I was struck by the ways in which the Shayk always asked about the particular circumstances and the broader context of the dreamer's life, drawing out further connections and gently, sometimes indicated a potential practical path to pursue further. That afternoon, as dream followed dream, we mainly shared oniric images of flying and constraint, which culminated in a young woman recounting a recurring dream she had of her dead mother whose presence to her was like a visitation. The intensity of her loss was palpable though, and the shadow of this personal loss fell over the group as a whole. She was comforted by a friend who had accompanied her there, and I also communicated my recognition of her mourning, before we moved back to more conventionally social interactions. We stayed on a while longer in the café, sharing coffee and sandwiches, later joined by two artists who lived nearby.

One thing that strikingly emerged is that where the different traditions of dream interpretation, from Ibn Sirin to Freud, converged was in how we agreed that the meaning of an image in one person's dream was not necessarily the same as that of an image in another person's dream. In Ibn Sirin's legacy of dream interpretation, a symbol achieves its sense from its context, the dreamer's circumstances. That said, the sharing of dreams came to reveal a collective mood pertaining to life in Cairo as a common circumstance. While the shared memory of the uplifting revolution of 2011 that brought people together remained vivid, the fact that this moment had left socio-economic difficulties unaddressed had led to feelings of hopelessness and disappointment, experienced both individually and in common. The young woman's dream of her lost mother may have acted here as a condensor or a shared metaphor for the group, and this sense of a profound unease, mourning and longing at the level of the social unconscious is what most strikingly emerged, and continued to be touchstones in a very different group that we held the following day.

The setting then was in a historic building in the process of renovation in El Moez street itself, where in addition to many of the participants in the first group, including Shayk Mostafa who came with a colleague, Shayk Ali, we were joined by members of the community, including women clad in niqabs, the buildings cleaners, male shopkeepers, a group of young schoolgirls who wandered in attracted by a poster outside the building announcing the work-shop, together with middle-class Egyptians in Western dress. It was immediately striking that this group was composed of people who otherwise do not get together to talk about themselves. The chairs had been positioned in a circle, a setting which by its very nature encouraged horizontal rather than hierarchical relations.

The exchanges took place this time entirely in Arabic, with a student assigned to translate for the two of us who didn't speak the language. A shy young woman who kept throughout to her role as interpreter, she nevertheless let me know that she also had a particular investment in the topic for she had read many dream manuals and most of her dreams had come true since she was eight. We began more formally with a prayer beautifully sung by Shayk Ali. The Shayks predictably held more authority in this group, and despite being introduced as an expert follower of Freud, I felt much more in the place of an observer. But, soon, dreams circulated around the room, as participants spoke up in a way that was unorchestrated yet seemed to follow the rhythm of the unconscious. Here, what was particularly interesting was the way we formally shared the space, in a horizontal way potentially subversive for both psychoanalysis and Islamic dream interpretation. The role of the expert was thus decentred, both by the arrangement of the chairs and by the unprescribed nature of the proceedings. One of the cleaners, who came in uniform in the middle of her shift, repeatedly challenged the Shayks claiming her own status as an experienced interpreter of dreams, and she held her own in a lively and sometimes humorous debate with Shayk Mostafa. When one of the young girls was visibly upset by her dream not being attended to in the way she may have needed, one of the participants encouraged her to draw it for us afterwards.

We did not necessarily agree on the interpretations, but what emerged from our experiment was the possibility of a new methodology. Sharing our dreams enabled us to speak to each other in ways we would not otherwise, ways that cut across social and cultural divisions without denying the imbalances of power and authority. In some respects, our common ground may have entailed a shared aesthetic language across cultures around the fact that dreams are seldom literal and allowed access to something beyond the manifest. The consideration that was raised was that we were not so much engaged in an anthropological approach to the social as in an imaginative approach to the social. As such, we spoke to each other in stories, symbols, metaphors, and also, more than once, produced dream drawings. While we began our session with a sung prayer, when we left, the Egypt's Living Heritage team sung popular songs in the car, by free association, across our cultural repertoires.

I will leave it at that, as an experiment, which stands in need of more reflection, as regards to its impasses, but also as to what it accomplished. And salient in that respect was that it was possible for a moment to come together and share a space, due to an effort of flexibility and openness, both on my part, as a representative of 'psychoanalysis' and on the part of Shayks Mostafa and Ali as representatives of 'Islam'. As we parted, I asked Shayk Mostafa with the help of the interpreter, what he thought of the experiment that we had shared over the last two days, and he said that what seemed especially valuable to him was simply the fact that we were able to come together.

To conclude, I would like to offer two quotations from two outstanding Egyptian writers, Baha Taher and Naguib Mafouz, both devout, irreverent humanists, both also attracted to Sufism, witnesses whose relevance resonates for us now. The first quotation is from Baha Taher's *Love in Exile* (1995 [2008]): 'People don't disclose their secrets to friends but to strangers, on a train or in the odd café. But that is not the issue now. The issue is I want to talk' (Taher, 1995 [2008], 63).

The second is from Naguib Mahfouz's short compendium, *The Dreams* (Mahfouz, 2004), in which he literally transcribed dream texts, a slow return to writing in old age after a long period of rehabilitation following an assassination attempt in a Cairo café in the mid-90s.

> This is a trial and this a bench and sitting at it a single judge and this is the seat of the accused [. . .]. But I grow confused when the dialogue between the judge and the leaders is conducted in a language I have never before heard, until the magistrate adjusts himself in his seat as he prepares to announce the verdict in the Arabic tongue. I lean forward to hear, but then the judge points at me to pronounce a sentence of death upon me. [. . .] I cry out in alarm that I'm not part of this proceeding and that I'd come of my own free will simply to watch and see—but no one even notices me scream.
>
> *(Mahfouz, 2004, 100)*

Of course, the task of psychoanalysis, whatever form it takes, is above all to notice. In the example of the Cairo dream workshops, it didn't matter whether we were religious, whether Islamic or not, or secularists, a space for talking, listening, and noticing was for a time opened up. And it is in this, after all, that lies the promise of the extensibility of psychoanalysis.

Notes

1 See my review of this book in the a forum devoted to it in *Politics, Religion and Ideology* (2016), 17:1, 101–109, for a more extensive account.
2 www.egyptianheritage.net/

References

Abdelkader, H. (2004) 'La psychanalyse en Égypte: entre un passé ambitieux et un futur incertain', *La Célibataire* 8: 61–73.

Ben Slama, F. (2002) *La psychanalyse a l'épreuve de l'Islam.* Paris: Aubier.

Ben Slama, R. (2010/2011) 'La psychanalyse en Égypte: Un problème de non-advenue'. *Topique* 110: 83–96.

Bion, W. (1961) *Experiences in Groups.* London: Tavistock.

Borossa, J. (1997) 'The Migration of Psychoanalysis and the Psychoanalyst as Migrant'. *Oxford Literary Review* 19: 79–104.

Borossa, J. (2012) 'The Extensions of Psychoanalysis: Colonialism, Post-Colonialism and Hospitality', L. Auestad (ed.), *Psychoanalysis and Politics: Exclusion and the Politics of Representation.* London: Karnac. 227–243.

Derrida, J. (1991) 'Geopsychoanalysis: . . . and the Rest of the World', D. Nicolson-Smith (trans.), *American Imago* 48:2 199–231.

El Shakry, O. (2017) *The Arabic Freud: Psychoanalysis and Islam in Modern Egypt*. Princeton: Princeton University Press.

Foulkes, S.H. (1964) *Therapeutic Group Analysis*. London: Allan & Unwin.

Freud, S. (1953 [1900]) 'The Interpretation of Dreams', J. Strachey (ed.), *The Standard Edition of the Complete Psychological Works of Sigmund Freud*. vol. V, London: Hogarth, 621.

Khanna, R. (2003) *Dark Continents: Psychoanalysis and Colonialism*. Durham: Duke University Press.

Lawrence, G. (2005) *Introduction to Social Dreaming: Transforming Thinking*. London: Karnac.

Lawrence, G. and Biran, H. (2002) 'The Complementarity of Social Dreaming and Therapeutic Dreaming', C. Neri, M. Pines & R. Friedman (eds.), *Dreams in Group Psychotherapy*. London: Jessica Kingsley Publishers.

Mahfouz, N. (2004) *The Dreams*. Raymond Stock (trans.), Cairo: AUC Press.

Massad, J. (2015) *Islam in Liberalism*. Chicago: Chicago UP.

Mittermaier, A. (2011) *Dreams that Matter: Egyptian Landscapes of the Imagination*. Berkeley: University of California Press.

Pandolfo, S. (2009) '"Soul Choking": Maladies of the Soul, Islam and the Ethics of Psycho-analysis', *Umbra: Special Issue Islam* 71–103.

Rooney, C (2015) 'Sufi Springs: Air on an Oud String', *CounterText* 1:1 38–58.

Taha, M., Mahfouz, R., and Arafa, M. (2008) 'Socio-Cultural Influences on Group Therapy Leadership Styles', *Group Analysis* 41:4 391–406.

Taher, B. (1995 [2008]) *Love in Exile*. Farouk Abdel Wahab (trans.), London: Arabia Books.

10

ISLAM, THE NEW MODERN EROTIC

Gohar Homayounpour

Using a psychoanalytic discourse, and thus using Freudian concepts such as phobia, fetish, repression, eroticization, perversion and the return of the repressed, I attempt to give an elaboration/translation of Islam as the modern erotic of our times, looking at new forms of Jihadists and fanatical Islamic groups inter alia. Islam is the religion Freud discarded from scrutiny because he, rather aptly, considered it a matter in need of further investigation. For better or worse, Islam would until recently be excluded from the psychoanalytic arena, both in Freud's works and those of other psychoanalysts to follow. This chapter aims to dive into this terra incognita while providing a review of current and rare psychoanalytic contemplations on the subject, regarding Islam as a potential subject, one which is possibly pregnant with issues that could lend themselves to current fanatical movements via a fundamentalist reading. In this regard, the question of Islam's problematic of language and translation is discussed, in the light of a brief comparative analysis between great monotheist religions in a historical context. This inherent untranslatability within Islam need not be its handicap but, on the contrary, my assertion is that if elaborated and looked at, it could provide a rainbow of possibilities. This untranslatability can indeed potentially allocate a marginalized and subversive space to Islam, where possibilities of becomings will be numerous. This is not far from a psychoanalytic discourse of the unconscious that must remain subversive and at times untranslatable and inaccessible, to allow the emergence of the autonomous subject. However, for such a shining possibility to emerge one must inevitably also look at the challenges of a Western liberal discourse imposed on Islam from various fronts, particularly within the spirit of our times.

As such this chapter also aims to bring into the light a respectively latent dialectic interplay that has been shadowed by contemporary Islamophobia, namely that of Islamo-fetisho-phobia. Taking a Freudian stance in delving into recent fundamental Islamic movements and its reception by the global community, this chapter reveals how Islam has become a somewhat-guilty alibi for a global symptom of our zeitgeist, that of the weakening of the name of the father, but also how it plays a role as an eroticized object. Attempting to give such dynamics a new translation will allow a new elaboration not only of Islamic fanaticism but also of the irrefutable contemporary emergence of the many faces of fanaticism, from ISIS all the way to Donald Trump.

Jihadism

The Jihadists, usually youngsters who commit to pledges that often carry them straight to their deaths, are wandering desperately, looking for any means of containment, remedies for deep narcissistic injuries, and in search of a paternal function where they can finally belong. The Jihadist is an alien in his family and his environment in general (Dumas, 2016), between internal and external, inside and outside, fantasy and reality; existing/not existing at the crossroad of alienation and emptiness. He is often an immigrant or the child of an immigrant who perceives his father as weak, as not belonging, as a castrated alien who often does not even speak the language of the host country's language very well. A trans-generational phenomenon of castrated men who do not 'speak,' who will learn the only option left to the psychic apparatus when one does not learn how to speak: they will *do* . . .

    This nightmare of the spirit of our times; our nightmare is someone else's failed dream, and the Jihadists go in search of roots. The 'radical' offer of radical Islamic groups, however, only grants them the possibility of roots in the sky, not on earth, not on firm ground. One should not forget that the noun 'radical' derives from late Latin *radicalis* 'of or having roots' from Latin *radix* (genitive *radicis*) 'root' (Skeat, 1980, p. 429; Dumas, 2016).

    In other words, their wish/fear to find the paternal function fails, as they can only meet an imaginary father, one who like familiar fathers of their own is not able to speak, one who yet again will represent a pure culture of the repetition compulsion, landing them in the imaginary of beyond the pleasure principle, of the death drive.

    The Jihadist is promised a super-life, but this seems to be only a means to hide his already-dead inner life. This way, the semi-suicidal act of the Jihadist becomes an attempt to regain his psychic aliveness on the one hand and to perform a homicidal act on the 'shadow of the object that has fallen upon the ego' (Freud, 1917). The new forms of terrorism are not to be understood as the once-upon-a-time Kamikaze (divine wind or spirit wind). The Kamikaze's suicidal act was in the name of real belief in ideology and defending one's country, and his inevitable death was the single possible method to destroy warships in the most effective way. 'Warship' is the keyword: they were not targeting innocent children, pedestrians. Their suicides could be even understood in terms of the life drive, but these new forms of terrorism are rebels without a cause. This is not a revolution, it is a gangbang ... teenagers without a cause within a pure culture of death drive, where their bodies are repeatedly exploded into a thousand tiny pieces, often near a garbage can.

It is also of interest to note the difference in the concept of martyrdom between Islam and Christianity (ibid.). The Christian martyr is not a fighter, but, as the etymology implies, a witness of God and does not die on the battlefield. As we find in the Gospel of Luke (14: 27): 'And whosoever doth not bear his cross, and come after me, cannot be my disciple.' Although one can find almost the same attitude within the Islamic tradition in a differentiation between the Greater Jihad (Jihad Al-Akbar: fighting one's own dark self and demons) and the Lesser Jihad (Jihad Al-Asghar: fighting the infidel), but the external or Lesser Jihad seems to prevail in the mind of radical Islamists in a somewhat Anti-Islamic manner. There's a large body of Hadith or sayings by the Prophet where he recognizes a man's Jihad with his self and his desires as the Greater Jihad and clearly places it above the Lesser Jihad (for instance, see: Ibn Hanbal, 1895, vol. 6, p. 22; Ibn Babewayh, 1993). In this regard, we can see how one of the cornerstones of Islam has been manipulated and is continuously ignored by the Islamic terrorist, and also within some psychoanalytic conceptualizations of the topic (Dumas, 2016).

Yet, as mentioned above, there is a difference between the Christian martyr who does not die armed, and the Muslim martyr who dies in many instances, especially after the First World War, defending the fatherland or while trying to restore the religion of his fathers (even the word Salafi means the one who returns back to his forefathers, from Arabic Salaf/سلف, meaning: 'forbears, ancestors, forefathers,' Wehr, 1976, p. 423). This hero never dies but he is alive and receives the most glorious rewards from God (Quran, 3: 169). This way, martyrdom is no longer a matter of mere fighting but a death in action. Death now becomes an initiation to life in the other world, making martyrdom an end in itself, and explaining its physicality, objectivity and brutality, as it becomes a passage from inner deadness to a wished-for aliveness.

This initiation and passing ritual points to another issue: that of a mélange between myth and reality (Benslama, 2016a). The Jihadist exposes himself to the collective belief of a mythical Islamic identity, far beyond any possible explanation or definition, turning a blind eye to the many minute differences between various schools of thoughts in Islam and taking this mythical, tribal and collective Islamic identity for granted. In this way he makes himself vulnerable to all sorts of abuse: political, economical as well as sexual (Benslama, 2016a). This mythical identity is fueled by the reality of war, rather like a self-fulfilling prophecy in which the Islamic mythical identity is under threat because its own believers are a threat to even other Muslims who do not share the same values and convictions. For instance, most Muslims do not believe in a worldwide Islamic Caliphate, the concept of one single world government. (Benslama, 2016a). Hence, the Jihadist mixes the real and the mythical to externalize a respectively mythical and archaic threat of degeneration and destruction. This mixture of myth and reality creates an impossible dead-end, (Campbell & Moyers, 1988) one that is extremely challenging to elaborate, re-translate and overcome.

This brings us to what I consider a crucial point within Islam regarding a potentially inherent untranslatability.

Untranslatability

Let us start from the Bible and the confusion of tongues in the Tower of Babel.[1] The story goes as follows: people who all speak one language, find 'a plain in the land of Shinar' (Genesis 11: 2). They then decide to build a city and a tower (note that the name 'Tower of Babel' does not appear in the Bible and it is referred to as 'the city and the tower' or simply 'the city'), tall enough to reach heaven, in order to make a name for themselves, so that they may not 'be scattered abroad upon the face of the whole earth' (Genesis 11: 4).

> And the Lord came down to see the city and the tower, which the children of men builded. And the Lord said, Behold, the people *is* one, and they have all one language; and this they begin to do: and now nothing will be restrained from them, which they have imagined to do. Go to, let us go down, and there confound their language, that they may not understand one another's speech.
>
> *(Genesis 11: 5–7)*

This well-known passage from the Book of Genesis, while it speaks of an archaic union in terms of language, also shows how the confusion of tongues and multilingualism results from the possibility of infringement or violation of the boundaries of heaven, something that one might read as missing from Islam's culture of pure submission which denies its believers the opportunity to rebel and hence, acquire the possibility of differentiation of language.

More from the Bible:

> And how hear we every man in our own tongue, wherein we were born? Parthians, and Medes, and Elamites, and the dwellers in Mesopotamia, and in Judea, and Cappadocra, in Pontus and Asia, Phrygia and Pamphylia, in Egypt and in the parts of Libya about Cyrene, and strangers of Rome, Jews and proselytes, Certes and Arabians, we do hear them speak in our tongues the wonderful works of God
>
> *(Acts 2: 8–11).*

Or: 'In my name shall they cast out devils; they shall speak with new tongues' (Mark 16: 17). And even more: 'If any man speak in an unknown tongue, let it be by two, or at the most by three, and that by course; and let one interpret' (Corinthians 14: 27), or in the story of Joseph, we find him talking to his brothers: 'For he spoke unto them by an interpreter' (Genesis 42: 23). We may see the embracement of the act of translation, inherent in the way the Bible deals with the issue of language. one who facilitates communication.

The earliest issues regarding translation are naturally grouped within the context of the translation of scriptures such as *the Targum*, the translation of the Hebrew Bible into Aramaic or the famous *Septuagint*, the primary Greek translation of the Old Testament. Different Abrahamic religions take different stances on this issue. Jews very early on decided that translation of the script is possible and permissible, and hence, the Hebrew Bible was translated into Aramaic, later into Greek and into other languages, especially Judaeo-Arabic, Judaeo-Persian and also Yiddish (Lewis, 2004). Even though when it comes to the problem of translation we distinguish Islam from both Christianity and Judaism (as the former never really produced esteemed translations such as *the Targum, Septuagint* or *King James's Version*, for instance), we should note that it is mostly a comparative analysis between Islam and Christianity that vividly underlines the very different paths taken by these two old traditions about the issue of translation and its potentials (leaving Islam and Judaism in a neighboring situation). Interestingly, with the ongoing and apparently endless Palestine-Israel conflicts in mind, some similarities between Islam and Judaism with regards to the dialectic of translatability/untranslatability sheds light on one possible aspect of the issue, which remains beyond the scope of this chapter.

In Christianity, not only is translation allowed, but it is even required (ibid.). It goes as far that we have translations which acquire the status of scriptures in their own right. *The Vulgate; the Syriac translation, the Ethiopic translation* and, one might add, *the Luther German Bible* and *the King James English Bible* are among the best-known examples of this status.

In Islam, a very different phenomenon is observed: 'translation of the Quran is not only not encouraged, it is expressly forbidden' (Lewis, 2004, p. 19). The text is considered a direct divine creation (Kalaam Al Allah or 'The Word of Allah'), inimitable (Quran, 17: 88), uncreated, eternal (Zaman, 1997) (Ghadim, as the term is in 'Elm Al Kalaam,' a branch of Islamic theology), and its translation was long recognized as an act of presumption and impiety (Azarnush, 1996, 2008; Lewis, 2004). Although many Muslims today do not understand Arabic and the text can be found in many different languages, this reproduced text is however mostly considered an interpretation and not a translation per se.

As the direct word of God can never be translated into the language of man, no translation could be considered the same as the sacred text. It is only the recitation of the Quran in Arabic that is recognized as a religious practice, regardless of the believer's mother-tongue: reading the so-called translation is just a way of contemplating on the meaning and not an act of worship or 'Sawaab' in particular. The same untranslatability applies to 'Salaat' or the every-day prayer. It is indeed unquestionable that no translation of the Quran has acquired the legitimate status of *the Vulgate* or *the Septuagint* or *the Targum* or *King James's Version*. In the Quran, we are reminded that the words of God were *revealed* to the Prophet Mohammad in Arabic (Quran, 12: 2; 13: 37; 16: 103; 26: 195; 20: 113; 41: 44). This goes as follows:

Had we made the Koran in a non-Arabic (language) they would have said: 'If only its verses were distinguished! Why in (a) non-Arabic (language, when the Prophet is) an Arab?' Say: 'To the believers it is a guidance and a healing. But to those who do not believe, there is a heaviness in their ears, to them it is blindness. They are those called from afar.'

(Quran, 39: 28; 46: 12; 42: 7; 43: 3; 41: 3)

Yet the Hebrew Bible does not mention that it is in Hebrew. On the contrary, the word Hebrew, meaning a language as distinct from its use as an ethnic designation, does not occur in the Hebrew Bible, which usually refers to the language used by the ancient Israelites as '*yehudit*' (Jewish) (2 Kings 18: 26 cf. Isaiah 36: 11; Nehemiah 13: 24; 2 Chronicles 32: 18) or Sefat Kena'an (language of Canaan) (Isaiah 19: 18) (Lewis, 2004, p. 20).

Through the spread of Islam, Arabic, being the language of God (Azarnush, 2008), became the one language that responded to society's every need, be it economical, political (Lewis, 2004), literal (Brown, 1908; Safa, 1976) and of course spiritual (Azarnush, 2008). The Quran also states that:

There is no crawling creature on the earth, nor a bird that flies with its two wings, but they are nations like you. We have neglected nothing in the Book. They shall all be gathered before their Lord.

(Quran, 6: 38)

Just one language meets all the needs, hence there is no more need to learn new ones. A medieval (probably tenth-century) Arabic writer explains:

The perfect language is the language of the Arabs and the perfection of eloquence is the speech of the Arabs, all others being deficient. The Arabic language among languages is like the human form among beasts. Just as humanity emerged as the final form among the animals, so is the Arabic language the final perfection of human language and of the art of writing, after which there is no more.

(Rasa'il Ikhwan al-Safa, III (Cairo, 1928, p. 152, quoted from Lewis, 2004, p. 22)

One can also highlight the noteworthy distinction between inspiration and revelation (Homer was inspired by the gods, but no one thought his words were those of gods! And such is the case with the Bible: the disciples were inspired by the life of Jesus Christ and wrote their Gospels and hence, the Bible is not considered to be the word of God in the same way as the Quran is in Islam).

This inherent untranslatability within Islam need not be its handicap but, on the contrary, my assertion is that if elaborated and looked at can become its rainbow of possibilities. This untranslatability, if looked at critically, can indeed potentially allocate a marginalized and subversive space to Islam, where possibilities of becomings will be numerous. This is not what has happened, and, instead, we see this potential untranslatability has led to a tragic fundamentalist reading of Islam, as well as the dialectic of Islamo-fetisho phobia later elaborated in this chapter. Untranslatable spaces have the outermost potential to become fearful and at the same time eroticized spaces. As psychoanalysts encountering the stranger of all strangers, the ultimate untranslatability of parts of the unconscious, the uncanniness of encountering parts of the unconscious via the psychoanalytic process, we are indeed familiar with how easily this discourse can become immensely feared, hated, misrepresented and ultimately desired.

Islam is not far away from the psychoanalytic discourse of the unconscious that must remain subversive and at times untranslatable and inaccessible, to allow the emergence of the autonomous subject to be a rare beacon of vagueness, of extreme creativity and playfulness. However; for such a marvelous possibility to emerge one must not only acknowledge this untranslatability but also cherish it, acknowledging its potentials and dangers, once again just as in one's encounter with the unconscious.

It should be repeated here that although the Quran has been translated into several languages, these translations are not regarded the same as the translations of the Bible and have never found the same status as, for example, the King James's Version. One should also recall how Islam was excluded both by Freud and later on by psychoanalysis. In his voluminous work, in which 'religion is omnipresent,' Freud 'refers to Islam directly only in his discussion of monotheism,' (Benslama, 2009, p. vii). In his last book, *Moses and Monotheism*, Freud postpones any elaboration of Islam as a subject for further investigation (Massad, 2015). In the discussion of his work, Freud (1939) writes:

> We have here dealt with only a single instance from the copious phenom-enology of religions and have thrown no light on any others. I must regretfully admit that I am unable to give more than this one example.
>
> *(p. 92)*

Even the word Islam does not appear in Freud's prose and he only refers to it as 'Mahommedan religion' which he believed to be 'an abbreviated repetition of the Jewish one' (ibid). This dismissal and lack of elaboration persisted long after Freud, which might be emblematic of a widespread Islamophobia, even among psychoanalysts and in psychoanalysis, but it could also have something to do with this 'untranslatability' inherent within Islam itself and thus the impossibility of addressing this closed network of one-language-for-all; all-for-one-language.

It goes without saying that some of this untranslatability is part and parcel of the carnivalesque and mysterious infrastructure of all monotheistic religions, but it is my assertion that there is an inherent and added insistence upon closing the possibility of a metaphorical translation in Islam. Clearly one cannot escape the dialectics of symptom creation between the other and Islam, and how this possible inherent quality has been used and abused in creating what I have termed Islamo-fetisho-phobia in the making of Islam into the modern erotic of our times. And so, having attempted to translate this inherent untranslatability in Islam, it also becomes crucial to elaborate this politics of fear/jouissance dialectically created within the zeitgeist our times.

If we adhere to the Freudian discourse, we know that what is repressed is that which is uncomfortable and fearful for our psychic structure. Where phobias are concerned, we repress the idea of an object both desired and feared: this conflictual affect is then displaced into a phobic object which is not the original object of the conflict. While the fetish object is formed as an attempt of a denial of castration, it comes out of the fear of castration. The fetish and the phobic object belong to the territory of fear, as well as both being part objects, where there is no possibility of full object relatedness. The idea of a part object allows the continuous de-humanization and de-subjectivization that contributes to the current state of affairs. At a socio-political level, we have been witnessing an Islamo-fetisho-phobia, where the phobic object, in this case, the Muslim, becomes the fetish object. What is most feared is in a sense what is intensely eroticized.

The fetish object

During the Boston Marathon on April 15, 2013, I noticed many Iranians were praying that the bombers would not turn out to be Muslims, saying afterwards 'Well, at least they were white, not very Muslim-looking, they looked like regular American college kids.' But, these are all the wrong concerns at the wrong time, as they shift the focus away from what is important to study and question at a time of a catastrophe. And why should one be put in the position of having to pray for the bombers not to be Muslims, is that not an attack on subjectivity and freedom? Does that not automatically lead to categorizations, namings, splitting and lead to a new set of problematics?

My Muslim patient in America told me how she feels like she has to be the one at her workplace to be the most critical of the bombers, as she was terrified of being mis-understood as defending the bombers just because she is Muslim, and she has chosen to wear the headscarf. She talked for her whole session about feeling guilty in front of her coworkers, as if she had done something wrong, and not being able to freely talk about her opinions regarding the matter, as she was terrified of being labeled as one of them. But, who are 'they' and what had she done wrong that would explain her guilt?

My patient's discourse got me thinking:

As the Boston Marathon events unfolded, I was thinking that through all this hyper-media coverage of the event, and the overexposure of the images, there were very specific images that were repetitively shown. One was of the American wife of the older brother, who had converted to Islam and wore the headscarf.

According to social media statistics, images of her were the most tweeted, watched and talked about images of the whole event. If one reads what is tweeted about her, we can clearly see that Katherine Russell has become the modern erotic. She is the pretty white American girl who was seduced by the big bad wolf, the sexual, dangerous Muslim man: and look what happened to her! But, Katherine Russell has clearly become a sexual object, the discourse around her is that of an erotic discourse, caught somewhere between the territory of a phobia and a fetish.

My patient and I both wanted to ask: how come Adam Lanza did not get the same celebrity treatment that the Tsarnaev brothers got. In which they were, after all, treated like reality stars. One of my American patients said it was the best action movie he had seen in a long time.

On December 14, 2012, Adam Lanza, 20, fatally shot twenty children and six adult staff members in a mass murder at Sandy Hook in Newton, Connecticut. Before driving to the school, Lanza had shot and killed his mother Nancy at their Newtown home.

The incident is the second deadliest mass shooting by a single person in American history (how come the deadliest shooting did not get such a deadly coverage as the Boston Marathon bombers?) after the 2007 Virginia Tech massacre. It is the second deadliest mass murder at an American elementary school, after the 1927 Bath School Bombings in Michigan. It is the deadliest school shooting in any public school in the United States.

Or we can think of another example:

> On July 20, 2012, a mass shooting occurred inside of a Century movie theater in Aurora, Colorado, during a midnight screening of the film *The Dark Knight Rises*. A gunman, dressed in tactical clothing, set off tear gas grenades and shot into the audience with multiple firearms, killing twelve people and injuring 58 others.

If we are honest and aware, we can admit that the compulsion to look at the images from the Boston Marathon bombing over and over again is not present in the other two cases just mentioned. For example, we keep looking at the images of the older brother's American wife under a tightly-worn black scarf and it does something to us at a visceral level. It is indeed the big bad wolf of an Other that has seduced our innocent little Red Riding Hood. It is the immediate effect of a phobic object, straight away producing disgust and fear in us. And yet it is also a fetish object that we can't help ourselves from compulsively looking at: it does, also, turn us on.

This is what has been referred to in the literature as Islamophobia, whereas I would like to expand the expression to Islamo-fetisho-phobia. We should not ignore the fetishistic aspect of a phobic object if we intend to fully understand it.

The Surmusulman

In Fakhry David's paper on Islamophobia (2006) he reports:
In the UK, the EU Monitoring Centre on Racism and Xenophobia reported:

> A significant rise in attacks on Muslims … numbers of incidents of violent assault, verbal abuse and attacks on property were noted, some … very serious. Muslim women wearing the hijab were easily identifiable and widespread targets for verbal abuse, being spat upon, having their hijab torn from them and being physically assaulted…Threatening and explicitly Islamophobic messages were also widely circulated over the Internet and through e-mails.

> [*Here I have to add that Muslims are at times more Islamo-phobic than non-Muslims and this is a very important point I would like to elaborate on. I can give, for instance, the example of the Iranian music reality show in the United States, in which they nominated the girl with the hijab as the winner. The amount of abusive media responses she got from Iranians was even surprising to me. (Abusive) telephone calls, anonymous post and threatening messages were also observed.*]

This pattern of intolerance was repeated throughout Europe and the United States with some local variation.

Taken together, they underline the fact that today's Muslim must not expect to be seen as 'one of us.' Instead, he is constantly under suspicion; and to be suspected is to be swiftly punished, the matter of guilt or innocence a mere academic afterthought (Davids, 2006, p. 3).

Again, quoted in Davids' paper is a line by Edward Said:

> Malicious generalizations about Islam have become the last acceptable form of denigration of foreign culture in the West; what is said about the Muslim mind, or character, or religion, or culture as a whole cannot now be said in mainstream discussion about Africans, Jews, or other Orientals, or Asians,
>
> *(Said, 1997, p. xii)*

This absence of elaboration which is so dominant in the discourse of the radical Islamic Jihadist, who looks for his roots in the heavens and disavows the earthly parlance, leads to nowhere other than a corporeal world of concrete metaphors, predominantly the body, which can also result in an attempt to destroy one's body in the field. Nevertheless I find fascinating Benslama's concept of '*Surmusulman*' (Benslama, 2016b), in which he highlights within the psychic apparatus of the Jihadist a perversion away from the Islamic ideal of submission inherent in the meaning of the word Islam (to submit), and the examples he provides (ibid.) such as terrorists shouting 'Allah Akbar,' a very famous Islamic motto, meaning God is greater. It is true that the terrorist uses this ideal of submission not in the usual and prescribed manner (to remember man's humility and submission to the omnipotent god), but as a way of attaching God's penis to himself and boasting of his Muslim-hood, creating what Benslama aptly names an 'Homme-Dieu incest' (Benslama, 2016a). But, one cannot generalize all such acts under the same perverse umbrella, for the Muslim person who recites his prayer in the street (in Hyde Park for example), may be neurotic in a way, but his symptom, like all symptoms, partly has an intention of working through something, it is an attempt to remember what has been forgotten. It is the return of the repressed. Perhaps he prays in Hyde Park to gain the recognition and acknowledgment of which he feels deprived. These street prayers, perhaps some of them, with their Islamic vestments, and over-emphasis on various symbols and memorabilia of Islam, is at times in my interpretation a mode, albeit a symptomatic method, of elaborating and translating the aforementioned reluctance to translation inherent within Islam. It is a way to say the unsayable, to remember what has been forgotten, what one is afraid will be forever forgotten. It is a compromise formation on the edge of the subject, on the edge of language.

Hence this attempt at elaboration and representation, although, I repeat, it is symptomatic, in my eyes, is a neurotic one and the 'negative of perversion' (Freud, 1905).

While this chapter points to the reluctance towards translation in its broad meaning within the Islamic tradition, this reluctance to elaboration is not *solely* an issue in Islam. One should expect that the repressed element's return is not greeted with open arms, as it recalls the hidden and disavowed desires inside, tickling the Muslim inside each of us! One should recall the Greater Jihad, as an endless endeavor to find and contain this inner Jihadist and Radicalist which reacts with all its might to keep the repressed back where it belongs, in the land of the repressed. But, this binary seduction and splitting will only prolong our nightmare. Let us consider the Trump phenomenon of our time: Trump is the return of the repressed, the uncanny return of that which is strangely, unbearably familiar, and this could be why people voted for him in secret ballots. They were unaware of why, but they were attracted to him like a butterfly to the candle, like the needle of the Sleeping Beauty, cursed, destined by the evil of the dark side. But, the dark will only become light when we speak, when we look into our mirrors and find our own dark shadows and grant them visas to come in. Otherwise, they will haunt us in the Oval Office when we don't even know why, when, and how we voted for Trump, hypnotized, following a part of ourselves we are so disgusted with that it has come back to haunt us as the Trump phenomenon.

Trump

The point is that Jihadists, the Trump phenomenon, Brexit and … all these phenomena should be understood dynamically and as various symptoms of a mind in conflict, of a body reacting psychosomatically, of a failure of a collective psychic apparatus to keep dreaming …

One may also consider these phenomena as a collective symptom of a fatherless zeitgeist of our era. The absence of the name of the father leaves behind orphaned children, children who, in the case of Islam, are prepared to go to extreme ends in order to find their roots and stay with their tribal, primordial father (Stein, 2010) and in case of the non-Muslim world, propels the public to vote for Trump as a mighty, rich daddy: is Trump not a *Surmusulman*? The super-muslim is the symptom of the spirit of our times. Our collective failed dream, the contemporary nightmare of the dislocated subject of *l'air du temps*.

Representing the lost narcissism of America, with the slogan of 'Let's Make America Great Again,' is not the Trump phenomenon (this dialectic will address also the people who voted for him) of a macho, rich, woman-grabbing, impulsive bully, who gets what he wants when he wants it: uncannily reminiscent of the popular cultural image of Jihadists of our times?

It could be that people voted for Trump because they have a strong wish to resurrect the lost paternal function of today's world. They want a rich daddy to stand up for them; they crave it, they need it but ah, they do not know that he is just a mirage in the desert, an absolute 'Sarab' as we say it in my mother-tongue.

The *Surmusulman* regards himself as being The Real Muslim or in Benslama's term, more Muslim than the ordinary, average Muslim (Dumas, 2016). He aspires to be part of a superior religious might, a superhuman power, which reveals his unconscious, internal threat of being an infidel and a nonbeliever. Hence it is not enough to simply be a Muslim (one who submits), but it becomes imperative to show the fact that one is a Muslim. This way, the term *Surmusulman* becomes 'a diagnosis of the psychic life, impregnated by Islamism, haunted by guilt and the need to sacrifice' (Benslama, in conversation with Dumas, 2016). These Muslims then show a profound guilt over religious matters and are tormented by not being Muslim enough (Benslama, 2016b). As such, they speak of fundamentalism and fanaticism. 'Not only these individuals are facing such internal requirements, but they have to bear the harassment of being accused of the worst of crimes by preachers who want them to prove that they were "good" Muslims' (Benslama, in conversation with Zarachowicz, 2016). These young Muslims try to overcome their shame and disgrace by identifying themselves with exemplary Muslim figures such as the Prophet, and they do their best to become much more Muslim than their parents and previous generations. For them, living by the ideal humility of Islam and inside the traditional Islamic structure does not suffice. They are on the verge of an ideological breakdown and here comes the radicalist movement, offering them a bandage for their pain, promising an omnipotence derived from the heroic Jihad and making them feel all-powerful through believing in an absolute and global cause (Benslama, 2016b; Zarachowicz, 2016). There is also the mythical and exotic Islam of the East with all its initiation rituals and its bewildering language, alphabet, culture and geography that seduces many European converts and Europe-born Muslim immigrants into taking this initiatory passage in the hope of finding some roots in the Islamic movement (Dumas, 2016).

Akhtar also points to this unconscious sense of guilt among the Muslim population, as he regards Islam as a demanding religion and considers that many Muslims find it very difficult to keep up with the expectations (Akhtar, 2018). Such guilty feelings, in turn, externalize themselves in an explosion of rage and a need for punishment, a need that Benslama conceptualizes as a motive for sacrifice (which is a plausible trajectory for the development of super-Muslims' furious desire for self-sacrifice). In his latest book, Akhtar also points to the many identity hazards faced by the young Muslim generation of the West who not only are rejected by their European neighbors as not being 'German-enough' or 'French-enough,' but also are not regarded as 'Algerian-enough' or 'Pakistani-enough' by their own parents (Akhtar, 2018). In this regard, the need to find roots in radical movements (Benslama, 2016a; Dumas, 2016) becomes even more immediate.

This perverse choice of target by fanatics like ISIS very much resonates with Stefano Bolognini's delineation of a certain type of empathy prevalent in the way mafiosos choose recruits to seduce (Bolognini, 1997, 2004) where the leader, in a very empathic manner, can distinguish his/her prey among those who are more vulnerable and thus, in my opinion, in need of a paternal function and who are in a sense, fatherless. Bolognini reminds us that being

> technically empathic does not automatically imply something good, benign, and benevolent: unfortunately, there are some occurrences in life where a perverse or criminal skill includes empathy regarding the psychic condition of the potential victim: a competence that can allow the aggressor to better circumvent or to condition the other, while perceiving exactly how the other is interiorly organized, how he feels and how he works.
>
> *(Bolognini, 2016, p. 3)*

With this in mind, one can distinguish the leaders (with the most probably pervert psychic structures) from the unconsciously guilt-driven soldiers who are looking to find some roots in a radical manner. This is how the soldier's guilt-ridden terrorist attack could actually be interpreted as a suicidal act. In *The Id and the Ego*, Freud writes:

> [the superego] rages against the ego with merciless violence, as if it had taken possession of the whole of the sadism available in the person concerned. [...] What is now holding sway in the superego is, as it were, a pure culture of the death instinct, and in fact it often enough succeeds in driving the ego into death, if the latter does not fend off its tyrant in time by the change round into mania.
>
> *(1923, p. 53)*.

This *pure culture of death drive* is what distinguishes today's guilt/death-driven terrorist from the ideology-driven terrorist of the past (e.g. Kamikaze pilots) who believed in their cause and had no other way to achieve their goal but to die.

As a result, we are facing this untranslatable subject, deprived of its possibility of symbolization, which faces annihilation anxiety rooted in an unconscious guilt. Following this matter, Akhtar (2017, p. 159) states at length:

> All this mobilizes annihilation anxiety (Klein, 1932, 1948; Winnicott, 1963; Hurvich, 2003); rage becomes the loyal lieutenant of efforts to ward off such anxiety. Hating Western nations and their way of life becomes a salve for the lacerations in the Muslim cultural identity. What might have been personally ego-dystonic (e.g. committing violence) now turns 'ethno-syntonic'.

This unconscious guilt, which speaks of a cruel and relentless paternal function, is not the only crisis of the untranslatability of Islam. There is also the Western other who surfs on this untranslatability and humiliation and aims to exclude Islam (Benslama, 2009) and to do whatever it can to keep it excluded. And that's where the term 'Islam . . . the new modern erotic' comes in. It is not for nothing that one can find ISIS in the seclusion of the dark net, in the neighborhood of pornography and guns. I tend to think that although Islam seems to be dwelling in an air of untranslatability, this forbidden-ness does not come only from within.

We have pointed to the seeming untranslatability, and perhaps the reluctance of Islam for communication within the realm of the other. It is also true that ISIS and other radical Islamic movements offer a promise of finding roots (Benslama, 2016a, 2016b; Dumas, 2016) to help cease an unconscious guilt (Akhtar, 2018) which, to tell the whole truth, leaves one with the image of ISIS as a grand orphanage for fatherless children, coming together with the wish/fear of finding a paternal function. With the recent Manchester attack in mind, we may more easily observe how this state of being fatherless, while on one hand promoting a search for roots, also pushes one to disgrace the father and in a sense, kill him in an endeavor driven by the Freudian death drive (one of the attackers was the son of a security guard!) We know from Freud that besides a wish for mastery within repetition compulsion (Freud, 1920), such deeds are also aimed to guarantee that the previous familiar state is bound to repeat and to be re-found; forbidding all possibilities of the emergence of a new event. In this regard, such terroristic acts lead to nothing more than disgracing the father (i.e. Islam) while brutally tearing his body to pieces, a homicidal wish becomes an act of suicide upon the interjected unstable and fragile shadow of the object, the fallen shadow upon the ego. In other words, these sons kill the symbolic father (Islam) in their search to find his lost function. More than anything, this process reveals the dynamic of submission and rebelliousness . . . that behind such submission, there lies a violent need for rebelliousness (Homayounpour, 2012).

We should also acknowledge this threat and terror posed on ourselves from both internal and external sources. Such a topic is not an easy one for a psychoanalyst, as

Islam is a 'terra incognita': in psychoanalysis there is a threat coming from such fanatics to scare us out of participating in such events which, in the final analysis, leads to a translation which seems far from the heart of the Islamic radical who prefers to stay untranslatable in a mythical, Homme-Dieu incest (Benslama, 2016a). They want to threaten us away from aiming for translation and into colluding with this somewhat psychotic unilingual state of being, which itself excludes the possibility of language. Elsewhere, I have noted how such marginalization may have delivered Islam to become a shining territory of calibanistic carnival (Homayounpour, 2012).

Thus as Carlos Padrón tells us in 'Discussion on "Psychoanalysis in Minor Language" by Mariano Horenstein' (2015):

> The Center exoticizes the Margins (as happened with 'Magical Realism,' once it became mainstream, or as happened, and continues to happen in Europe, in considering the so-called New World as the haven or paradise of the bon sauvage, where the Margins become an object of desire for the Center because it contains the magical reverse of what the Center does not have and thus craves for: an enigmatic and sexy secret.

How can we escape from this logic to the point where the essential Otherness of psychoanalysis, or what Padrón calls psychoanalysis as the safeguarder of an Otherness to come, becomes possible?

In the struggle between the Master and the Slave for recognition (the struggle to be recognized by the Other), the Master might exoticize (make more desirable or idealize) the Slave, so as to experience, to its maximum, the recognition by the Slave's (the Margin's) desire, once it happens. Yet, the opposite effect might also occur: the Slave (Margins) might self-exoticize himself or herself so as to receive the maximum amount of gratification once he is recognized by the Master's (the Center's desire).

These are also the problematics of Islam today, in its appointed role as the modern erotic Caliban chosen by Prospero.

But, is it not true that as psychoanalysts we are only interested in that which is subversive? The unconscious is inherently subversive. Nothing can remain subversive in the daylight of the mainstream; it is in the carnival of the masks of the Margins, in the unofficial time of the night that we find our way to Alice's rabbit hole and back. It is in the Margins, in this playground of subversion, that Islam's marginality is not a handicap but its possibilities. Islam becomes like psychoanalysis itself this way, sharing a delightful marginality that has the potential of becoming its rainbow of possibilities.

However; due to the mentioned threats and problematics in this chapter, a sort of internal untranslatability, on the one hand, an Islamo-fetisho-phobia on the other (an eroticization with mutual benefits for both subjects involved), this did not happen.

Saying the unsayable

We should attempt to say the unsayable. We should believe in the magic of words, of the Margins, and believe that it is only via such encounters that we can reach over this yawning gap created by the terrorist who wants to stay with the aforementioned untranslatability; and it is to this demand that we should not give in. Giving up will guarantee the absolute mutation of any possibilities of dreaming for all of us, it will assure the dictatorial ruling power of nightmares for generations to come.

At the same time, we should not be afraid of the Muslim who prays in Hyde Park and discard him as a pervert with regard to the Islamic ideal of submission. We need to bear in mind that Islamophobia or, let's call a cat a cat, Islamo-fetisho-phobia, also excludes the possibility of an encounter. Although we can claim there are some issues within the Islamic mode of thought that contribute to current events, we should also recognize that there is a Muslim inside every one of us. In this regard, Islam seems to have a touch in activating our disconcerting, untranslatable parts (only because of its exclusion which, as I already mentioned, could have made far more interesting for psychoanalysis), since, in our *air du temps*, we are all dislocated subjects. Such issues oblige us to face parts of our own split-off minds. Though frightening and anxiety-provoking, this moment is an opportunity for translation, an attempt at making Islam representable and not merely presentable. I state again that this is not just an issue with Islam and Muslims as, *à la fin*, we're all interconnected. I propose to think of this issue as a swollen part of the whole body called human, as an injury to the human subjectivity in the broadest of sense. Our zeitgeist needs ISIS, as it represents an injured part of itself. A dreadful trauma of our own.

We should continuously be aware of this seductive need for splitting, categorizing and un-hospitable identifications. It is true that we name ISIS as a materialized symbol of such need, but in doing so, we're seduced into taking sides and falling into a discourse of crime and punishment or a superficial, humanitarian discourse which, in my mind, seems to be far from the language of the psyche and an analytic discourse. Such seductions deprive us of the opportunity to elaborate and encounter these dark, dangerous waters. It is true that there are severe issues with the Islamic fundamentalist, which I shall once again recall and point to. But, we shall not forget that Islam is part of the human world at large as well.

If we consider that it is only radicalism's quest to retrieve its roots and to look for a paternal function by idealizing and promoting a super-Muslim mentality (Benslama, 2016b) (though simultaneously killing the father in the act), then we are in danger of missing how this issue is a quality of our era, and we would risk failing to see how ISIS' promise of making Islam great again might correspond to Trump's 'Make America Great Again.' Such a split discourse traps us in that uncanny untranslatability and deludes us into missing that Trump is also a super-Muslim in almost the same way as the term might apply to a fundamentalist fanatic. This matter is certainly beyond the problematics of Islam, and hence it is even more important than ever not to succumb to binary conceptualizations that split 'us' from 'them.' As psychoanalysts, we know very well that events do not take place in isolation. In order to gain an understanding of Trump and the super-Muslim, we should aim to understand our internal Trumpist and refrain from such splitting, which destroys the opportunity for these extremely uncomfortable encounters.

The conference on which this book is based was held at the end of Ramadan (the holiest Muslim month), Muslims all over the world had just celebrated *Eid-al-Fitr*, and we managed to meet in Manchester after a horrifying terrorist attack, after recent terrorist attacks in my country and in the UK. All of our Iranian students were denied the visa for entry into the UK and were therefore unable to be here with us. But, their papers were read thorough the voices of their colleagues; and yet we managed to be at the conference to attempt to elaborate, with a Derridaean hospitality, a marginalized discourse, not in order to bring it into daylight but to assign it its rightful place within a subversive discourse, away from binary politicizations, eroticizations and territorializations.

Given everything I have said above, one can recognize this very conference as a challenge of establishing a transcription, a challenge of encounter, and saying the unsayable which, one should never forget, has its own hazards, impediments and reluctances, even or specially among psychoanalysts.

'Our dreams failed, and we woke with angst into nightmares; if we ever want to dream again, if we ever want an invitation by our psychic apparatus in the playground of dreaming,' we must unequivocally remain faithful to our most cherished conviction of saying the unsayable, of translating that which refuses to be translatable, of seeing that which we cannot bear to see. And Derrida on the taste of a dream: 'I was terrorized, he was welcoming' (in Cixous, 2007, pp. 128–129).

Acknowledgements

This chapter is dedicated to Lorena Preta for being the magician of translating that which refuses to be translated.

Note

1 Etymologically speaking, the name Babel (also the Hebrew name for Babylon) comes uncertain, but it may derive from *bab-ilum*, meaning 'gate of God' (Day 2014). As the Bible says, the city received the name 'Babel' from the Hebrew word *balal*, meaning to jumble or to confuse (Genesis 11:9).

References

Akhtar, S. (2018). *Mind, culture and bloodshed: psychoanalytic reflections upon current global unrest.* London: Routledge.
Azarnush, A. (1996). *A history of translation from Arabic to Persian: the case of quran translation* [Taarikhe Tarjome Az Arabi be Faarsi: Tarjome haaye Qoraan]. Tehran: Sorush Publishing.

Azarnush, A. (2008). *The challenge between Persian and Arabic in the first centuries* [Chaalesh Miane Farsi ve Arabie Sadehaaye Nokhost]. Tehran: Ney Publishing.

Benslama, F. (2009). *Psychoanalysis and the challenge of Islam*. Minneapolis, MN: University of Minnesota Press.

Benslama, F. (2016a). 'Assimiler la radicalisation Islamiste à un phénomène sectaire pose problem.' *Le Monde*. Published 11 June 2016. www.lemonde.fr/religions/article/2016/05/10/assimiler-la-radicalisation-islamiste-a-un-phenomene-sectaire-pose-pro bleme_4917030_1653130.html.

Benslama, F. (2016b). *Un furieux désir de sacrifice. Le surmusulman*. Paris: Le Seuil.

Bolognini, S. (1997). 'Empathy and "empathism".' *The International Journal of Psycho-Analysis* 78(2): 279.

Bolognini, S. (2004). *Psychoanalytic empathy*. London: Free Association Books.

Bolognini, S. (2016). 'The humanizing function of psychoanalytic empathy,' 43rd Freud lecture. Presented at the Freud Museum: Vienna.

Brown, E. G. (1908). *A Literary History of Persia: From the Earliest Times until Firdawsi*. London: T. Fisher Unwin.

Campbell, J., & Moyers, B. D. (1988). *The power of myth*. New York: Doubleday.

Cixous, H. (2007). *Insister of Jacques Derrida*. Edinburgh: Edinburgh University Press.

Davids, F. (2006). 'The Impact of Islamphobia.' *Psychoanalysis and History*, 11(2): 175–191.

Day, J. (2014). *From Creation to Babel: studies in Genesis 1-1*, Vol. 592. London: Bloomsbury Publishing.

Dumas, C. (2016). 'Fethi Benslama: En tuant les autres, le terroriste acquiert une toute-puissance de désastre/Interview with Fethi Benslama.' *Liberation*. Published 20 May 2016. www.liberation.fr/debats/2016/05/20/fethi-benslama-en-tuant-les-autres-le-terroriste-acquiert-une-toute-puissance-de-desastre_1454047.

Freud, S. (1905). *Three essays on the theory of sexuality*. In J. Strachey (Ed. & Trans.). *The Standard Edition of the Complete Psychological Works of Sigmund Freud*, Vol. 7, (pp. 123–246). London: Hogarth Press.

Freud, S. (1917) Mourning and Melancholia. In J. Strachey (Ed. & Trans.) *The Standard Edition of the Complete Psychological Works of Sigmund Freud*, Vol. 9. London: The Institute of Psycho-Analysis and Hogarth Press.

Freud, S. (1920). *Beyond the pleasure principle*. In J. Strachey (Ed. & Trans.). *The Standard Edition of the Complete Psychological Works of Sigmund Freud*, Vol. 18, (pp. 3–64). London: Hogarth Press.

Freud, S. (1923). *The id and the ego*. In J. Strachey (Ed. & Trans.). *The Standard Edition of the Complete Psychological Works of Sigmund Freud*, Vol. 19, (pp. 3–66). London: Hogarth Press.

Freud, S. (1939). *Moses and monotheism*. In J. Strachey (Ed. & Trans.). *The Standard Edition of the Complete Psychological Works of Sigmund Freud*, Vol. 23, (pp. 3–137). London: Hogarth Press.

Homayounpour, G. (2012). *Doing psychoanalysis in Tehran*. Cambridge, MA: MIT Press.

Hurvich, M. (2003). 'The place of annihilation anxieties in psychoanalytic theory.' *Journal of the American Psychoanalytic Association* 51: 579–616.

Ibn Babewayh, A. (1993). *Maeaani Al-Akhbaar*. Qom: Daar Al-Kotob Al-Islamiyah.

Ibn Hanbal, A. (1895). *Al-Mosnad*. Cairo: Matba'at al-Sa'adah.

Ibn Hanbal, A. (2000). *Mosnad-i Ahmad Ibn Hanbal*. Beirut: Moassesa Al-Risala.

Klein, M. (1932). *The psychoanalysis of children*. New York: Free Press. 1975.

Klein, M. (1948). 'On the theory of anxiety and guilt.' In M. Klein (Ed.). *Envy and Gratitude and Other Works: 1946–1963*, (pp. 25–42). London: Hogarth Press. 1975.

Lewis, B. (2004). *From Babel to Dragomans: interpreting the Middle East*. Oxford: Oxford University Press.

Massad, J. A. (2015). *Islam in liberalism*. Chicago, IL: University of Chicago Press.

Padrón, C. (2015), *Discussion on "psychoanalysis in minor language" by Mariano Horenstein*. New York.

Safa, Z. (1976). *The history of Iranian literature* (Taarikhe Adabiaate Iran). Tehran: Tehran University Press.

Said, E. (1997). *Culture and Imperialism*. London: Random House.

Skeat, W. W. (1980). *A concise etymological dictionary of the English language*. New York: Piergee Press (Originally published: 1882).

Stein, R. (2010). *For love of the father: a psychoanalytic study of religious terrorism*. Stanford, CA: Stanford University Press.

Wehr, H. (1976). *A dictionary of modern written Arabic*. New York: Spoken Language Services (SLS).

Winnicott, D. W. (1963). The development of the capacity for concern. In *The maturational processes and the facilitating environment (1965)*, (pp. 73–82). New York: International Universities Press.

Zaman, M. Q. (1997). *Religion and politics under the early 'Abbāsids: the emergence of the Proto-Sunnī elite*. Brill.

Zarachowicz, W. (2016). 'De l'islamisme au surmusulman: quand la psychanalyse se penche sur les parcours sacrificiels'/Entretien avec Fethi Benslama. *Telerama*. Published 16 May 2016. www.telerama.fr/idees/de-l-islamisme-au-surmusulman-quand-la-psychanalyse-se-penche-sur-les-parcours-sacrificiels,142381.php

11

ENDURING TROUBLE

Striving to think anew

Amal Treacher Kabesh

Islam and psychoanalysis are two discourses and practices that overlap; they are seemingly distinct and yet they share concerns as well as socio-cultural-psychic preoccupations in relation to what makes us human. In this chapter, I want to explore some of the inter-connections between Islam and psychoanalysis in order to draw out a few shared preoccupations between these two seemingly distinct discourses and practices. There is, as Joseph Massad points out, a difficulty with knowing what Islam is and what it has come to mean; does Islam, he asks, name a 'religion, a geographical site, a communal identity?' (2009, p. 193). A similar question can be asked of psychoanalysis: is it a religion, an ideology, a theoretical framework and/or clinical practice? I understand Islam and psychoanalysis as belief systems, ideologies and discourses that involve practices and rituals.

While there is agreement that there are different versions of psychoanalysis and similarly that Islam is practised differently according to geographical location, to date there has been little attention paid to the question of whether there exist specific connections between Islam and psychoanalysis

Attending to this question will hopefully unsettle commonplace perceptions that there is little overlap between the West and the Rest and this chapter is an attempt to prise apart these concrete – and frequently resolutely held – opinions. We need to ensure that Islam and psychoanalysis speak to each other while simultaneously recognising their different conceptualisations of socio-cultural systems and their contrasting understandings of human beings.

Within a psychoanalytic framework we have to endure and tolerate that there is always a gap – a chasm, indeed – between who we desire to be and who we are as we are perpetually riven with conflict, aggression, hate and indifference. Within an Islamic discourse, human beings are conceptualised also as struggling with the basic instincts of egotism, aggression, excessive self-regard and arrogance. The message of

Islam is that individuals are agents of their moral beliefs and actions and are continually responsible before an omniscient and omnipresent God.

One focus of the overlap between Islam and psychoanalysis is an implicit preoccupation with endurance: as an ethical position, struggling with aspects of the self that are unpalatable and unacceptable and persisting with other human beings no matter the obligations that they demand.[1] Endurance can be understood as practice, as ritual and as an implicit aspect of the philosophical frameworks of both Islam and psychoanalysis. Psychoanalytic and Islamic practices both offer a space to be endured and to endure, an interval to tolerate that life cannot be what we desire no matter how fervently we may wish it to be otherwise. Psychoanalysis and Islam punctuate a state of mind, a mood and the overwhelming preoccupations of everyday living.

This chapter addresses one aspect of my wider intellectual project to understand the inter-relationships between the West and the Middle East (specifically the UK and Egypt). This preoccupation came into focus following 9/11/2001 when the discourse of a 'clash of civilisations' took hold. This powerful discourse persists and is difficult to shift, no matter the evidence or arguments to the contrary. Exploring people's perceptions of Jamaica and the UK, the Jamaican cultural theorist Stuart Hall writes the idea that:

> because I moved – irrevocably as it turned out – from one world to the other, from colony to metropole, there were no connections between them has always seemed inconceivable to me. But others have tended to see these worlds as much more compartmentalised. And to someone who doesn't know the interior life and spaces of the colonial formation, and how its antinomies were forged, the connections may not appear to be evident ... their interdependence is what defines their respective specificities; in everything they reverberate through each other but how these interconnections take place, are felt and thought through is challenging to elucidate and trace through.
>
> *(2017, p. 11)*

There are various understandings of the inter-relationship between the Middle East and the West, as found, for example, in Samuel Huntington's problematic 'clash of civilisations' thesis (1996) and in the work of Bernard Lewis (2002), both of whom argue that these two geo-political regions are resolutely different and irreconcilable. Huntington's and Lewis' arguments arise from, and perpetuate, the value-laden assertion that the West is politically, culturally and socially superior to the inferior Middle East.

Joseph Massad (2015), Edward Said (1997), and Marina Warner (2002, 2012), however, elucidate and illuminate the complex inter-relationships that exist between the Middle East and the West. Said's influential book *Orientalism* (1997) explores the nuanced inter-connections that have persisted politically, socially and as importantly – affectively. Warner focuses on the possibilities for a hopeful interchange but does not avoid thinking through the exploitation of the Middle East as an object of fascination, while Massad and Said are more worried, if not angry, about the uses made of the Middle East by the West for political and military gain. Massad's stringent analysis explores how the very conception of liberalism itself is built upon the notion of Islam as autocratic and restrictive of freedom and democracy. In order to reinforce the illusion of democracy and freedom in the West, Massad writes, the Middle East is positioned as a region that is resolutely patriarchal and autocratic (2015). On this account and in short, those who inhabit the West are the luckiest people on earth, while other human beings who live elsewhere are hapless and unfortunate.

The discourses that position the Middle East and the West as founded on inevitably divergent and irreconcilable differences are prevalent. Embedded within these discourses is the view that these chasms are natural and inescapable. There are, however, different historical accounts that challenge these established discourses. Here, I could draw upon an account of the crusades but this is familiar territory and in the attempt to think anew we must be cautious that we do not adhere to a particular version of events that forecloses knowledge of other histories. The inclusion of a socio-historical account is important because, first, it can let us know (or alert us to the historical reality) that these divisions have not always existed and, second, it can reveal to us that there are other ways of being and relating to the other that do not rest on denigration and exclusion.

The commonplace account of the crusades underlines a history of conflict, war, aggression and domination. Jerry Brotton, however, begins his account of the relationship between Elizabethan England and the Islamic world with an account of a Moroccan ambassador's time in London (2016).[2] The ambassador was in London to negotiate trade agreements and a political alliance that would unite English Protestants and Moroccan Muslims against their common enemy – Catholic Spain. Elizabethan England was close in its diplomatic, commercial and military politics to the Moroccan dynasty. The Protestant and Islamic worlds formed a strong alliance against Catholicism and while, as Brotton points out, this now seems fanciful, such was the power from the Moroccan ruler that it was given serious consideration (2016, p. 7). This political and military alliance extended to the various ways that English men and women came to understand their place in the sixteenth-century world: what they ate, how they dressed and furnished their homes (Brotton 2016, p. 8). The influence from the Islamic world went back to Henry VIII as he and his court wore Ottoman clothing and imported commodities such as cotton, rhubarb, currants, sweet wine and intricate textiles, as well as copious amounts of sugar (Brotton 2016, p. 8).

As early as the 1550s Englishmen were doing business in Muslim countries especially Morocco and Syria. These commercial transactions did not exist just within the sphere of commerce as these businessmen returned to England bringing with them new experiences, new encounters and new words – sugar, crimson, mascara, zero – words that have become embedded within ordinary language (Brotton 2016, pp. 8–9). As Warner maintains, the cross-fertilisation that has taken place 'between our own culture and cultures which have been deemed irrational and unenlightened has been more pervasive and influential than has been acknowledged or understood' (2012, p. 25).

History is a palimpsest made up of layers upon layers of events, interpretations and conceptualisations that are contradictory and pull in different directions. Before we get carried away with the romance of Elizabethan England and imagine that this was a time of only tolerance and respect, simultaneously there was disgust and distancing from the Islamic world and this may be due to the resonance from the crusades. There was no attempt to understand Islam on its own theological terms; 'instead throughout the Tudor period a powerful set of misrepresentations, misconceptions and misunderstandings developed which defined relations between the two faiths' (Brotton 2016, p. 9). The amicable relationship that prospered briefly arose from expediency and *realpolitik*. Yet, as Brotton points out, that relationship gave rise to a variety of unintended consequences. By the eighteenth century, Brotton asserts, the Muslim world had become remote, rejected and expelled, so Samuel Johnson commenting on a monumental 1,200-page survey focusing on the Ottoman Empire reveals a typical Georgian indifference to the Islamic region, asserting that 'no-one desires to be informed' (Brotton 2016, p. 11).

By the eighteenth century there was a resolute distancing by England towards the Islamic world especially in the political, economic and military spheres, but, in the field of culture, there was a rather different response to Islam by the West. For example, *The Arabian Nights* was celebrated, albeit, with different responses that ranged from appreciative enjoyment to horror. This medieval Arabic story collection 'became established in Europe as a masterpiece of imagination, inventiveness and wit, and took its place as a supreme fiction' (Warner 2012, p. 20). Histories, along with affective responses, are always intricate, nuanced and contrary. As Warner points out:

> Pursuing the well-rehearsed racial and negative values of the past does not contribute to opening a dialogue; uncovering a neglected story of reciprocity and exchange can make for a greater understanding. And one place where the conversation between East and West took a different shape was fiction, especially fabulist stories, packed with wonders, elastic in handling time and space, and plotted according to the different laws of fate and magic.
>
> *(2012, p. 26)*

There is never a clear fit between the political, cultural, social and affective spheres and we must endure what we do not know and tolerate that nothing ever dovetails together neatly. In her first Reith Lecture *The Day is for the Living* (2017), Hilary Mantel stresses, that we must resist the temptation to use history as a way of organising our ignorance of the past. It is when we think that we have understanding in our grasp that we should be at our most vigilant to that which is inevitably pulsing away underneath the surface.

Towards understanding belief systems

An understanding needs to take place focused on the place of religious beliefs in the lives of many people whatever their faith, as religious beliefs require to be taken seriously. Terry Eagleton points out that most contemporary cultural theorists pass 'over in silence some of the most vital beliefs and activities of billions of ordinary men and women' (2016, p. ix), and this absence sits alongside the declaration of a wholehearted commitment to diversity. I understand religion as a source of solace and simultaneously as an ideological system that constrains human beings as religious faith binds people into the socio-political order. This viewpoint adheres to Marx's opinion that religion 'is the sigh of the oppressed creature, the heart of a heartless world, and the soul of soulless conditions. It is the opium of the people' (1844/1970). It is important to take seriously religion's place in the yearning to belong. We have to be respectful of various belief systems based on the recognition that all religious systems are based on and founded in ideology. In short, no belief system is neutral and that includes both secularism and psychoanalysis.

It is commonplace to understand the word Islam as meaning 'surrender', Massad, however, prefers the phrase 'giving oneself over' (2015). Islam is a religion based on discipline; furthermore, and as Geaves points out Islamic law prescribes all human activity: diet, dress, hygiene, prayer, commerce, relations with others and the rules of warfare (2010, p. 46). By professing their faith, Muslims accept a structure based on a direct personal relationship with God and the Message of the last Prophet Mohammed (Muslims believe in the existence of Jesus Christ but not that he was the last Prophet). The pillars of faith, ritual practice, social obligations, moral codes and prohibitions define Islam as a religion. The pillars are: there is no god except God, Muhammed is his Messenger, daily prayer, paying zakat – charitable contributions and fasting during Ramadan, which is perceived as having a threefold function: spiritual, physiological and social. Ramadan is a month to turn inwards towards introspection and reflection. The last pillar of Islam is to perform Hajj but only if there are financial resources to undertake a pilgrimage.

In Cairo, where I live for some of the time, religion saturates everyday life: for example, the call for prayer (adhan) fills the soundspace. Everyday talk is replete with religious belief – thanking God for everything including misfortune. The rituals and habits of everyday living, including cleanliness, prayer and diet, are undertaken according to the Qur'an and the hadith. This is a world in which it is impossible to avoid religion, and within which atheism cannot be imagined. I was brought up within the Muslim faith and despite identifying as secular I do find myself throwing up prayers (if they can be called that) into thin air rather frequently in the hope that they land somewhere (they hardly ever do). My mother and stepfather were both devout Christians. I know the value of religion and what it provides in relation to consolation, belonging and as an emotional and social glue.

As Massad points out, Islam is often positioned as the counter-point to liberalism (2015) and a prevalent belief that liberalism and liberal values will rescue Muslims from a rigid and overly strict ideology dominates in the 'West', where an often-expressed aim 'is to convert *Muslims and Islam* to Western liberalism and its value system as the only just and sane system to which the entire planet must be converted' (Massad 2015, p. 3). The apparently sacred values of freedom, liberty and equality are the only route to a different salvation. Secularism as a belief system that consoles and reassures is bypassed through this unthinking faith in a particular liberal framework.

We need to be attentive to, and cognisant of, the ways in which psycho-analytic theory and practice can dovetail too neatly into liberal ideologies. Psychoanalysis, after all, is also a belief system that can ensure an illusion of coherence, understanding and access to a distinctive matrix of knowing the world and human beings. Massad provides an essential challenge that perturbs a liberal (psychoanalytic?) viewpoint that Muslim subjectivities should be reliant on Western beliefs of what constitutes exemplary maturity, rationality and autonomy (Massad 2009, 2015).

Eagleton argues that secularism has its roots in a material history including the expansion, during the eighteenth/nineteenth centuries of European commer-cialism and more recently, the rapid growth of international monopolies as well as the impact of new technologies (2016). Interwoven with these massive shifts in the economic and material spheres was the partial dissolution of traditional hierarchies and as Eagleton asserts it was not so much God but priests that were the site of criticism for the task 'was not so much to topple the Supreme Being as to replace a benighted version of religious faith' (Eagleton 2016, p. 6). It was reason and not God that should be the all-powerful and self-determining power and while the 'Enlightenment sought to reconstruct morality on a rational basis … [but] the morality in question remained largely Christian in provenance' (Eagleton 2016, p. 9). It is crucial to understand that 'although secularism is often defined negatively – as what is left after religion fades – it is not itself neutral. Secularism should be seen as a presence. It is *something*' (Calhoun et al. 2011, p. 5).

Perhaps one reason that the commonplace assumption that secularism is value-free and without basis in ideology arises from a fear and distrust of excess. As Adam Phillips writes, 'nothing makes us more frightened, more furious, more despairing than other people's extreme commitment to political ideals or religious beliefs' (Phillips 2009). Phillips explores this horror of excess as based on fear and despair of our own longings and desires and these emotions are provoked when we judge someone as holding excessive beliefs (the basis on which a judgement is made of what is believed to be excessive, out of proportion, intemperate is always complex). I have no conscious desire to blow myself up and simultaneously I can identify with the wish to make an impact and the need to go out with a bang and not an ordinary whisper. Feeling flooded by anxieties about excess can lead to either a pretence of tolerance and/or proselytising against excessive religious beliefs. Jean Bethke Elshtain carefully explores Charles Taylor's distinction between tolerance and proselytising, writing that proselytisation occurs when a person

> knowingly and determinedly sets out to change someone else's mind about something basic to his or her identity and self-definition, like religious belief. Toleration requires that (I) learn to live with deep differences even though (I) may disagree profoundly with another's beliefs and identity.
>
> *(2004, p. 130)*

Full respect entails recognising that we inhabit and transmit different histories and these histories are active as they form our belief and value systems, our perceptions and responses to other human beings. A crucial aspect of recognition is understanding that though histories and lived experiences are not congruent, that does not undermine the necessity of respect. Iris Marion Young writes that within 'a stance of moral respect, each party must recognise that others have irreducible points of view, and active interest that respectful interaction must consider ... such mutual acknowledgment is the meaning of moral equality' (1997, p. 351). Respect entails accepting that people can express their religious beliefs differently and indeed publicly. Far too frequently, people declare the following: 'people can believe what they want as long as they keep it hidden' (Bethke Elshtain 2004, p.131). Some Islamic practices are public: for example wearing the veil, praying in the street if circumstances require it and the call for prayer. The private/public divide does not hold the same importance for all societies.

Sayeeda Warsi[3] writes poignantly about what her Islamic faith means to her:

> My faith is about who I am and not about who you are. It's a rule-book for me, not a forced lecture series for you. Its strength is a source of peace for me not ammunition with which to fight you. It's a ruler I have chosen to measure myself against, not a stick with which to beat you. It allows me to question myself, not to judge you. And recognizing myself, being sure of who I am, being comfortable in my identity, does not mean having to downgrade, erase or reject who you are.
>
> *(Warsi 2017, p. 270)*

This passage can be understood as a description and as a reassurance both that Warsi will not proselytise and force anyone to convert, and as a calm resistance to relentlessly being positioned as a religious fanatic.

The moral endeavour to respond to and tolerate the other is at the core of Islamic and psychoanalytic discourses. Both frameworks argue that we all have to give ourselves over to the demands of the other and propose that enduring the other human being is central to the effort of being a moral human being. For psychoanalysis, we have to endure the other and withstand that other human beings are never as we want them to be as they never provide unconditionally and meet our desires without reservation. While for psychoanalysis the moral code is the relationship between one human being and another, within Islam morality entails the profound relationship with God. The relationship of a Muslim with God is a conscious and voluntary submission to the will of God and it provides a degree of intimacy between God and the human being (Geaves 2010, p. 47). Islamic ethics are linked primarily to the ideal of being virtuous and are based, as Geaves points out, on a strong sense of social justice. Muslims have to prepare for divine judgement by striving to right the wrongs of social injustices and political injuries (Geaves 2010, p. 48).

Of equal importance to the discourses of Islam and psychoanalysis is the proposition that ethical and moral conduct requires self-discipline on the part of the individual. Endurance is ethical as it entails not forcing the other to be who we wish them to be and necessitates the endeavour to avoid being coercive and colonising other/s (Butler 2005). Interwoven with enduring the other, there are the vexed difficulties of acknowledgement and recognition. Entwined with acknowledgement and recognition is the necessary capacity for empathy which I understand as allowing the other into the self so that the other person makes a difference to who we are (Young-Breuhl 1998). Emotions, however elusive, weak and slippery they may be, have effects that are, in contradiction, powerful as they pulse through, and between, human beings. As Kathleen Stewart writes, ordinary affects 'highlight the question of the intimate impacts of forces in circulation. They're not exactly "personal" but they sure can pull the subject into places it didn't exactly "intend" to go' (Stewart 2007, p. 4–5).

Emotions and fantasies can pull us away from our best intentions as embroiled in self-other relationships, there is always the use of the other. Winnicott explores the necessity of the use of another person and material objects as crucial aspects of finding the self (1970). As part of the ritual of prayer Muslims roll out a rug that is used only for prayer and it is worth registering, if not pondering on, the symbolism of Freud's oriental rug that lies across his couch. Many patients lie on couches that, I hazard a guess, are covered in oriental rugs. Lynda Marinelli writes in her catalogue to the exhibition – *The Couch: Thinking in Repose* – that Freud's choice of 'examination bed' opens a wide spectrum of experience between dreaming and waking, dissoluteness and moral control. It serves as a therapeutic instrument, as a site of free association and as a vehicle of poetic production (Marinelli in Warner 2012, p. 411). In order to free associate, to start edging towards speaking that which is illicit and socially forbidden, and to begin to know the 'stranger within',[4] that which is unwelcome and alien we lie on an object that comes from elsewhere.

To use an object fully, however, as Warner points out, is to allow it to exist in all its foreignness and strangeness (2012, p. 49). The object frequently takes on a religious allure and Warner draws attention to how visitors to the Freud Museum behave as if there is 'something holy about the room, elicit exchanges in hushed voices and referent behaviour turning the visitors into pilgrims' (2012, p. 412).

There are two (minimum) ethical endeavours that need to occur. First, there is the essential knowledge that an object that we use comes from outside of ourselves and arrives from somewhere foreign and distant. Second, we also have to struggle with the abject knowledge that we are dependent on the other for our very existence (Winnicott 1970). Our reliance on the other is dependent on a belief that other human beings are on the whole trustworthy and simultaneously we have to acknowledge our tendencies to exploit, colonise and manipulate other people. Enduring dependency and knowing that we are reliant on other human beings can lead to paying back the debts incurred to other human beings whether known, familiar or not.

Need, desire, fantasy

In thinking through the relationship between psychoanalysis and Islam, there is the crucial matter of temporality. Psychoanalysis emphasises the relationship between the past and the present while for Islam it is the future that holds the promise of an ideal life in paradise. I could let the matter rest there, except it is not that straightforward for two reasons. First, temporalities are fused as the past, present and future are intertwined in a complex knot of temporalities, experiences and identities (Treacher Kabesh 2011). Second, as Adam Phillips explores, all our lives are lived through that which we continue to wish had taken place (2013). We live our lives through that which has been but is now absent and that which has never occurred, as well as through our wishes and desires for a different life. We dream that if we had had another life – had actually been someone else – then this life would be smoother and more fulfilling and with fewer disappointments/frustrations/regrets. It would be a life of ease and satisfaction.

Much of our mental life is about the lives we are not living, the lives we are missing out on, the lives we could be leading but for some reason are not (Phillips 2013, p xi). What we fantasise about and yearn for are people and experiences that are absent and needless to say we 'also learn to live somewhere between the lives we have and the lives we would like' (Phillips 2013, p. xi). We learn, albeit reluctantly, to inhabit the reality principle and 'our lived lives might become a protracted mourning for, or an endless tantrum about, the lives we were unable to live' (Phillips 2013, p. xiii). A crucial aspect of the reality principle is that we have to endure life in all its frustrations, irritations, challenges, pleasures and joys. We pay the price and make a reluctant choice about whether to believe that God will ensure us the ideal life in the hereafter or that through undergoing an analysis our lives will improve in the here and now. Phillips writes that Darwin showed us that everything in life is vulnerable, ephemeral and without design or God-given purpose … Belief in God (and providential design) was replaced by belief in the infinite untapped talents and ambitions of human beings (and in the limitless resources of the earth) (2013, p. xiv). A profound belief of neo-liberal societies is that people can achieve their potential, be productive and make use of the opportunities available. Standing still is never an option let alone passing our sell-by date. Baumann argues throughout *Liquid Life* (2005) that people in the West are meant to possess a life of choice, individuality and fluidity, and are supposed to be in a process of an endless remaking of identity.

Stephen Frosh underlines that endurance is a generous state of mind. He writes, psychoanalysis 'reminds us that there is something important about stillness, about remaining with a situation until it organises itself under the pressure of its own desire; it reminds, us, that is to say, of the virtues of endurance' (Frosh 2015, p. 157). Waiting for someone either literally or emotionally can offer another human being a lifeline. Waiting for someone also entails having to endure that something or someone is more important than oneself and being willing to give oneself over to another human being is a crucial aspect of our humanity.

Within neo-liberal discourses, waiting can too easily be seen as passive, irrational, and too simplistically perceived as fatalism. Muslims become positioned as passive dependents who are overly dependent on divine will and are not autonomous or reasoning beings. There is a spiritual humility in the knowledge that we must give of ourselves and if you are a practising Muslim to know that your fate has been preordained by God. This is not a passive fatalism. We should not assume, as I did until recently, that fate is equivalent to passivity because it does take courage, patience, fortitude, to accept one's fate which after all is another way of accepting who one is. In any case, as Freud points out, it takes an awful lot of energy to be passive (1905/1953). To think psychoanalytically about fate leads to questioning the belief in the value of autonomy as a sign of maturity and an interrogation of a belief that rationality and reason can exist without the workings of the unconscious. We have to be wary that the unconscious does not become another implicit form of fate so that the unconscious works in this way: nothing to do with me, it's my unconscious.

During the Enlightenment and beyond, rationality became an important value, and this entailed, as Eagleton points out, the imperative to deny failure, disorder or vulnerability prevailed (2016). Islam and psychoanalysis perpetuate the fiction, either overtly or covertly, that if human beings place their faith in their particular system then doubt and ambivalence will be alleviated. In seeming contradiction, however, psychoanalysis stresses the importance of enduring our fragmented and broken identities (one reason why psychoanalysis is unpalatable for many). Within psychoanalytic theory, release is never readily available while within an Islamic framework redemption will take place on Judgement Day.

Islam and psychoanalysis as discourses and as practices stress the importance of thinking as a verb and both frameworks emphasise the necessity of thinking anew and the struggle of understanding. The word jihad circulates in the contemporary Western geo-political region. It evokes fear if not terror, anxiety if not dread, troubling wordless affect if not horror. The word – jihad – probably, I hazard a guess, is what most non-Muslim people associate with Islam and the association of a war against the other is its most simplistic connection. It is worth pointing out that in the over 80 accepted definitions or understandings of jihad only one refers to war and this with strict stipulations and conditions: war is legitimate only in self-defence and if it is necessary due to aggression or colonisation (Ramadan 2017, p. 161).

Jihad means 'effort' and is an injunction to the self to carry out a perpetual struggle to overcome negative thinking, emotions and behaviour. It is a command that every human being should resist temptation: sexual, material, whatever corrupts, and to overcome the negative impulses within ourselves and in society. Jihad, the effort required, is twofold as it focuses on resistance *and* reform. Jihad within Islam resonates with the psychoanalytic injunction to continually re-think, exert effort and struggle with our aggression, hatred, envy, selfishness and apathy – in short, our negative impulses. Psychoanalysis in this reading *is psychoanalysis as jihad*.

Atmospheres are ambiguous, for as Ben Anderson writes, on the one hand, 'atmospheres are real phenomena. They "envelop" and thus press on a society "from all sides" with a certain force. On the other, they are not necessarily sensible phenomena' (2009, p. 78). Atmospheres are indistinct and simultaneously equivocal as they shift 'between presence and absence, between subject and object/subject and between the definite and indefinite – that enable us to reflect on affective experience as occurring beyond, around, and alongside the formation of subjectivity' (Anderson 2009, p. 77). The tone and atmospheres of a society can be enigmatic, elusive and have material effects on subjectivities and subjective experience. There are various demands that are made on Muslims to be legitimate and to become like a Western subject while simultaneously remembering that this is impossible.

Perhaps a starting place is to scrutinise how all human beings strive to be legitimate subjects because as Ferguson pithily asserts 'subjection is preferable to abjection' (2013). The perpetual question that has to be persistently asked is: how is the other always being exploited in order to ensure that our (my) place in the socio-political order is secure? This exploitation takes place through disavowal, distancing, direct or in-direct racism or through what Bourdieu describes as symbolic violence (1991). Accountability, following Butler (2005), is based on knowing that we internalise and perpetuate the socio-political orders that we live by and we cannot wish that away. There is the necessary and persistent matter of how we can be hospitable and respectful to other human beings. This pertinent challenge applies to individual subjects of whatever faith, to Islam and psycho-analysis as systems of belief, and to societies from whichever geo-political region. Knowing the value of our inter-connections is one way forward to being hospitable and respectful.

Notes

1 I am indebted to Stephen Frosh for his essay 'Endurance' (2015).
2 It is worth reading the novel *Leo Africanus* by the Lebanese author Amin Maalouf (1992) that is based on a Renaissance man who travelled extensively and explores how Islam and Christianity are inter-related.
3 Sayeeda Warsi is a lawyer and a member of the House of Lords in the UK.

4 Julia Kristeva's book *Strangers to Ourselves* (1991) is an exploration of the foreigner in society and the foreigner within ourselves – the unconscious.

References

Anderson, B. (2009) Affective Atmospheres. *Emotion, Space and Society*, 2, 77–81.

Baumann, Z. (2005) *Liquid Life*. Cambridge: Polity Press.

Bethke Elshtain, J. (2004) Toleration, Proselytizing, and the Politics of Recognition. In Abbey, R. (ed.) *The Self Contested in Charles Taylor*. Cambridge: Cambridge University Press, pp. 127–139.

Bourdieu, P. (1991) *Language and Symbolic Power*. G. Raymond & M. Adamson (trans.). Massachusetts: Harvard University Press.

Brotton, J. (2016) *This Orient Isle, Elizabethan England the Islamic World*. London: Penguin Books.

Butler, J. (2005) *Giving an Account of Oneself*. New York: Fordham University Press.

Calhoun, C. et al. (eds) (2011), *Rethinking Secularism*. Oxford: Oxford University Press.

Eagleton, T. (2016) *Culture and the Death of God*. New Haven and London: Yale University Press.

Ferguson, J. (2013) Declarations of Dependence: Labour, Personhood, and Welfare in South Africa. *Journal of the Royal Anthropological Institute*, 19(2), 223–242.

Freud, S. (1905/1953) *Three Essays on Sexuality*. Volume 7. In *The Standard Edition of the Complete Psychological Works of Sigmund Freud* J. Strachey (trans.). London: Hogarth Press & The Institute of Psychoanalysis.

Frosh, S. (2015) Endurance. *American Imago*, 72(2), 157–175.

Geaves, R. (2010) *Islam Today: An Introduction*. Bloomsbury: London.

Hall, S. with Schwarz, B. (2017) *Familiar Stranger, A Life between Two Islands*. London: Allen Lane.

Huntington, S. (1996) *The Clash of Civilisations and the Remaking of the World Order*. New York: Simon and Schuster.

Kristeva, J. (1991) *Stranger to Ourselves*. Leon S. Roudiez (trans.). New York: Columbia University Press.

Lewis, B. (2002) *What Went Wrong? The Clash between Islam and Modernity in the Middle East*. New York: Perennial.

Maalouf, A. (1992) *Leo Africanus*. P. Sluglett (trans.). Lanham, MD: New Amsterdam Books.

Mantel, H. (2017) *The Day is for the Living*. The Reith Lectures. London: BBC.

Marx, K. (1844/1970) *A Critique of Hegel's Philosophy of Right*. Cambridge: Cambridge University Press.

Massad, J. A. (2009) Psychoanalysis, Islam and the Other of Liberalism. In Borossa, J. & Ward I. (eds). *Psychoanalysis and History*, 11(2), 193–208.

Massad, J. A. (2015) *Islam in Liberalism*. Chicago, IL: Chicago University Press.

Phillips, A. (2009) Insatiable Creatures. *The Guardian*, 8th August 2009.

Phillips, A. (2013) *Missing Out: In Praise of the Unlived Life*. London: Penguin Books.

Ramadan, T. (2017) *Islam: The Essentials*. F. Reed (trans.). London: Pelican, Random House.

Said, E. W. (1997) *Orientalism*. New York: Pantheon.

Stewart, K. (2007) *Ordinary Affects*. Durham and London: Duke University Press.

Treacher Kabesh, A. (2011) On Being Haunted by the Present. *Borderlands*, 10(2), 1–21.

Warner, M. (2002) *Fantastic Metamorphoses, Other Worlds Ways of Telling the Self*. Oxford: Oxford University Press.

Warner, M. (2012) *Charmed States and the Arabian Nights*. London: Vintage Books.

Warsi, S. (2017) *The Enemy Within: A Tale of Muslim Britain*. London: Penguin.

Winnicott, D. W. (1970) *Playing and Reality*. London and New York: Routledge.

Young, I. M. (1997) Asymmetrical Reciprocity: On Moral Respect, Wonder, and Enlarged Thought. *Constellations*, 3(3), 340–363.

Young-Breuhl, E. (1998) *Subject to Biography, Psychoanalysis, Feminism, and Writing Women's Lives*. Cambridge, MA/London: Harvard University Press.

INDEX

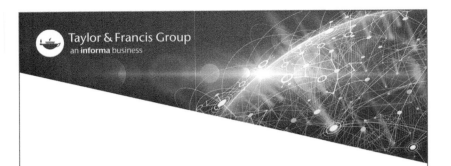